strategic brand management

strategic brand management

RICHARD ELLIOTT

LARRY PERCY

OXFORD

UNIVERSITY PRESS

OXFORD

UNIVERSITY PRESS

Great Clarendon Street, Oxford OX2 6DP

Oxford University Press is a department of the University of Oxford.
It furthers the University's objective of excellence in research, scholarship,
and education by publishing worldwide in

Oxford New York

Auckland Cape Town Dar es Salaam Hong Kong Karachi
Kuala Lumpur Madrid Melbourne Mexico City Nairobi
New Delhi Shanghai Taipei Toronto

With offices in

Argentina Austria Brazil Chile Czech Republic France Greece
Guatemala Hungary Italy Japan Poland Portugal Singapore
South Korea Switzerland Thailand Turkey Ukraine Vietnam

Oxford is a registered trade mark of Oxford University Press
in the UK and in certain other countries

Published in the United States
by Oxford University Press Inc., New York

British Library Cataloguing in Publication Data

Data available

Library of Congress Cataloging-in-Publication Data

Elliott, Richard.
  Strategic brand management / Richard Elliott, Larry Percy.
    p. cm.
  ISBN 978-0-19-926000-3
  1. Product management. 2. Strategic planning. I. Percy, Larry. II. Title.
  HF5415.15.E43 2007
  658.8'27—dc22   2006033911

Typeset by Newgen Imaging Systems (P) Ltd., Chennai, India

Printed in the UK by CPI William Clowes Beccles NR34 7TL

ISBN 978-0-19-926000-3

10 9 8 7 6 5 4

■ ROAD MAP

 # PREFACE

'Creating a true brand is one of the most powerful things any company can do to enhance its market power' (*Financial Times*).

Successful branding adds customer value and can provide protection from price competition and pressures towards commoditization. This involves complex processes of authenticity, reassurance, the development of meaning, the transformation of experience, and differentiation which eventually move from satisfying a basic human need for control and assurance to becoming a medium of social exchange and social structuration in advanced societies. The subject is growing in importance as financial services, politicians, celebrities and even religions come to be recognized as brands that can and should be managed.

The theoretical base for the book comes from the research of the first author into brands and symbolic meaning, identity and emotion; and that of the second author into brands and advertising. It also draws on the communication and positioning models covered in the companion text (*Strategic Advertising Management*) and therefore integrates brands and advertising in a unique fashion not covered elsewhere.

The book takes a socio-cultural approach which draws on contemporary sociology, cultural studies, anthropology and social theory rather than relying on just the cognitive, information-processing approach to branding. We believe it moves the subject field forward in intellectual terms. However, the wide experience of both authors in consulting with industry and teaching on demanding MBA and executive development courses around the world means that these complex and exciting ideas are firmly grounded in managerial implications and applications.

CONTENTS

▦ LIST OF FIGURES

■ LIST OF TABLES

The Socio-Cultural Meaning of Brands

This section locates brands in relation to consumer behaviour and the growth of consumer culture, drawing on psychology, sociology and anthropology.

Understanding the Social Psychology of Brands

KEY CONCEPTS

1 Brands exist in the mind of the market, so brand management is the management of perceptions.

2 Brands can be separated into those that are primarily functional and those that are primarily emotional.

3 We review the ways in which consumers make choices between brands and emphasize the key role played by involvement.

4 In low-involvement situations, top-of-mind awareness may be the single most important factor.

Introduction

In building brand value 'perception is more important than reality' (Duncan and Moriarty, 1998), and as brands only exist in the minds of customers then the management of brands is all about the management of perceptions. The power of a brand to influence perceptions can transform the experience of using the product. In a double-blind trial, patients taking a branded analgesic perceived it to be more effective in treating pain than a chemically identical unbranded analgesic (Branthwaite and Cooper, 1981). In order to manage brands strategically we need to understand how perceptions are organized, how they influence behaviour and how a brand can compete in the battle for 'mindspace' (Corstjens and Corstjens, 1995).

The organizing framework for this book is constructed by the separation of the concept of the brand into a functional domain and an emotional/symbolic domain. In the functional domain, the basic brand attribute is a product that keeps its promises of performance. As expressed in a TV ad for Ronseal woodstain in the UK: 'It does exactly what it says on the tin'. The very basic consumer benefit a brand provides is replicability of simple satisfaction of a functional need, the solving of a problem. At a more abstract level we can say that it brings some certainty in an uncertain world and this delivers a prime benefit for the consumer: it makes choice easy, simplifying the world for us. This develops into habitual behaviour, because once we find something that works, we can just keep buying it and don't have to think, or worry, or process information other than to remember the brand.

Ronseal - your guide to beautiful wood, click here

Ronseal - your guide to specialist paint, click here

Ronseal - your guide to metal paint, click here

Welcome to Ronseal. Does exactly what it says on the tin®

© 2004 Ronseal Limited

http://www.ronseal.co.uk/

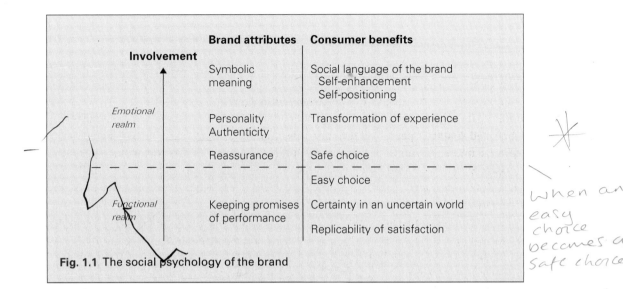

Fig. 1.1 The social psychology of the brand

[Handwritten margin note: When an easy choice becomes a safe choice]

The border between the two domains is expressed by a dotted line because we cross into an emotional/symbolic domain when an easy choice becomes a safe choice. The difference is due to increasing levels of risk, both functional and symbolic. As risk increases, a consumer choice has to be more than just easy, we have to develop a trust relationship with the brand. As we become more involved with a purchase decision our choice becomes increasingly driven by emotional processes and so the consumer benefit of the brand becomes a safe choice. In Chapter 2 we will be examining emotion-driven choice and the development of trust in brands, and it is this trust as a fundamental component of brand equity which is examined in Chapter 5. As we become more involved with the brand still, then its symbolic meaning becomes of prime importance as it transforms our lived experiences and may become part of how we build and communicate our social and cultural identities. The symbolic meaning of a brand is discussed in Chapter 3 and the cultural communication process is discussed in Chapter 4. But before we come to the specifics of brand meaning and how it is used by consumers, we need to locate brands in formal models of consumer behaviour.

Understanding consumer behaviour

The traditional approach to understanding consumer behaviour is as a sequence of stages through which the buyer moves, gathering information and evaluating competitive offerings before reaching a decision and acting upon it. This is an idealized model which has its origins as a cognitive psychological model of how a rational purchaser *should* make purchase choices and only rarely describes how people actually behave. See Fig. 1.2.

This shows the consumer moving through a series of psychological states and sequences of action before reaching a choice decision. It is an information-processing model which assumes that the consumer is sufficiently motivated to invest the mental and physical

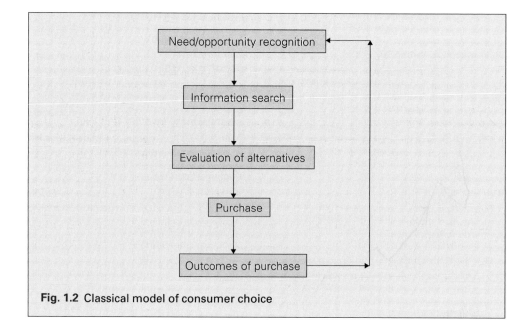

Fig. 1.2 Classical model of consumer choice

effort required to search out and process information. However, if we examine what consumers actually do through the various stages, we find wide divergence from the classical model.

Need/opportunity recognition

Consumers recognize a need or an opportunity for a product when they perceive an important gap between their current state and their ideal or desired state, either because of a change for the worse in their actual state—need recognition; or because their ideal or desired state becomes further away—opportunity recognition. For example, much simple demand is a result of a need recognition because of running out of stock of a product, or of a product failing to deliver satisfaction. Opportunity recognition occurs when life changes or advertising prompt a change upwards in expectations, and this represents much of the growth of consumer product and service markets. However, the level of motivation required to prompt a purchase may be at a much lower level than this suggests. For example, much consumption is driven by a desire to emulate other people, and this may often be at a sub-conscious level, thus the emphasis on a process initiated by conscious perception may be overstated. Also low levels of simple curiosity may be sufficient to prompt purchase.

Information search

Having recognized that a product will satisfy a need or an opportunity gap, the consumer will search for information with which to make a decision. Searching for information may involve an internal search of memory and/or an external search of the environment for information. For most consumers of most products an internal search of memory substitutes for external search, and as we shall see, awareness alone may be sufficient to effect choice. Studies of external information search and actual shopping behaviour for consumer durables have found wide differences between individual search behaviour, such that 25% of people visited four or more shops, while 37% bought at the one and only shop they visited; 32% only considered one brand while 16% considered four or more; 52% obtained no independent information, while 11% consulted two sources (Beatty and Smith, 1987). Even for the purchase of new cars, more than 30% of people considered only one make of car and visited only one car dealer prior to purchase (Punj and Staelin, 1983). The conclusion seems to be that even for expensive goods most consumers only visit one shop, do not gather additional information from advertising and generally process very little information. The extreme of minimal information search may lie with fast-moving consumer goods (fmcgs) where consumers purchasing detergents were found to spend a total of 13 seconds from entering the supermarket aisle, walking to the area where the brand is located and selecting the chosen brand. Over 70% looked at only one package, and only 11% looked at more than two (Hoyer, 1984).

Evaluation of alternatives

In order to choose between competing brands the consumer must decide which evaluative criteria will be used and employ some form of decision rule. The evaluative criteria (sometimes called choice criteria) are the product attributes, functional, symbolic and emotional, on which the relative performance of the competing alternatives will be compared. The decision rule is the strategy the consumer uses to deal with the information available and arrive at a choice. However, consumers also use certain tangible attributes as surrogate indicators, or signals, of less tangible attributes. In particular, price and brand name are often used as surrogate indicators of quality and this appears to be a cultural universal (Dawar and Parker, 1994). Decision rules can be categorized as either compensatory or non-compensatory. Compensatory rules allow poor performance on one attribute to be offset by good performance on another attribute, while non-compensatory decision rules are simpler strategies in which consumers use one single standard and eliminate those alternatives which do not measure up to it. Rules are developed by experience and stored in memory and can be retrieved when necessary; at other times consumers may construct rules as they go along, using fragments of rules stored in memory to make an on-the-spot choice (Payne *et al.*, 1992). For example, we may make a choice between two brands of instant coffee based partly on knowledge about the comparative prices, the colour of the packaging and a vague memory of a taste preference.

It has become clear in recent years that human information-processing limitations greatly affect the way in which consumers make purchase decisions. In conjunction with the dominant perspective of humans as 'cognitive misers' who will always seek to reduce cognitive effort and will be content to merely satisfice rather than maximize their decision outcomes, the study of decision rules has moved towards the study of various simplifying decision heuristics or 'rules-of-thumb' used by consumers to shortcut the cognitive process of choice. It has been argued that some of these 'rules-of-thumb' are efficient and accurate, such as the equal weight rule which examines all of the attributes and all of the data but simplifies the process by ignoring the relative importance or probability of each attribute.

However, most 'rules-of-thumb' used by consumers seem either to be inaccurate strategies or to lead to severe and systematic bias when compared with the rational decision-making model of economic theory. Consumers may use simple counts of good or bad features or rely on rules such as 'buy the cheapest brand' or 'buy what my parents buy' or the simplest habit rule, 'buy the brand I bought last time' (Hoyer, 1984). Perhaps the most ubiquitous is when the consumer retrieves pre-formed evaluations from memory and the one with the highest level of overall liking is chosen. We shall consider this simple use of emotion to drive the choice process in Chapter 2. Consumers also appear to use inferences based on experience of the market place to help them cope with information. For example, it appears that many consumers cannot handle the arithmetic needed to compare prices across different quantities, and instead use a 'market belief' such as that 'if an item is on price promotion then it must be a better buy' (Alpert, 1993). These consumer market beliefs incorporate such brand beliefs as 'own-label brands are just the same as brand leaders sold under a different label at a lower price', and 'all brands are basically the same', and shop beliefs such as 'the more sales assistants there are in a shop, the more expensive are its products', and 'larger shops offer better prices than small shops'.

A class of 'rules-of-thumb' that are more general in their applicability and seem to operate over a wide range of decision areas and to reflect some inherent biases in human judgement are three judgement rules: representativeness, availability, and anchoring (Kahneman and Tversky, 1979). Representativeness refers to the tendency to judge the probability that an object belongs to a category based on how typical it appears to be of that category, ignoring the statistical probability. This is linked to the 'law of small numbers' and the 'gambler's fallacy' in which people seem to not only believe that small samples can accurately represent large populations, but also expect random sequences to look random. Of more direct relevance to consumer decisions is the availability rule, which refers to the tendency for an event to be judged more probable in terms of how easily we can bring it to mind. For example, the performance of products with unusual brand names is more likely to be judged as a failure than the same product performance with less distinctive brand names. A further judgemental bias is the 'framing effect', in which the way in which product attributes are framed with either a positive or a negative label will affect consumer evaluations. Consumers who were presented with minced beef that was labelled '75% lean' had much more favourable evaluations of the meat than when the beef was labelled '25% fat'. However, this effect was reduced after actually tasting the meat (Levin and Gaeth, 1988).

Purchase

Two important aspects of the purchase stage are the extent to which the purchase is actually pre-planned, and the choice of outlet to buy from. There are a range of factors which will intervene between a formed purchase intention and actual purchase. The major factor is time, in that the more time between intention formation and behaviour, the more opportunity exists for unexpected factors to change the original intention.

However, in many instances a conscious purchase intention is not formulated prior to the purchase act. In supermarket shopping, the displays of products can act as a surrogate shopping list and prompt a type of impulse purchase (Cobb and Hoyer, 1986). This would be more accurately termed a partly planned purchase as, although no specific intention is formed, a general intention to purchase exists, and it is not a true impulse purchase which involves a sudden strong urge to purchase with diminished concern for the consequences. A large US study of supermarket purchase decisions found that the majority of brand decisions are made in-store, with 83% of snack food choice being decided upon in the shop (Meyer, 1988).

Rather than a choice between brands, for many people and many types of product, shops form the group of brands from which choice is made, and brands may only be chosen once the shop decision has been made. For the increasing number of people for whom shopping is a recreational activity, browsing can lead to many unplanned purchases but is itself a pleasure-giving activity for a significant proportion of the population (Elliott, 1994).

Outcomes of purchase

The essence of post-purchase evaluation is whether the consumer is satisfied or dissatisfied with the product. The major cognitive approach in this area is the Expectancy Disconfirmation Model, which points to the importance of prior expectation as determining how we will interpret experience with the product post-purchase. If we have low expectations then poor performance will not cause much dissatisfaction. If, however, we have high expectations then poor performance will result in high levels of dissatisfaction. The opposite is true for satisfaction, in that if we have low expectations and the product performs well then we will be satisfied. However, recent research has emphasized the extra role of emotional aspects in achieving satisfaction versus the purely instrumental aspects of dissatisfaction.

Although dissatisfaction with purchases is common, relatively few consumers actually make complaints. Complaint behaviour seems to be determined largely by individual factors, only 38% of people being likely to take direct action and 14% likely to take no action (Gilly and Gelb, 1982).

The ability of the consumer to learn from the experience of purchasing and using products is subject to a number of limitations and cognitive biases. In particular, if not highly motivated, consumers may limit learning by relying on previously learned schemas, which can often be derived from advertising. In general, it is suggested that consumer learning from experience can be managed, with market leaders having much to gain by impeding learning. The principal method used is to encourage ambiguity by avoiding direct comparisons, and by attempting to control the attribute agenda by suggesting belief structures or schemas which consumers can use to interpret consumption experiences (Alba and Hutchinson, 1988). Heinz Tomato Ketchup set the attribute agenda for sauces by adopting the claim of 'thickness', which could be easily verified and used to judge competing brands. It was left to the consumer to draw the inference that thickness equals flavour. Heinz have now moved to focus on different attributes because of their move to top-down plastic bottles.

Consumer involvement

The concept of involvement is pivotal in consumer psychology as it attempts to describe aspects of the relative personal relevance or importance that a product or brand has for an individual. Fundamentally, involvement can be seen as the motivation to search for information and to engage in systematic processing, and it is a motivational state which affects many of the key aspects of consumer behaviour such as decision making, responses to persuasion and processing of advertisements. Although it should properly be understood as a continuum running from very low to very high, it is useful to refer to high versus low involvement as a structural aid in locating different individuals' subjective perceptions of the personal relevance of a product, a brand, a purchase decision, or an advertisement. There are a number of different definitions of involvement and several alternative measurement methods but there is some agreement that involvement is a function of three sources of importance: the consumer, the product, and the situation (Richins *et al.*, 1992). Individual differences in the characteristics of the consumer include the self-concept, values, personal goals and needs. Product characteristics which will affect the level of involvement include the price, how frequently it is purchased, the symbolic meanings associated with the product and their social visibility, the perceived risk of poor performance or potential for harm, and the length of time one will have to commit to the product once it is purchased. The situational variables include aspects of the purchase situation itself, such as the amount of time available, whether the purchase is made privately or in the presence of others; and more importantly, aspects of the intended use situation such as whether the product is intended as a gift, or will be used in an important social situation. It must always be remembered that involvement is person/product/situation specific, and while we can classify products as high or low involvement for ease of application, no product is low involvement for every person at all times. The key elements of this model of involvement are shown in Figure 1.3.

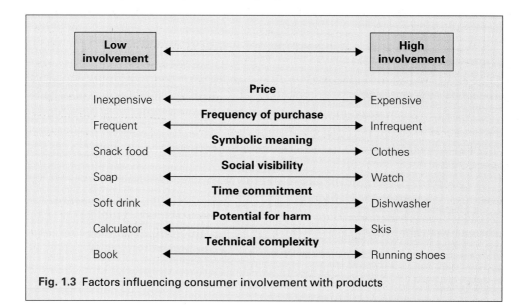

Fig. 1.3 Factors influencing consumer involvement with products

The classical model of consumer decision making usually only applies to high-involvement products and/or when there are important situational factors. In these cases consumers may often seek extensive information prior to purchase. However, a qualification of the simple 'More involvement equals more information search' hypothesis is only true of functional products, those which satisfy by their physical performance. Expressive or symbolic products, those which help the consumer express their personality or self-concept, are at once both highly involving and purchased with little information search, as the psychosocial interpretation of these products is less susceptible to explicit information search as it is largely idiosyncratic. This will be addressed when we consider emotion-driven choice in Chapter 2. But what do we know about how consumers make purchase choices when they are not involved with the product?

Low-involvement choice

By combining data from a wide range of studies we can build a picture of the low-involvement consumer. It seems clear that consumers have very little knowledge about the differences between brands and perceive them as all very similar. If they hold any beliefs about an individual brand then these are likely to be very weak, and thus easily changed. Avoidance of mental and physical effort seems to be the key motivation as consumers are seeking to be satisfied, not necessarily delighted. Perhaps the major criterion is that the choice be the one least likely to give them any problems. It has been suggested that for much of the time, consumers are paying little or no conscious attention to the information environment, but are relying on past behaviour as a guide. In most cases awareness of a brand is a key predictor of purchase, in that brands in 'top-of-mind' awareness are the only ones consumers are likely to choose from, unless some situational factor at point-of-sale draws a new brand to their attention. We know that consumers have a very limited number of brands in any category which they can recall from memory, usually 7 plus or minus 2, and in low-involvement categories nearer to 4 plus or minus 1. So building top-of-mind awareness is a crucial task for marketing communications in low-involvement categories. However, the major route to awareness is through past behaviour (Ehrenberg, 1974). You will recall that one of the factors that predicts that a product will be low involvement is frequent purchasing, so that once a consumer has purchased a brand several times and found it reasonably satisfactory, they can fall back on habit from then on. On the first purchase occasion, consumers may use trial as a low-risk method of evaluating the brand, before forming any judgements about it. This model of low-involvement choice is shown in Fig. 1.4.

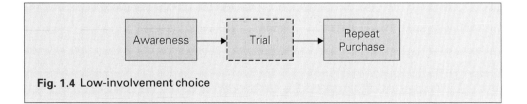

Fig. 1.4 Low-involvement choice

So far we have considered the extent to which the consumer engages in mental effort in choosing a brand, that is the extent of information processing that is carried out. But many products and services are not thought about coolly and rationally, so what happens when choice is under the control of emotional processes? We will be considering the combination of emotion and high involvement in the next chapter, but now let's look at the combination of low involvement and low levels of emotion.

Low-involvement choice and emotion

When consumers are not so involved with the product or service but it is still an area where judgement is largely driven by emotional factors, then studies of the effects of emotion on judgement have shown that even slightly positive emotional states lead to less thought, less information seeking, less analytic reasoning, less attention to negative cues and less attention to 'realism'. In this state we can consider consumers as seeking a mild sense of warmth, rather than hot emotion, and seeking to choose the brand which they simply feel best about. This feeling of warmth may derive from a number of factors. There is a large amount of experimental evidence that far from 'familiarity breeding contempt', mere exposure to a brand name over time can result in the development of a non-rational preference. Emotional responses can be used as a signal, in particular a basic emotional signal is that of rejection or dislike. The 'refusal of other tastes' may well be a fundamental process in that we first reject everything we dislike, and that left must be what we like. Also emotional responses can carry information, in that we can consult our feelings for information for a choice decision: 'Well, how do I feel about it?' Because we are not so involved with the choice we may not be motivated to justify our choice with rational arguments, but some people still feel the need to seek out information that justifies their choice, although this may be a rather more passive operation than that when choice is driven by emotion. This low-emotion model of choice is shown in Fig. 1.5.

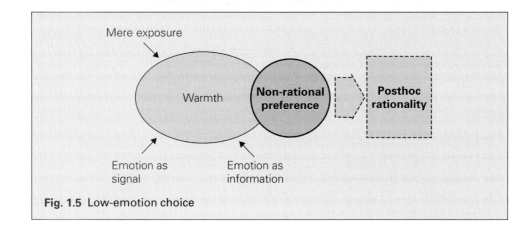

Fig. 1.5 Low-emotion choice

Brands and low-involvement choice

When people are not involved with a purchase, then the brand becomes an heuristic for making choices and our mental resources are barely involved in processing information, rather, we learn passively by subconscious processing that places brands in our memory with little or no processing. It is this low-involvement processing that is 'the glue that holds the entire world of brands together' (Heath, 2000). Choice between brands is driven largely by simple associations between the brand and attributes or emotions usually created and sustained through advertising. Consumers will even construct causal inferences about a brand and its functional attributes which need have no basis in reality. The evidence suggests that meaningful brands can perhaps be built from meaningless differentiation on irrelevant attributes (Carpenter *et al.*, 1994), and we will be developing the ways in which a low-involvement brand can be differentiated from the competition in Chapter 8.

But brand associations can also be constructed to emotional responses without the need for conscious awareness through the processes of conditioning and 'mere exposure'. Classical conditioning requires the repeated pairing over time between brand and a positive emotional stimulus (e.g. a beautiful picture of a sunset) and eventually the brand alone will automatically evoke the pleasant emotional response (Shimp *et al.*, 1991). The mere exposure effect is where repeated exposure to a brand name in the absence of any other stimulus can eventually evoke mild positive emotional responses (Bornstein, 1989). Both of these processes have been demonstrated to successfully influence brand choice, even against competitors with superior performance characteristics (Baker, 1999). We will be discussing how these emotional processes can be built into brand strategy in Chapter 8.

CHAPTER SUMMARY

In this chapter we have demonstrated that perceptions of brands must be the focus of managerial action. We have reviewed what is known about how consumers make choice decisions between brands and identified the critical role played by levels of consumer involvement. We suggested that in conditions of low involvement, achieving top-of-mind awareness might be the primary management goal. We went on to explore how even low-involvement brands may be associated with low levels of emotion and non-rational preference.

DISCUSSION QUESTIONS

1   Why are perceptions so important in developing brand strategy?

2   How does risk separate the functional from the emotional domain?

3   To what extent do consumers make thoughtful, rational choices between brands?

4   How can the attribute agenda used by consumers be influenced by market leaders?

5 Why is involvement a pivotal concept in consumer psychology?

6 What is the role of past behaviour in building brand awareness?

7 How can emotions be linked to low-involvement brands?

CASE STUDY

De Beers: Romancing the Stone

De Beers is a leading brand in the diamond business. Diamond sales are inextricably linked to the fortunes of any country's economy. In 1995 Europe was not yet fully out of recession. Facing weaker consumer demand, De Beers Europe cut its marketing budgets across Europe. With the decline in marketing budgets, however, De Beers planned for a more ambitious target with profit maximization.

Without as much marketing support as before, De Beers needed a new strategy that was more focused and more hard-hitting in order to achieve its aggressive targets. As purchases of diamond jewellery were less frequent, De Beers found that they could make more money by selling larger diamonds. While two rings could sell for the same price, the one with fewer, larger stones could be worth up to four times the profit to De Beers. Therefore, De Beers decided to encourage consumers to trade up to larger stones: Solitaire, the largest diamond.

Solitaires, pieces with a single diamond, simply epitomize diamonds. However, qualitative research showed that they were seen to be very old-fashioned, like a grandmother's engagement ring. They were also almost entirely associated with the traditional 'claw set' ring. To women, Solitaires were seen as a predictable, boring choice, and, without the benefit of design, lacking in individuality. Despite these negative views, Solitaires were also seen to possess a simple purity and an uncluttered beauty. They are large enough for one to see deep into the stone, each revealing its own unique sparkle and colour. They are 'proper' diamonds—not chips off a block. Moreover, every Solitaire is believed to be unique. Each has its own history and story to tell.

'Everyone knows that every diamond is unique . . .'
Susan Bell Research, Australia, July 1995

'When you think about the stone, then you remember there is no other like it.'
Added Value, UK, February 1995

This uniqueness matched what diamonds symbolize in the eye of women. Women were looking for something that could uniquely reflect their relationship and their individual sense of style. Such symbolism meant a piece of jewellery with a strong design element.

'I don't want to see my ring on someone else. It's mine.'
Studio Paven, Italy, March 1995

'I want something different. Something that belongs to me.'
Added Value, UK, February 1995

Nevertheless, research suggested that 80% of diamonds were bought by men. The main motivation was the gift of love. In discussion, men proudly expressed how they picked out the gift themselves—the ultimate gift being the surprise gift. Surprisingly, however, a more searching investigation revealed that women have a much greater influence than we imagined and that the surprise gift is usually a myth.

Women admitted to a shared conspiracy on diamond purchases: a long campaign of subtle and not-so-subtle hints. There are the jewellery brochures left open on the coffee table, the casual comments over the washing up, the pause outside the jeweller's window, with the innocent '*just looking, darling*'. Yet when they receive a diamond they are genuinely surprised. (At last he has done it!) Every woman seems to have her own ways of letting her man know exactly what she wants. Women have the strongest influence on what gets bought. This insight was brought to life more vividly by the psychologist, Dr. Sam Cohen.

> '*Women need to express their need for a diamond and also disguise it. A woman would never say "Oh, twentieth anniversary. You know what I want darling". Why not? To some extent she is looking for pseudo-surprise. Not an actual surprise, but some feeling that something has been given to her. She also feels she needs to protect her pride, and for him to feel a sense of ownership and pride. So coding and de-coding messages between the couple becomes extremely important.*'

Dr. Sam Cohen Nation-wide Reporting

Subsequent discussions with retailers confirmed this finding.

> '*Women enter the shop with a very clear idea of what they want in their heads. Part of my job with her is to help the man feel he has a role to play beyond simply signing the cheque.*'

> '*Men do come in on their own. However, more often than not, I have already seen their wives.*'

UK Jewellers

Women, therefore, became the target audience. This was the first time in the history of the brand in Europe that a message had been aimed exclusively at women and concerned solely with their motivation. So, De Beers needed to find a compelling link between the woman and her choice of diamond—Solitaire.

The conventional approach to advertising diamonds had been to dramatize them as the ultimate gift of love. However, could a Solitaire really claim to be the ultimate of what was already the ultimate? Every time anyone buys a diamond they are buying a part of the dream De Beers has created. However, diamonds are capable of evoking immense excitement and powerful emotion, beyond the moment of giving. (We have all witnessed the flurry of excitement in the office as the girls surround someone who has recently become engaged.) Women draw strength from their diamonds. They make them feel special, confident and attractive.

'*I am suddenly 2 feet taller.*'
Added Value, UK, February 1995

'*I feel the world is looking at me.*'
Studio Paven, Italy, March 1995

'*I can do anything wearing my diamonds.*'
Susan Bell Research, Australia, July 1995

Others admit to behaving in a more exaggerated way.

'*I am inclined to run my hand through my hair more often than I would normally.*'
Millward Brown, Spain, July 1995

'*I try and catch my diamond in the light.*'
Added Value, UK, February 1995

Maybe it was time to leave this dream intact. As a result, De Beers stepped outside the language of love and focused on the woman herself and her experience of wearing a diamond. Every diamond is unique—no two are the same. Obviously, this is also true of people. De Beers explored the link between these unique, extremely individual emotions and the uniqueness of a Solitaire. They wanted to convey the unique feelings and joy a woman experiences when wearing her diamond. Thus the Solitaire became an expression of individuality. The central idea was that **no one is the same—neither the woman herself nor her solitaire diamond.**

We have explained how women are looking for something individual and that a Solitaire is perceived to fall short of this. Yet we also knew that every diamond was considered unique. Each has its own history and story to tell; each has its own particular way of playing with light. De Beers successfully transferred a woman's desire for unique design to the uniqueness of the stone.

First, the advertising tells the woman's own story alongside the unique geological story of the diamond itself. This genuine uniqueness is then captured by giving it the owner's name. De Beers put the two facts together and said: There is nothing else like it in the universe. And, because it is yours, it legitimately bears your name. Like Elizabeth Taylor and Sarah Millington in the UK and Valeria Martin in Italy, women are asked to believe that they too can claim and name their diamond as their own.

Second, real women show genuine joy and excitement. De Beers portrayed this emotion through a range of different, real women interacting with their diamond. The models were shown as themselves, unglamourized. The woman's emotion comes from her relationship with the diamond, not with the giver. The emotion is joy: the joy of ownership. The contrast of real women and this joy shines amongst the clutter of posed, perfect models that dominate most women's press advertising.

Lastly, De Beers talked to women in a private medium in order to take part in the conspiracy and influence women's desire for a particular piece. Women's press seemed the natural choice. It lends itself to a one-to-one conversation. It allows De Beers to focus on her thoughts and feelings. Besides, the woman's decision is not made overnight. It evolves. Inspiration and ideas are collected from a myriad of different sources. It could be something she has seen in a magazine, something she saw someone wearing, or simply from gazing into the jeweller's window. De Beers needed to talk to women more often than they could afford to do on television, their traditional medium, best able to create the romance and fantasy of diamonds.

This is, in many ways, a unique story. It illustrates how conventional wisdom and a superficial look at research can easily lead you in the wrong direction. The creative planning input was based on a more thorough investigation of the consumers' true motivation and behaviour. This led De Beers to break some of the conventions of diamond advertising.

Sources: WARC, Creative Planning Awards 1997, De Beers: Romancing the Stone, by Vanella Jackson
Edited by Hazel H. Huang

Discussion Questions

1 Why did De Beers change its audience to women, instead of men, who are the main purchasers of diamonds? Discuss the differences between the targeting of women and targeting of men in terms of communication strategy.

2 What are the difficulties in the brand moving from symbolizing a love relationship to one focusing on the woman herself?

3 What are the implications for the brand strategy of the complex psychological relationship between couples?

4 How could De Beers maintain their sales of traditional less expensive diamonds while focusing the brand on Solitaires?

FURTHER READING

- There is a vast amount of experimental evidence about the consumer decision-making process based on the cognitive information-processing model and a very comprehensive source is Franzen, G. and Bouwmen, M. (2001), *The Mental World of Brands*, Henley-on-Thames: WARC.

- A radical alternative to the cognitive model which instead emphasizes the primary role of behaviour and its ability to be used to mathematically model consumer choice is proposed by Ehrenberg, A. (1988), *Repeat Buying*, London: Charles Griffin.

- A comprehensive discussion of low-involvement processes is by Heath, R. (2001), *The Hidden Power of Advertising: How Low Involvement Processing Influences the Way We Choose Brands*, London: NTC Publications.

REFERENCES

Alba, J. and Hutchinson, W. (1988), 'Dimensions of consumer expertise', *Journal of Consumer Research*, 13, 411–54.

Alpert, F. (1993), 'Consumer market beliefs and their managerial implications: an empirical examination', *Journal of Consumer Marketing*, 10, 2, 56–70.

Baker, W. (1999), 'When can affective conditioning and mere exposure directly influence brand choice?' *Journal of Advertising*, XXVIII, 4, 31–46.

Beatty, S. and Smith, S. (1987), 'External search effort: An investigation across several product categories', *Journal of Consumer Research*, 14, 83–95.

Bornstein, R. (1989), 'Exposure and affect: overview and meta-analysis of research, 1968–1987', *Psychological Bulletin*, 106, 265–89.

Branthwaite, A. and Cooper, P. (1981), 'Analgesic effects of branding in treatment of headaches', *British Medical Journal*, 282, 1576–8.

Carpenter, G., Glazer, R., and Nakamoto, K. (1994), 'Meaningful brands from meaningless differentiation: the dependence on irrelevant attributes', *Journal of Marketing Research*, XXXI, 339–50.

Cobb, C. and Hoyer, W. (1986), 'Planned versus impulse purchase behaviour', *Journal of Retailing*, 62, 384–409.

Corstjens, J. and Corstjens, M. (1995), *Store Wars: The Battle for Mindspace and Shelfspace*, Chichester: John Wiley.

Dawar, N. and Parker, P. (1994), 'Marketing universals: consumers' use of brand name, price, physical appearance, and retailer reputation as signals of product quality', *Journal of Marketing*, 58, 81–95.

Duncan, T. and Moriarty, S. (1998), 'A communication-based marketing model for managing relationships', *Journal of Marketing*, 62, 1–13.

Ehrenberg, A.S.C. (1974), 'Repetitive advertising and the consumer', *Journal of Advertising Research*, 14, 2, 25–33.

Elliott, R. (1994), 'Addictive consumption: function and fragmentation in postmodernity', *Journal of Consumer Policy*, 17, 159–79.

Gilly, M. and Gelb, B. (1982), 'Post-purchase consumer processes and the complaining consumer', *Journal of Consumer Research*, 9, 323–28.

Heath, R. (2000), 'Low-involvement processing', *Admap*, March, 14–17.

Hoyer, W. (1984), 'An examination of consumer decision making for a common repeat purchase product', *Journal of Consumer Research*, 17, 141–48.

Kahneman, D. and Tversky, A. (1979), 'Prospect theory: an analysis of decision under risk', *Econometrica*, 47, 263–91.

Levin, I. and Gaeth, G. (1988), 'How consumers are affected by the framing of attribute information before and after consuming the product', *Journal of Consumer Research*, 15, 374–79.

Meyer, M. (1988), 'Attention Shoppers!' *Marketing and Media Decisions*, 23, 67.

Payne, J., Bettman, J., and Johnson, E. (1992), 'Behavioral decision research: a constructive processing perspective', *Annual Review of Psychology*, 4, 87–131.

Punj, G. and Staelin, R. (1983), 'A model of consumer search behaviour for new automobiles', *Journal of Consumer Research*, 9, 366–80.

Richins, M., Bloch, P., and McQuarrie, E. (1992), 'How enduring and situational involvement combine to create involvement responses', *Journal of Consumer Psychology*, 1, 2, 143–53.

Shimp, T., Stuart, E., and Engle, R. (1991), 'A program of classical conditioning experiments testing variations in the conditioned stimulus and context', *Journal of Consumer Research*, 18, 1, 1–12.

Emotion and Brands

 KEY CONCEPTS

1 Emotions are social and cultural as well as psychological so it is vital to understand the socio-cultural environment in which a brand is marketed.

2 The symbolic meaning of consumption is prime motivation for emotion-driven choice.

3 Non-rational preferences involve holistic perception and non-verbal imagery.

4 People may justify an emotional choice by post hoc rationalization.

5 Trust is very important for reducing perceptions of purchase risk and involves a reliance on emotion.

6 Trust is most important for symbolic brands and involves consumer-brand intimacy.

7 The emotional significance of a brand will influence how much attention is paid to it.

8 It is possible to 'emotionalize' a product that has little rational connection with emotions.

Introduction

In this chapter, we shall be dealing with the importance of emotions both to choosing brands and to evaluating and forming opinions about them. The predominant model of consumer choice process is based upon cognitive information processing, even though this cognitive framework has rarely managed to explain more than 20% of the variance in global evaluation measures of behaviour (Obermiller, 1990). Emotion informs cognitive processing, yet is too often ignored by those trying to understand consumer behaviour. But the consumption experience is replete with emotion, often of a high degree of intensity. In the area of impulse buying, consumers describe a compelling feeling that was 'thrilling', 'wild', 'a tingling sensation', 'a surge of energy', 'like turning up the excitement volume' and a study of the everyday consumer experiences of women yielded descriptions of making purchases in a 'dreamlike' way when they were 'captivated' by a product and gave an impression of an almost seamless flow of events unpunctuated by 'stopping to think'. In addition, emotion is a critical part of the consumer evaluation of brands. There are emotional associations linked to brands in memory, and these will influence how new information about a brand is processed, as well as mediate judgements about it during purchase.

What is emotion?

To begin with, when considering emotion, a frequent source of confusion is the tendency to think about emotion and feelings as the same thing; they are not. Feelings are part of the emotional language that describes the subjective feeling component of emotion (Bradley and Lang, 2000). Emotion is made up of a number of components, most often considered within the context of the so-called 'reaction triad' of psychological arousal, motor expression, and subjective feeling (Scherer, 2000). As Damasio (1999) has put it: 'The full human impact of emotions is only realized when they are sensed, when they become feeling, and when those feelings are felt. That is where they become known, with the assistance of consciousness'. It is this aspect of emotions that concerns us.

Everyone experiences these 'feelings'. But the concept of emotion goes beyond this, and is perhaps best understood within the context of something called affect program theory (Griffiths, 1997). In its modern form, the affect program theory deals with what are generally considered the six basic, or primary, emotions following Ekman (1992): surprise, anger, fear, disgust, sadness, and joy. These affect program states are phylogentically ancient, and informationally encapsulated reflex responses that appear to be independent of cultural considerations. This is important, because it means that when one is dealing with a primary emotion, it will be the same for everyone, regardless of social situations or culture.

However, while primary emotions are a basic part of our being human, there are many others, for example embarrassment or guilt, that are to some extent acquired, and are triggered by things people have come to associate with that emotion through experience.

These are the so-called secondary or social emotions (cf. Damasio, 1999, and others), are informed by cultural schemas and are part of social construction notions of emotion. Importantly, they are part of higher-order cognitive processes and they will differ across cultures owing to the role culture plays in psychological development.

In summary, we might think of emotion in two fundamental ways. First, there are of the six primary emotions that comprise the affect program theory, and which are basic to all humans. While they are triggered by a cognitive system, it is one that does not freely exchange information with other cognitive systems, and they are basically short-term responses of the autonomic nervous system. Second, there are all the other emotions, which are associated with the social constructionist literature, and are informed by experience. In this chapter, we are primarily concerned with the latter.

Emotion and consumer choice

Traditional models of consumer behaviour have assumed a hierarchy-of-effects in which cognitive activity is followed by emotional evaluation in the formation of an attitude, which ultimately results in behaviour. This assumes that cognition mediates emotion and directs it, while emotion mediates behaviour. Although the growing recognition of the existence of low-involvement purchasing produced such concepts as affect-referral and spontaneous attitude accessing, these were assumed to be a result of previous cognitive processing which were stored in memory. A major challenge to this orthodoxy was made by Zajonc (1980), who proposed that emotion is not only a separate processing system which does not involve cognition, but also the primary influence on the development of preferences and sometimes actually precedes cognition. He defined some of the other characteristics of emotion as: inescapable; irrevocable; judgements which implicate the self; are difficult to verbalize; and are independent of cognition.

While this idea was seriously challenged by Lazarus (1982) at the time, the real issue according to Griffiths (1997) is the *degree* to which the information-processing system responsible for emotional response is independent of, or a part of, the same system that is involved in longer-term, planned behaviour. There is no question that the system dealing with emotion in the brain (principally the pre-frontal cortex and amygdala) can perceive and store information that does not reach conscious attention, yet it does engage the declarative memory system (Eichenbaum, 2002). It is the declarative memory system that is home to the cognitive processing we are talking about here. But a separate pathway seems to be involved (Yamasaki *et al.*, 2002) with emotion.

Even Zajonc, in later work (Murphy and Zajonc, 1993) dealing with priming effects, suggests that only simple valenced judgements are likely to occur without more involved cognitive processing. As Lane (2000) has pointed out, while it is possible to make positive or negative judgements about subliminally primed stimuli, they are crude judgements. More refined preference judgements are not possible without conscious awareness. What all this means is that while most decisions involve higher-order cognitive processing, some do not; and even higher-order cognitive processes may be mediated by unconscious emotional responses.

An interesting example of a non-cognitive way of looking at the role of emotion in consumer choice is offered by Mittal's (1988) affect choice model. This model applies to the purchase of expressive products (products with symbolic meaning) and suggests that emotion-based choice is holistic, self-focused and unable to be verbalized. Holistic choice means that consumers are unable to separate out the individual attributes or 'preferenda' but form an overall impression. For example, one may not be able to break down a preference for a perfume into specific attributes. Choice is self-focused in that emotional judgements of expressive products involve the judge directly. That a car is 'too flashy' reflects the values and personality of the judge more than any inherent property of the car. Emotional judgements are made almost instantaneously and reflect basic subjective feelings which may not have verbal descriptors, and thus emotion relies much more on non-verbal channels of communication.

Another concept of 'extraordinary experience' has been used to describe a special class of unusual hedonic consumption which is intrinsically enjoyable and involves high levels of emotional intensity. A study of white-water river rafting demonstrated that despite the vivid recall of retrospective reports of the intensity of the emotional experience, participants did not appear to want to engage in very much cognitive recall as the magic was 'best preserved if the associated feelings and sensations are not examined too closely' (Arnould and Price, 1993).

Social perspectives on emotion

A major issue with the conceptualization of emotion used in much consumer research is that it refers to a personal and individual phenomenon, when in fact the many important aspects of emotion are social. This is reflected in the social constructivist models of emotion (Harré, 1986, Shweder, 1993). They posit that the *meaning* of emotion is generally constructed by socio-culturally determined behaviour and value patterns. Social constructivist models view emotions not as natural responses elicited by natural features in a situation, but as socio-cultural constructions which serve a situated social function, so that the meaning of an emotion is located within the socio-cultural system in which it is culturally appropriate: an emotional response is a function of shared expectations regarding appropriate behaviour.

Advocates of social constructivist models do not deny the psychobiological reaction components of the reaction triad, but they consider this secondary to the meaning derived from socio-cultural context. They are very concerned with the ways in which emotions are labelled in a language, believing that this reflects the emotional meaning structure in a particular culture (Scherer, 2000). Interpersonal communication theory follows this idea, suggesting that 'emotion is constructed on-line as part of the developing relationship emerging from a real-time encounter between people' (Parkinson, 1995). Emotions are not simply internal events but are communicative acts addressed to specific audiences, and are thus partly defined according to conventional cultural representations.

Cross-cultural studies have shown that cultural differences in the conceptualization of the self can play a central role in shaping emotional experiences. For example, Asian cultures that insist on the fundamental relatedness of individuals to each other, result in different experiences of such emotions as pride, guilt and anger in comparison with Western cultures which are more focused on the individual and inner attributes (Markus and Kitayama, 1991). Thus the cultural context of consumption will lead to socially constructed emotional responses, under the direction of situational norms. Hochschild (1983) describes how we learn the local 'Feeling Rules' in a social situation so that our emotions are appropriate to local circumstances and meet the expectations of other people.

While primary emotions are fixed biologically and some componens of emotion may be fired by evolutionary pressure, and specific secondary emotions can certainly be the result of individual emotional development, nevertheless there is much evidence that pronounced social and cultural variations exist not only in the representation of secondary emotions but also in the ways in which people experience, express, and regulate them (Parkinson *et al.*, 2005). This is why it is so important to understand the socio-cultural environment within which a brand is marketed. It will be that environment that informs the extent and manner in which emotions will influence both consumer decision making and brand evaluation.

Emotional response

While we have just seen how important the socio-cultural context is to understanding and defining emotions and emotional responses, this does not mean that knowing the socio-cultural context will make it easy to predict an emotional response. A way to approach understanding emotional response is to assume that emotions are grounded in mechanisms which are not voluntary and are under only limited human control. These principles, which are basically empirical regularities, have been framed as laws by Frijda (1988), who proposed eleven laws of emotional responding, four of which are crucially important in understanding the consumer.

The law of concern

Emotions arise in response to events that are important to the individual's goals, motives, or concerns. This links values and situations by stating that hidden behind every emotion is a more or less enduring disposition to prefer certain states of the world. This is a key issue for understanding consumer emotions as it is the law of concern which links our motivations and emotional responses and underpins consumer involvement and thus drives much consumption. A prime source of emotional involvement is the search for identity in postmodern society where the individual is threatened by a number of 'dilemmas of the self' (Giddens, 1991, p. 201): fragmentation, powerlessness, uncertainty and a struggle against commodification. These dilemmas are driven by the 'looming threat of personal meaninglessness' as the individual endeavours to construct and maintain an identity which will remain stable through a rapidly changing environment. Although the individual may on the one hand fear mass commodification because it threatens to remove choice and replace it with standardization, in fact, through ever-growing plurality of consumer choice the individual is offered resources which may be used creatively to achieve 'an ego-ideal which commands the respect of others and inspires self-love' (Gabriel and Lang, 1995, p. 98). Thus it is likely that goods which can be used as resources to construct and maintain identity will involve emotion-driven choice. The symbolic meaning of goods will be explored in Chapter 3.

The law of apparent reality

Emotions are elicited by events appraised as real, and their intensity varies accordingly to the level of reality attributed. In this regard, 'knowing means less than seeing'. Vivid imagination also has the power of 'reality' and is capable of eliciting strong emotions; in this respect 'feeling means more than knowing'. The law of apparent reality accounts for the weakness of reason as opposed to the strength of passion as it suggests that imagination and fantasy can overwhelm reason and that the consumer can create their own 'reality'.

The law of closure

Emotions tend to be closed to probabilities and likelihoods, and to be absolute in their judgements and have control over the action system. It may be that the cause of an emotion may be relatively minor but emotional response may not recognize this and be a total experience. When one is very angry the thing that happened is felt to be absolutely bad, and the person involved to be intrinsically bad too. Verbal expressions of emotion tend to reflect this absoluteness in quality and time: 'I could kill him' or 'I cannot live without her'. The absoluteness of feeling and thinking tends to be reflected in behaviour and to override other concerns. The law of closure may be considered the essential feature of emotion, in that it captures the involuntary nature of strong emotional impulses and urges. Desire for a consumption object can be a totally overwhelming sensation which drives out all other aspects of the environment and entails complete absorption in the shopping experience.

The law of the lightest load

There is a tendency to view any situation in a way that minimizes negative emotional load. People tend to avoid and deny unpleasant knowledge and will seek to interpret a situation in a way which maximizes emotional gain. This suggests that emotion can drive our interpretation of a situation in such a way that we can make it more pleasing to us and that we are motivated to develop strategies of emotion management. Individuals may be motivated to preserve a positive emotional state by using mood maintenance strategies, and to alleviate negative emotional states through strategies of mood repair. Mood repair has been found to be the prime motivation maintaining addictive consumption, in that the shopping experience is a very effective short-term solution to feelings of unhappiness and stress (Elliott, 1998). It is likely that mood repair is a major motivation underlying a broad range of compensatory consumption behaviour. Strategies of mood maintenance may include the common social behaviour of going out to dinner after a pleasant occasion and then going on after that for a drink.

So despite their cultural and local situational contingency, emotions may be law-like in their effect upon us. The law of apparent reality states that once events are subjectively perceived to be real, often through imagination and fantasy, then the emotional responses overwhelm objective evidence; and the law of closure proposes that emotions are blind to reason and that they 'know no probabilities . . . they do not weigh likelihoods' (Frijda, 1988). In this sense then, preferences really do direct inferences and emotion does dominate cognition (Zajonc, 1980).

Consumption and the symbolic meaning of goods

As soon as a product's ability to satisfy mere physical need is transcended, then we enter the realm of the symbolic meaning of goods. The functions of the symbolic meanings of products operate in two directions, outward in constructing the social world: *Social-Symbolism*, and inward towards constructing our self-identity: *Self-Symbolism*. This will be explored further in Chapter 3.

If consumers 'identify themselves by the formula: I am = what I have and what I consume' and it is symbolic meaning that is used in the 'search for the meaning of existence' (Fromm, 1976, p. 36), then we can think of the extraction of symbolic meaning from consumption as a powerful motivational force. Symbolic interpretation is essentially non-rational improvization that does not obey the codes of language but operates at the unconscious level. A Jungian analysis goes even further and suggests that the full significance of a symbol cannot be grasped in purely intellectual terms; if it becomes fully definable in rational terms it is no longer a true symbol (Storr, 1973). This suggests that perhaps the function of emotion is to make up for the insufficiency of reason (O'Shaughnessy, 1992) and to help us carry out the vital task of symbolic interpretation so that we can effectively construct an identity and communicate it to others. Thus the symbolic meaning of consumption can be seen as a potent and perhaps prime motivation for emotion-driven choice.

A conceptual model of emotion-driven choice

We can now begin to construct a conceptual model of the process of emotion-driven choice as being motivated by the interpretation of symbolic meaning and the construction of self and social identity. The model is illustrated in Fig. 2.1.

Emotion and preference formation

Self-illusion

The law of apparent reality suggests that imagination and fantasy can overwhelm reason and that the consumer can create their own 'reality'. Campbell (1987) has suggested that modern consumption is active pleasure-seeking, often carried out in a state of 'self-illusory

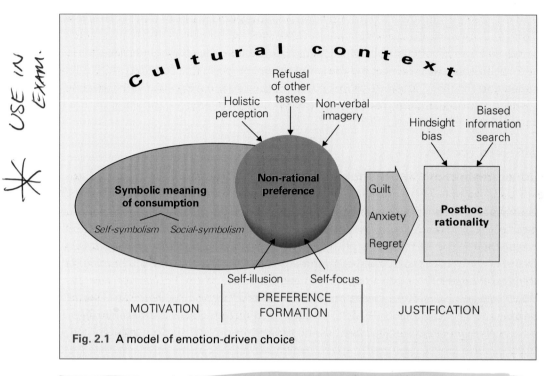

Fig. 2.1 A model of emotion-driven choice

'hedonism', characterized by daydreams where we can 'know something to be false but feel it to be true'. In this state of self-illusion rational beliefs are suspended because they are not strong enough to prevent us enjoying ourselves.

Self-focus

Emotional judgements implicate the self, in that our assessment is more about us than it is about what is being assessed. When evaluating an item of clothing the consumer is likely to be imagining how they would look in the clothing rather than features of the clothing itself. In addition, individuals may frequently use their own emotional state at the time of judgement as a piece of information in a 'How do I feel about it?' heuristic. Rather than computing a judgement on the basis of cognitive evaluation, individuals may instead rely on their present feelings to guide a judgement, such that if they feel positive they make more positive evaluations than when they feel negative. This is particularly likely when the emotional judgement is considered to be overly complex, if it is based on information processing, when there are time constraints, and when there is little other information available.

Holistic perception

The formation of a non-rational preference involves holistic perception, in that we reach an overall evaluation which need not be traceable back to some component attributes. Also when making emotional judgements people tend to 'form sweeping global impressions' rather than engage in analytic reasoning (Schwarz, 1990). In large part, the holistic nature of emotion-driven choice may be a result of our inability to verbalize the reasons for our feelings: 'there simply aren't very effective verbal means to communicate why we like people and objects or what it is about them that we like' (Zajonc, 1980). The way in which we directly experience the world through emotions is different from the system of arbitrary symbols (language) we use to make verbal descriptions. With 'the articulation of our feelings through words we acquire a distance from them, so it is possible to act with respect to our emotions rather than expressing them directly' (Radley, 1988).

Non-verbal imagery

The communication of emotion relies heavily on non-verbal channels, especially facial expression which may have elements of pan-cultural universality (Ekman and Friesen, 1971). The 'vividness effect' evoked by pictures has much more effect on attitudes and behaviour than verbal reports of the same events (Fiske and Taylor, 1984). The iconicity of advertising images (the ability of an image to represent reality by partial similarity or by analogy) means that they can be 'soaked with meaning' by their association with a rich variety of emotions to which we are already attuned through our interactions with our social and natural environments (Messaris, 1997). Thus imagery can allude to many of our past experiences and cultural learning with a potency unavailable to the more restricted channel of language. Imagery interpretation processes are 'subconscious and private in nature' and have 'a latent content that does not appear in overt verbal reports' (Holbrook and Hirschman, 1982).

Refusal of other tastes

Bourdieu (1984) suggests that the basic element in the forming of preference may not be a positive emotional response but a negative one, not to choose that we like most but to reject those that we most dislike. This 'refusal of other tastes' is a powerful force: 'disgust provoked by horror or visceral intolerance (sick-making) of the tastes of others'. When they have to be justified, tastes are asserted purely negatively; and taste is the basis 'of all that one has—people and things—and all that one is for others, whereby one classifies oneself and is classified by others'. The rejection of other people's consumption lifestyles may be one of the strongest barriers between social classes, and is proposed as a fundamental factor in establishing and maintaining social class distinctions. So perhaps consumer choice may often follow from rejection of disliked alternatives, leaving those not rejected as the preferred option. This is particularly likely to be so in the case of goods which carry high levels of social-symbolic meaning. The consumption of these goods is proposed to involve the accumulation of symbolic capital by demonstrating an understanding of class-appropriate style and taste.

Justification of emotion-driven choice

Post hoc rationalization

Zajonc and Markus (1982) have argued that decision research has consistently overestimated the role of cognition in choice because many people believe that they should act rationally and therefore report rational judgement activities that they did not actually use. This ever-present tendency for people to engage in post hoc rationalization is similar to the proposition that 'hedonic consumption acts are based not on what people know to be real but on what they desire reality to be' (Holbrook and Hirschman, 1982).

Another form of post hoc rationalization is described by Zajonc (1980), who suggests that people form a preference first based on emotional response and then justify it to themselves cognitively. It is proposed here that this process, if it occurs at all, is driven by attempts to cope with post-decisional and/or post-purchase feelings of guilt, anxiety and regret.

Guilt, anxiety and regret

The subjective emotional experiences of regret, remorse and self-blame after purchase are facets of consumer guilt (Lascu, 1991). Unfortunately the whole area of post-purchase theory and research is 'still at an early stage' (Gardial *et al.*, 1994) and the role played by emotions has tended to focus on rather simplistic taxonomic and dimensional analyses of consumer satisfaction. Two exceptions are studies of impulse buying which have shown that many impulse buyers subsequently experienced feelings of anxiety and guilt (Rook, 1987), and that when asked about their mood following a recent impulse purchase just as many respondents said they were anxious and guilty (24%) as said they were feeling pleasure and excitement. Consumer guilt has been used in advertising through 'guilt appeals' which attempt to arouse feelings of guilt (or fear of such feelings) and then offer a guilt-reducing solution. Alternatively, advertising may attempt to diminish the importance of guilt by the promotion of a 'guiltless hedonism' (Lascu, 1991). Guilt is a culturally constructed emotion and varies according to the cultural location and the local feeling rules in relation to the self, society and the interdependence of the two (Markus and Kitayama, 1991). Opinions differ as to whether there has been a general decrease in the occurrence of feelings of guilt in response to consumption of luxury goods (Lunt and Livingstone, 1992) or in contrast, an increase in feelings of guilt associated with postmodernity (Giddens, 1991). At the moment there is insufficient data on the subject, but it seems likely that the global growth of consumer culture is associated with a reduction in feelings of guilt, anxiety and regret and as a consequence in the frequency of post hoc rationalization.

Hindsight bias and biased information search

The theory of Motivated Choice (Kunda, 1990) proposes several mechanisms through which post hoc rationalization may affect judgement and choice. Building on evidence that in testing hypotheses people rely on a positive test strategy, that is they seek out instances which are consistent with the hypothesis rather than seeking instances which are inconsistent, it is proposed that a hypothesis-confirmation bias operates and people search out evidence which supports their desired outcome, and will ignore or 'forget' evidence which might disconfirm their hypothesis or desired outcome. A second mechanism is that of hindsight bias, where people maintain a belief that events that happened were bound to happen. In both cases, the underlying mechanism seems to be resistant to the provision of 'rational' information and people will make considerable efforts to defend their emotional judgements against contradictory arguments and go to great lengths to construct seemingly reasonable justifications for their conclusions.

The process of emotion-driven choice

When driven by emotion the process of choice is non-linear in that non-rational preference is formed holistically and faster than cognitive processing, in fact, almost instantly. It may then be followed by attempts at post hoc rationalization. The formation of preference may be driven by the deriving of symbolic meaning for use by the individual in their project of identity construction, or it may be a negative drive emanating from a refusal of other tastes. Once the non-rational preference is formed it tends to drive out further rational evaluation as the emotional responses overwhelm objective evidence and dominate consumer behaviour.

The apparent absence of thoughtful decision-making and unbiased reasoning when consumer choices are driven by emotion may not necessarily be detrimental. It may actually be beneficial, not least because unrealistically positive views of the self and the social environment are often very adaptive. There is evidence that actually thinking about the reasons for preferences may have disruptive effects leading to less optimal choices, and to people being less satisfied with their choices (Wilson and Schooler, 1991).

Emotions and trust

'The ultimate goal of marketing is to generate an intense bond between the consumer and the brand, and the main ingredient of this bond is trust' (Hiscock, 2001), but trust is an elusive concept. A wide variety of conceptualizations have resulted 'in a confusing potpourri of definitions applied to a host of units and level of analysis' (Shapiro, 1987). For Deutsch (1973), trust is a person's willingness to be dependent on another party in the belief that the party will not intentionally disappoint them. Dwyer and Oh (1987) maintain that 'trust refers to a party's expectation that another desires coordination, will fulfill its obligations, and will pull its weight in the relationship'. Bagozzi (1975) sees trust as the degree of perceived validity in the statements or actions of one's partner in a relationship. Shapiro (1987) defines trust as a social relationship in which principals invest resources, authority, or responsibility in another to act on their behalf for some uncertain future return, while Powell (1990) views trust as cooperation that emerges from mutual interests with behaviour standards that no individual can determine alone. Ring and Van de Ven (1994) interpret trust as faith in the moral integrity or goodwill of others and Gulati (1995) defines trust as a type of expectation that alleviates the fear that one's partner will act opportunistically. For Gronroos (1996) trust is cooperation or commitment to a mutual cause.

A sociological theory of trust has been proposed by Luhmann (1979), who argues that there are three modes of asserting expectations about the future based on personal experiences and cultural meaning systems: familiarity, confidence, and trust. Familiarity is a precondition of trust: 'Trust is only possible in a familiar world, it needs history as a

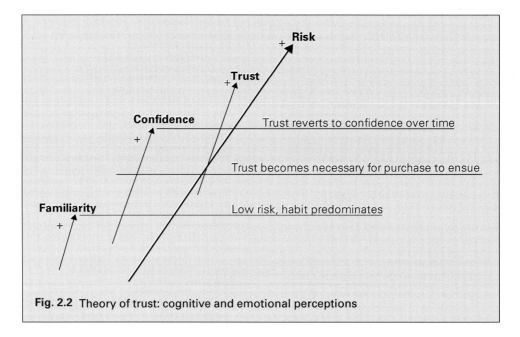

Fig. 2.2 Theory of trust: cognitive and emotional perceptions

reliable background' (p. 20). But trust is required only in situations of high perceived risk; at other times confidence or mere familiarity will suffice for action to ensue. 'One who trusts takes cognizance of the possibility of excessive harm arising from the selectivity of others' actions' and 'a fundamental condition of trust is that it must be possible for the partner to abuse the trust and that the partner must have a considerable interest in doing so' (Luhmann, 1979, p. 24).

In order to relate the active investment of trust to expectations about the future, Möllering (2001) argues that a further element is required to enable the proverbial 'leap of trust', and this is 'suspension'. Suspension is the mechanism of 'bracketing the unknowable', thus making expectations of the future 'momentarily certain'.

Translating this approach to consumer brands, when faced with purchase decisions involving low levels of perceived risk, familiarity (which is a binary division as things are either familiar or they are unfamiliar) will suffice for purchase. At higher levels of perceived risk, confidence is required and this is a mix of cognitive and emotional perceptions, largely based on experience. At high levels of perceived risk trust becomes necessary for purchase to occur and this involves emotional judgements rather than cognitions, and for suspension of fear of the unknowable. With repetition over time risk perceptions reduce and trust reverts to confidence. This is illustrated graphically in Fig. 2.2.

Trust in human relationships

Psychological theory allows us to further model how trust in brands develops over time with experience by analogy with the way that we develop trust within human relationships. Trust in people is seen to evolve out of past experiences and prior interaction and

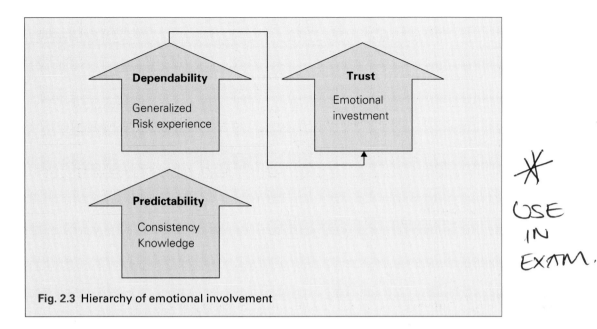

Fig. 2.3 Hierarchy of emotional involvement

develops in stages moving from predictability, to dependability, to trust and eventually sometimes to faith (Rempel *et al.*, 1985). This represents a hierarchy of emotional involvement which reaches trust when people make an emotional involvement in another person. The basic requirements for predictability are some experience of consistency of behaviour from which we can build a knowledge base. Dependability requires further experience and involves a move away from specific behaviours to a more generalized set of beliefs which are invested in the person. This move is likely to depend heavily on the accumulation of evidence from a limited and diagnostic set of experiences involving risk and personal vulnerability. Trust requires a move from reliance on rational cognitions to reliance on emotion and sentiment and a developing intimacy which leads to an investment of emotion in the person. See Fig. 2.3.

A model of trust and confidence in brands

We can draw these models of social trust and human relationships together into an integrative model of trust and consumer brands. See Fig. 2.4.

We can see that the concept of trust is particularly relevant to symbolic brands, with high involvement due to high perceptions of purchase risk.

Functional brands, at the lowest level of perceived risk if they are familiar provide an *easy choice* based on predictability and credibility. With increased risk functional brands provide a *safe choice* through confidence which allows consumers to depend on them. Symbolic brands in markets with high perceived risk need to provide *trust*, which is achieved through developing perceptions of consumer-brand intimacy and emotional investment, and this will be discussed further in Chapter 7.

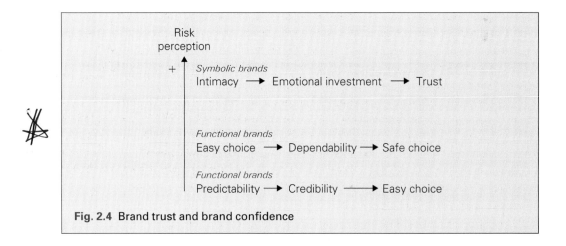

Fig. 2.4 Brand trust and brand confidence

Emotional brand associations

Up to this point we have been concerned with the role of emotion as socially or culturally constructed, and its mediating effect upon choice and behaviour. Now we will address the role emotional associations *with* brands play in informing effective strategic planning. Everyone holds in non-declarative emotional memory emotional associations with memories. This means people have emotional associations with brands that have grown out of their experiences with them, and they are linked in memory to those brands.

When a memory is recalled, all the component parts of that memory, including the emotional associations, are reunited. When a person thinks about a brand, they will be drawing from memory not only its cognitive associations such as benefits or features, but also their emotional 'feelings' about the brand. Measuring the emotions associated with a brand provides the manager with a powerful tool for better understanding their brand because these emotional associations will inform how people process information about the brand.

We discussed earlier that emotion is likely to be part of a neural system that is independent of those generally associated with higher-order cognitive processes. But as it happens, secondary emotions appear to be highly integrated with cognitive processes. Primarily, emotion is centred in the amygdala, which is an important part of the limbic system. It is here that the link to higher-order cognitive process is made. The limbic system, while sometimes debated in the specific, is generally understood to be the controlling factor in processing both emotional and cognitive information. Within the limbic system, the hippocampus is concerned with cognitive processing and the amygdala with emotional processing.

Emotion, interacting with declarative memory (what we are conscious of), plays a role in motivating deliberate plans of action rather than triggering the rapid, reflex-like responses that proceed out-of-consciousness. They are likely to be integrated into cognitive processing that leads to more long-term planning or decisions. In a sense, this is consistent with the evolutionary neuropsychology idea that there is an adaptive value in having such emotional feelings because they can be important to long-term planning, explicit processing systems, especially where there are too many factors to be easily handled at a cognitive level (Rolls, 1999). So, even though emotions are not a part of cognitive neural systems, they are nonetheless integrated into the cognitive processing of information. In a very real sense it is emotion that 'frames' conscious cognitive processing.

An interesting study using functional magnetic resonance imaging (fMRI) investigated the influence of implicit memory (i.e. unconscious, non-cognitive memory) on brand choice (Deppe *et al.*, 2005). What they found was an integration of previous emotional experience with a brand into ongoing decision processing. In fact, when someone made a choice of their favourite brand, it was characterized by reduced activation of the cognitive areas of the brain associated with working memory and reasoning and increased activation in areas involved in processing of emotions. Later in Chapter 5 we will be discussing another study using fMRI that shows when someone is choosing between Coke and Pepsi, and they know what they are drinking, those whose favourite brand is Coke are only using those areas of the brain associated with emotional memory when stating their preference. But when people do not know what they are drinking, only those areas of the brain involved with taste are active. There is no doubt that emotion is involved in brand choice.

While positive emotional memories will never override negative cognitive associations in brand choice decisions, in all other cases the emotion will provide a positive feeling as information about a brand is being processed, or when someone is thinking about it. As a result, the emotional significance of a brand will influence how much attention is paid to it, and how much someone will elaborate upon its significance. It also means that emotional associations with brands will determine what information is potentially available for recall when making brand choice decisions.

Fortunately, it is possible to measure the emotion associated with a brand (Percy *et al.*, 2004). With that information in hand, a manager is better able to address issues of positioning and marketing communication because the emotional associations with a brand will inform how people will process information about it. Consider the results of a study that measured the emotional associations with three shampoo brands shown in Table 2.1. The numbers in the table reflect the overall strength of the emotional associations (other data identified the specific emotions involved).

Table 2.1 Emotional intensity measures for shampoo brands

Brand	Net Strength
Dove	0.742
Head & Shoulders	−0.099
Sanex	1.281

Table 2.2 Emotional intensity measures for shampoo brands: users vs. non-users

Brand	Net Strength
Dove User	0.910
Dove Non-User	0.832
Head & Shoulders User	2.650
Head & Shoulders Non-User	−0.525
Sanex User	1.694
Sanex Non-User	1.133

There are strong emotional associations with Sanex and Dove, but a negative emotional association with Head & Shoulders. But if we look at the strength of the emotional associations with each brand broken out between users vs. non-users of each brand, we see something much different (Table 2.2).

We see that *users* of Head & Shoulders, far from holding negative emotional associations with the brand, hold very strong positive feelings. On the other hand, the emotional strength for Sanex and Dove does not differ significantly between users and non-users. Strategically, this has critical implications. It suggests that attracting switchers to Head & Shoulders will be very difficult until the negative associations held by non-users are changed. But with Sanex and Dove, because everyone holds positive feelings for these brands, switching will be much easier.

Implications for brand strategy

As emotion is socially constructed, we learn the feeling rules appropriate for our culture through the socialization process. One of the social roles of advertising is in educating consumers how to feel about products and services, and this is exemplified in the current move towards 'emotionalizing' many product categories. For example, instant coffee and luxury ice-cream have both been repositioned successfully as products with romantic/ sexual connotations. This suggests that it is possible to 'emotionalize' products which have little rational connection with powerful emotions. This will be discussed in relation to symbolic brand strategy in Chapter 7. However, when marketing across borders, care must be taken to ensure that an emotional positioning strategy is culturally appropriate.

As emotion-driven choice is an almost instantaneous process, it is imperative for marketers to ensure that there are no impediments to immediate purchase. In some cultures, and with some product categories, it may be necessary to provide consumers with rational evidence to support their emotion-driven choice, either during or post-purchase. This will be discussed in relation to low-involvement brand strategy in Chapter 8.

As already noted, the emotional associations with a brand that people hold in memory will influence how they process information about that brand. Profiling the emotions linked to a brand vs. competitors will help guide the development of more effective positioning and marketing communication programmes for that brand. The ability to measure these emotional associations also means managers can track changes in them, or their strength in response to marketing and communication programmes.

CHAPTER SUMMARY

In this chapter we have explored the complexity of emotions and how the symbolic meaning of consumption is fundamental to understanding the ability of brands to communicate social, psychological and cultural messages. Trust is an emotional factor in brands and we have shown how it develops over time. It is possible to emotionalize a product or service that has little rational connection with emotions, and we explore these issues further in the next two chapters.

DISCUSSION QUESTIONS

1   Why is it important to understand the socio-cultural environment in which a brand is marketed?

2   Why might the symbolic meaning of brands be a prime motivation for emotion-driven choice?

3   How is the formation of non-rational preference influenced by perception?

4   How is the 'refusal of other tastes' involved in consumer choice?

5   How might post hoc rationalization reduce feelings of guilt?

6   Why and how do consumers invest trust in a brand?

7   How do consumers build emotional associations with a brand?

CASE STUDY

Glenfiddich: Starting over

Glenfiddich is the leading malt whisky in the UK and has shown considerable growth in the past decade. Although Glenfiddich sales had plateaued within the context of the imperilled whisky market, the future looked rather grim.

Glenfiddich had an insurmountably strong position. The brand had world-wide ubiquity; it had Scottish authenticity; it commanded admiration from many consumers; the name was evocative; the pack was distinctive; and the parent company, William Grant & Sons, was well regarded. However, Glenfiddich's strengths could also paradoxically be taken as failings: it was too well known to be a malt drinker's malt and too precious to be a blended drinker's drink. It therefore hung in between these two categories, lacking a clear, identifiable persona. Despite the brand having a distinctive identity, it lacked the emotion that provides personality. More significantly, Glenfiddich was unavoidably tied to the ailing world of whisky. The category was losing its 'younger' entrants and some of its existing loyalists.

Whisky has a challenging taste: a taste that conventionally is acquired over time. This is even more visible in the case of malts because malt drinkers are likely to be old. Given that young spirit drinkers are particularly promiscuous and are not inclined to give a product any length of time, malt whiskies are not likely to be included in their repertoire. In addition, malt brands have traditionally been wary of extending their reach beyond the confines of the niche malt market. Most have battled to occupy this territory, employing conservative strategies based on heritage and tradition. Advertising innovation and radicality was rare. In the end they perpetuated the market's problems: malt whisky was not only in decline but also particularly unable to touch the drinkers' heart.

Glenfiddich's research confirmed this fact and showed how respondents seemed resistant to extend their perceptions and usage of malt whisky. To be included in a spirits portfolio a brand needs identity, authentic credentials, appropriate packaging, a perceived usage and image benefit, and a differentiated personality. Consumers, even though identifying a Glenfiddich image, could not offer a usable personality because the brand's imagery was irrelevant at best and anachronistic at worst. Respondents had little to gain by, or to feel from, being seen with the brand. Glenfiddich was suffering from an increasing irrelevance to younger drinkers.

To attract younger drinkers Glenfiddich could have simply taken the existing product and brand attributes and represented them in a contemporary form. However, it would be counter-productive to try *too hard* to change pre-ordained attitudes to whisky. There were two potential problems with this. First, there was a credibility gap, such that the consumer would not accept the new claim. And second, the strategy was too obvious, communicating desperation rather than renaissance. Glenfiddich had to remain true to the brand. A better solution was to accept the deeply held truths that exist about the product (and this brand) and turn them (via a powerful emotional connection) into something motivating and 'moving': to get the consumer *emotionally* involved.

What Glenfiddich was looking for was a deep-seated and relevant emotion that could credibly be linked to Glenfiddich. This linkage, it was felt, might allow the brand to gain the sort of appropriate personality and imagery-edge currently lacking or misplaced. In order to find the proper linkage, Glenfiddich needed to focus on the mind-set of its target audience. The primary target group was BC 1 males, aged 25–40. They didn't feel as old as their birth certificate would say they were and in their hearts they felt as if they were in their mid 20's and just in the beginning of their lives. Whisky and its imagery had never touched their lives and they would feel awkward if ordering a Glenfiddich.

> 'Glenfiddich is not for me. It was for my father, it is for older men. Maybe one day it will be my drink but for the moment, I've no reason to be making the effort.'

However, the exploration of masculinity in search of a universal emotional truth found that it was not the product that was questionable but rather the male psyche in every form. On the other hand, their actual life (steady jobs, marriage, children, etc.) reflected the fact that a youthful spirit could coexist with responsibility and maturity. The fact that they were growing up was no longer treated with regret, provoking them to desperately reach for the badges of youth, but rather inspired a calm and collective enthusiasm about having entered a new chapter in their lives. It is at this juncture that they began examining the badges of the older generation with caution and suspicious acceptance.

The universal truth that emerged from Glenfiddich's trip into the male psyche was that sons don't get to know and really value their fathers as men until it's late on in life. When they do, they become frighteningly aware of their mortality. Many men assume that the reason they gradually become friends with their fathers is because their fathers have changed and suddenly become 'younger' in outlook. However, it is their own maturity that allows them to see their fathers as real men. The tragedy of discovering the man behind the father after his death is a constant theme in popular culture. 'The wasted years' is a phrase closely associated with the father–son relationship. Effectively, tolerance and pride towards one's father is a sign of personal pride, confidence, and maturity.

'And in this new light, all of a sudden a lot of things that he values make sense now. They're not the dated totems of a father, there for rejection by the son: they're simply the tastes and habits of a man like me. And that's a very good reason to get to appreciate them for myself while I've got time.'

Glenfiddich can be credibly attached to this myth: it is seen as the drink of our fathers, a symbol of their values that we come to cherish. *Because it's your father's drink, it should also mean something to you.* More importantly, it is credible to attach the brand to an optimistic, even aspirational definition of maturity. *Coming to appreciate your father is a sign of maturity and confidence so the faster it happens, the better.*

In this sense Glenfiddich was making the product relevant to the male mind-set not by challenging the conventional wisdom about it but rather by reversing the negative connotations attached to that conventional wisdom. It is all a matter of perspective conditioned by emotion versus sentiment.

The creative strategy was to capture the drama and emotional intensity of a key moment in the father–son relationship imbued with the realization of mortality and attach to it the Glenfiddich brand. The ad had the filmic values of quality contemporary cinema but also employed the cinematic legacy of whisky (dark, misty, exuding a broody emotional feel). The brand merely attached itself in a background role to the ad just as Jack Daniel's had attached itself to countless films which have touched our lives. It was through this subtle association that the brand would be imbued with the qualities of the occasion-experience itself. There would be no need to explicitly integrate the product in the ad as long as the tone of the ad reflected the nature of the product.

After the ad was on the air, agreement with the key statement 'a brand I can see myself drinking nowadays' increased from 0.60 to 0.79 in the test region, but declined from 0.73 to 0.51 in the control non-advertised region. Advertised regions saw a higher increase in rate-of-sale. This result demonstrated that the ad worked quite well. Glenfiddich and its values remained unchanged but the context in which it was placed illuminated the product and these values from a new angle.

Source: WARC, Creative Planning Awards 1997, Glenfiddich: Starting over, Author: not credited

Edited by Hazel H. Huang

Discussion Questions

1 What are the advantages and disadvantages of keeping Glenfiddich's brand values and of changing its brand/product perceptions completely?

2 Why did Glenfiddich decide to remain 'true' to its brand, as opposed to reviving the brand by abandoning the whisky traditions?

3 What is the symbolic interpretation of drinking Glenfiddich before and after its advertisement focusing on the father–son relationship?

4 Glenfiddich emphasized emotional relevance for its creative strategy. Why is relevance important to consumers' emotional bonding with a brand? How did it work in Glenfiddich's case?

FURTHER READING

- A review of the role of emotion in a wide range of information-processing activities is provided by Chaudhuri, A. (2006), *Emotion and Reason in Consumer Behaviour*, Oxford: Butterworth-Heinemann.

- The psychology of emotion is explored in detail by Strongman, K. (2003), *Psychology of Emotion: From Everyday Life to Theory*, London: John Wiley.

- The evidence that reason and emotion are closely linked is argued from a solid base in neuroscientific research by Damasio, A. (2006), Descartes' Error: Emotion, Reason and the Human Brain, London: Penguin.

REFERENCES

Arnould, E. and Price, L. (1993), 'River magic: extraordinary experience and the extended service encounter', *Journal of Consumer Research*, 20, 24–45.

Bagozzi, R. (1975), 'Marketing as exchange', *Journal of Marketing*, 39, 4, 32–40.

Bourdieu, P. (1984), *Distinction: A Social Critique of the Judgement of Taste* (R. Nice, trans.), London: Routledge.

Bradley, M.M. and Lang, P.J. (2000), 'Measuring emotion: behaviour, feeling, and physiology', in R.D. Lane and L. Nalel (eds.), *Cognitive Neuroscience of Emotion*, Oxford: Oxford University Press, pp. 242–76.

Campbell, C. (1987), *The Romantic Ethic and the Spirit of Modern Consumerism*, Oxford: Blackwell.

Damasio, A. (1999), *The Feeling of What Happens*, New York: Harcourt.

Deppe, M., Scheindt, W., Kugel, H., Plassman, H., and Kenning, P. (2005), 'Nonlinear responses within the medial prefrontal cortex reveal where specific implicit information influences economic decision making', *Journal of Neuroimaging*, 15, 171–82.

Deutsch, M. (1973), *The Resolution of Conflict: Constructive and Destructive Processes*, New Haven: Yale University Press.

Dwyer, F.R. and Oh, S. (1987), 'Output sector munificence effects on the internal political economy of marketing channels', *Journal of Marketing Research*, 4, 347–58.

Eichenbaum, H. (2002), *The Cognitive Neuroscience of Memory*, Oxford: Oxford University Press.

Ekman, P. (1992), 'Facial expressions of emotion: new findings, new questions', *Psychological Science*, 3, 1, 34–38.

—— and Friesen, W.V. (1971), 'Constants across cultures in the face and emotion', *Journal of Personality and Social Psychology*, 17, 124–29.

Elliott, R. (1998), 'A model of emotion-driven choice', *Journal of Marketing Management*, 14, 1–3, 95–108.

Fiske, S. and Taylor, S. (1984), *Social Cognition*, New York: Random House.

Frijda, N. (1988), 'The laws of emotion', *American Psychologist*, 43, 5, 349–58.

Fromm, E. (1976), *To Have Or To Be*, London: Routledge and Kegan Paul.

Gabriel, Y. and Lang, T. (1995), *The Unmanageable Consumer: Contemporary Consumption and Its Fragmentations*, London: Sage.

Gardial, S., Clemons, S., Woodruff, B., and Burns, M. (1994), 'Comparing consumers' recall of prepurchase and postpurchase product evaluation experiences', *Journal of Consumer Research*, 20, 548–60.

Giddens, A. (1991), *Modernity and Self-Identity: Self and Society in the Late Modern Age*, Cambridge: Polity Press.

Griffiths, P.E. (1997), *What Emotions Really Are*, Chicago: The University of Chicago Press.

Gronroos, C. (1996), 'Relationship marketing: strategic and tactical implications', *Management Decision*, 34, 3, 5–15.

Gulati, R. (1995), 'Does familiarity breed trust? The implications of repeated ties for contractual choice in alliances', *Academy of Management Journal*, 38, 1, 85–112.

Harré, R. (ed.) (1986), *The Social Construction of Emotions*, Oxford: Basil Blackwell.

Hiscock, J. (2001), 'Most trusted brands', *Marketing*, March, 32–33.

Hochschild, A.R. (1983), *The Managed Heart: Commercialization of Human Feeling*, Berkeley: University of California Press.

Holbrook, M. and Hirschman, E. (1982), 'The experiential aspects of consumption: consumer fantasies, feelings, and fun', *Journal of Consumer Research*, 9, 132–40.

Kunda, Z. (1990), 'The case for motivated reasoning', *Psychological Bulletin,* 108, 480–98.

Lane, R. (2000), 'Neural correlates of conscious emotional experience,' in R.D. Lane and L. Nadel (eds.), *Cognitive Neuroscience of Emotion*, Oxford: Oxford University Press.

Lascu, D. (1991), 'Consumer guilt: examining the potential of a new marketing construct', *Advances in Consumer Research*, 18, 290–95.

Lazarus, R.S. (1982), 'Thoughts on the relation between emotion and cognition', *American Psychologist*, 37, 1019–24.

Luhmann, N. (1979), *Trust and Power*, Chichester: John Wiley & Sons.

Lunt, P. and Livingstone, S. (1992), *Mass Consumption and Personal Identity*, Milton Keynes: Open University Press.

Markus, H. and Kitayama, S. (1991), 'Culture and the self: implications for cognition, emotion, and motivation', *Psychological Review*, 98, 2, 224–53.

Messaris, P. (1997), *Visual Persuasion: The Role of Images in Advertising*, Thousand Oaks: Sage Publications.

Mittal, B. (1988), 'The role of affective choice mode in the consumer purchase of expressive products', *Journal of Economic Psychology*, 9, 499–524.

Möllering, G. (2001), 'The nature of trust: from Georg Simmel to a theory of expectation, interpretation and suspension', *Sociology*, 35, 2, 403–20.

Murphy, S. and Zajonc, R. (1993), 'Affect, cognition, and awareness: affective priming with suboptimal and optimal stimuli', *Journal of Personality and Social Psychology*, 64, 723–39.

Obermiller, C. (1990), 'Feelings about feeling state research: a search for harmony', *Advances in Consumer Research,* 17, 590–3.

O'Shaughnessy, J. (1992), *Explaining Buyer Behavior: Central Concepts and Philosphy of Science Issues*, New York: Oxford University Press.

Parkinson, B. (1995), *Ideas and Realities of Emotion*, London: Routledge.

Parkinson, B., Fisher, A.H., and Manstead, A.S.R. (2005), *Emotions in Social Relations*, New York: Psychology Press.

Percy, L., Hansen, F., and Randrup, R. (2004), 'How to measure brand emotion', *Admap*, November, 32–34.

Powell, W.W. (1990),'Neither market nor hierarchy: network forms of organizations', *Research in Organizational Behavior*, 12, 295–336.

Radley, A. (1988), 'The social form of feeling', *British Journal of Social Psychology*, 27, 5–18.

Rempel, J., Holmes, J., and Zanna, M. (1985), 'Trust in close relationships', *Journal of Personality and Social Psychology*, 49, 1, 95–112.

Ring, P.S. and Van de Ven, A. (1994), 'Development processes of cooperative interorganizational relationships', *Academy of Management Review*, 19, 90–118.

Rolls, E.T. (1999), *The Brain and Emotion*, Oxford: Oxford University Press.

Rook, D. (1987) 'The buying impulse', *Journal of Consumer Research*, 14, 189–99.

Scherer, K.R. (2000), 'Psychological models of emotion', in J.C. Borod (ed.), *The Neuropsychology of Emotions*, New York: Oxford University Press, pp. 139–62.

Schwarz, N. (1990), 'Feelings as information', in E.T. Higgins and R. Sorrentino (eds.), *Handbook of Motivation and Cognition: Foundations of Social Behavior*, Vol. 2, New York: Guildford Press.

Shapiro, S.P. (1987), 'The social control of impersonal trust', *American Journal of Sociology*, 93, 623–58.

Shweder, R.A. (1993), 'The cultural psychology of emotions', in M. Lewis and J.M. Haviland (eds.), *Handbook of Emotions*, New York: Guilford Press, pp. 417–34.

Storr, A. (1973), *Jung*, London: Fontana.

Wilson, T.D. and Schooler, J. W. (1991), 'Thinking too much: introspection can reduce the quality of preferences and decisions', *Journal of Personality and Social Psychology*, 60, 2, 181–92.

Yamasaki, H., Labor, K., and McCathy, G. (2002), 'Dissociable prefrontal brain systems for attention and emotion', *Proceedings of the National Academy of Sciences USA*, 99, 11447–51.

Zajonc, R. (1980), 'Feeling and thinking: preferences need no inferences', *American Psychologist*, 35, 151–75.

—— and Markus, H. (1982), 'Affective and cognitive factors in preferences', *Journal of Consumer Research*, 9, 2, 123–32.

The Symbolic Meaning of Brands

→ **KEY CONCEPTS**

1 Brands can be used as symbolic resources for the construction and maintenance of identity/identities.

2 Advertising can build symbolic meaning through narratives.

3 Brands can help establish and communicate some of the fundamental cultural categories.

4 Brands can also be used to counter some of the threats to identity posed by postmodernity.

5 Brands can acquire deep meaning through the socialization process.

Introduction

Contemporary social theory has begun to focus on consumption as playing a central role in the way in which the social world is constructed and developments in post-structural anthropology have led to a renewed interest in the relationship between society and material culture. These trends can be subsumed into the development of postmodern theories of consumer culture which focus on aspects of cultural practice in the construction of consumer society rather than just on consumption itself. The implications for the marketing of brands under conditions of postmodernity are that many assumptions about the consumer and consumption require fundamental reassessment.

The postmodern consumer and symbolic meaning

Central to postmodernism is the recognition that the consumer does not make consumption choices solely from products' utilities, that is, what they actually do, but also from their symbolic meanings, that is, what they communicate. The functions of the symbolic meanings of brands operate in two directions, outward in constructing the social world: *Social-Symbolism,* and inward towards constructing our self-identity: *Self-Symbolism.* The social-symbolic meanings of brands can be used to communicate to other people the kind of person we wish to be seen as. For example, an ad for Seiko watches says very plainly: 'It's not your shoes, it's not your tie, it's not your car, it's your watch that says most about who you are'. More subtly and with a touch of postmodern irony, Volkswagen ran a TV campaign for the Golf in the UK which showed a series of vignettes where a man showed off a large gold watch with the subtitle 'I'm loaded', a man sat at a pavement café reading a serious book with the subtitle 'I'm an intellectual', a skinhead was seen with a ferocious dog with the subtitle saying 'I'm hard'. The final scene was a young man in jeans and a t-shirt getting into a Golf with the subtitle 'I'm just going down the shops'. The sign-off was 'VW Golf, a car not a label'. The self-symbolic meaning of brands is what their usage communicates to us about who we are or want to be. For example, an ad for Baldessanini men's fragrance from Hugo Boss says 'Separates the men from the boys'. As consumption plays a central role in supplying meanings and values for the creation and maintenance of the consumer's personal and social world, which is one definition of what constitutes a consumer society, so advertising is recognized as one of the major sources of these symbolic meanings. These cultural meanings are transferred to brands and it is brands which are often used as symbolic resources for the construction and maintenance of identity.

This semiotic perspective of products as symbols (which is explored in more detail in Chapter 4) raises difficult questions about the location of cultural meaning. The term symbol itself can relate to the product that carries meaning or to the meaning it carries, and the interpretation of meaning is a complex product of what is contained in the representation and what the individual brings to the representation. Symbolism can be analysed semiotically by examination of the system of signs and what they signify; however, it has been realized that this leads to an infinite regress as one sign leads to another without there

IT'S NOT YOUR SHOES.

IT'S NOT YOUR TIE.

IT'S NOT YOUR CAR.

IT'S YOUR WATCH THAT

SAYS MOST ABOUT WHO YOU ARE.

ARCTURA
KINETIC
CHRONOGRAPH
TITANIUM

POWERED BY THE MOVEMENT OF YOUR BODY.
NEVER NEEDS A BATTERY.
TITANIUM CASE AND BRACELET.
STRONGER THAN STEEL AND 40% LIGHTER.

SEIKO

www.seiko.co.uk
01628 770988

Image supplied by Seiko UK Limited

ever being anything 'real' outside the system. All meaning is socially constructed and there is no essential external reference point, so ultimately 'There is nothing outside the text' (Derrida, 1977). To complicate matters further, symbolic interpretation is essentially non-rational improvization that does not obey the codes of language but operates at the subconscious level. A Jungian (or unconscious) analysis goes even further and suggests that the full significance of a symbol cannot be grasped in purely intellectual terms, for if it becomes fully definable in rational terms it is no longer a true symbol. This implies that a brand may be imbued with a particular symbolic meaning by the organization but that this is not necessarily what consumers interpret the brand as meaning. As we discuss in Chapter 4, consumers may even appropriate the meaning of a brand to serve their own sub-cultural purposes.

Consumption of the symbolic meaning of products is a social process that helps make visible and stable the basic categories of a culture which are under constant change, and consumption choices 'become a vital source of the culture of the moment' (Douglas and Isherwood, 1978). The meanings of consumer goods are grounded in their social context and the demand for goods derives more from their role in cultural practices rather than from the satisfaction of simple human needs. Consumer goods, then, are more than just objects of economic exchange, 'they are goods to think with, goods to speak with' (Fiske, 1989) and are an important part of the symbols and signs which we use to locate ourselves in our society. Consumption as a cultural practice is one way of participating in social life and may be an important element in cementing social relationships, whilst the whole system of consumption is an expression of the existing social structure through a seductive process which pushes the purchasing impulse until it reaches the 'limits of economic potential' (Baudrillard, 1988). It is within this social context that the individual uses consumer goods and the consumption process as the materials with which to construct and maintain an identity, form relationships and frame psychological events. Thus we need to understand ecology of a brand, how it integrates with the wider social and cultural experiences of the consumer. We will discuss brand ecology further in Chapter 7.

The postmodern consumer and identity

The self is conceptualized in postmodern consumer culture not as a given product of a social system nor as a fixed entity which the individual can simply adopt, but as something the person actively creates, partially through consumption. The consumer exercises free will to form images of who and what s/he wants to be, although, paradoxically, 'free will' is directed by values which are probably also a social product. Thompson (1995, p. 210) describes the self as a *symbolic project*, which the individual must actively construct out of the available symbolic materials, materials which 'the individual weaves into a coherent account of who he or she is, a narrative of self-identity'.

The individual visualizes her/his self according to their imagined possibilities of the self. Markus and Nurius (1986) suggest that 'an individual is free to create any variety of possible selves, yet the pool of possible selves derives from the categories made salient by the individual's particular socio-cultural and historical context and from the models, images, and symbols provided by the media and by the individual's immediate social experiences'. Thus the nature of the self-concept is complex: the consumer may possess a variety of actual selves (or roles) and a variety of possible or ideal selves. If the consumer possesses a multiplicity of role identities, how can these multiple selves coexist in harmony? How does each identity develop? And how does the consumer express each self in a particular social situation? We live in a symbol-rich environment and the meaning attached to any situation or object is determined by the interpretation of these symbols. Through the socialization process the consumer learns not only to agree on shared meanings of some symbols but also to develop individual symbolic interpretations of his/her own. The consumer uses these symbolic meanings to construct, maintain and express each of her/his multiple identities. Here lies enormous potential for brands to offer an identity or self image that a consumer can buy into by adopting the brand as being symbolic for them, saying something that they want to be associated with.

Narrative identity theory suggests that in order to make time human and socially shared, we require a narrative identity for our self, that is, we make sense of ourselves and our lives by the stories we can (or cannot) tell. Thus we come to know ourselves by the narratives we construct to situate ourselves in time and place. This task can be greatly aided by symbolic resources; the main one articulated by Ricoeur (1977) is literature which gives structure and meaning to the complexity and confusion of life by providing a causal model for the individual by linking disparate life events into a coherent sequence. However, advertising can also be used as a symbolic resource for the construction of narratives to give sense to our life history and personal situation: the soap opera is still a mainstay of advertising executions which situates the brand and the consumer in a powerful representation of narrative sequence. This is exemplified in the Love over Gold case study.

The development of individual self-identity is inseparable from the parallel development of collective social identity, and this problematic relationship has been described as the *internal-external dialectic of identification* by Jenkins (1996), who maintains that self-identity must be validated through social interaction and that the self is embedded in social practices. This means that there is always a social dimension to a brand; an individual may love a brand's image, but will want his/her important others to like it too. This is particularly true of adolescents who are actively building their identity in relation to their peer group and are very sensitive to peer-group approval or disapproval. Endeavours to create the consumer's self-identity often involve the consumption of products, services, and media and there is always a tension between the meanings we construct for ourselves and those we are exposed to socially; this dialectical tension requires active negotiation of meaning. Dittmar (1992) comments that 'material possessions have a profound symbolic significance for their owners, as well as for other people and the symbolic meanings of our belongings are an integral feature of expressing our own identity and perceiving the identity of others'. The key point here is that not only do we interpret the symbolic meanings of other people's possessions but at the same time they are interpreting ours in a complex process of symbolic meaning construction and communication. Although McCracken (1988) suggests that ritual is the prime means for the transfer of symbolic meaning from goods to the person, the complex social practices of consumer culture extend far beyond the concept of the ritualistic, and entail a reciprocal, dialectical relationship between the individual and her/his cultural milieu.

Identity and self-symbolic consumption

All voluntary consumption carries, either consciously, subconsciously, or unconsciously symbolic meanings; if the consumer has choices to consume, s/he will consume things that hold particular symbolic meanings. These meanings may be idiosyncratic or widely shared with other people. For example, using recycled envelopes may symbolize 'I care for the environment', going to classical concerts may symbolize 'I am cultured', while supporting gay rights may signify 'I am open-minded', or buying unbranded detergent may mean 'I am a clever consumer'.

A considerable literature suggests that the consumer is what s/he has, since her/his possessions are viewed as major parts of her/his extended self (Belk, 1988). Csikszentmihalyi and Rochberg-Halton (1981) suggest that the consumer invests 'psychic energy' such as effort, time, and attention in an object. This energy and its products are regarded as a part of the self because they have grown or emerged from the self. To an extent, then, our possessions are as much a part of us as our limbs or our ideas. The symbolic meanings of the consumer's possessions may portray essences of her/his individuality, or reflect her/his desirable connections with others (Kleine *et al.*, 1995), and symbolic consumption helps the consumer to categorize her/himself in society, to ease her/his self-transitions and to achieve her/his sense of continuity and eventually preparation for death. How people dispose of their possessions through wills and direct gifts is an important part of preparing to die and the symbolic meaning of a gift from a now-dead relative lives on in many of our homes with items of pure sentimental value.

Possessions can also be part of a process of symbolic self-completion, where individuals who perceive themselves as lacking a personal quality attempt to fill this gap using symbolic resources (Wicklund and Gollwitzer, 1982). This offers huge potential for brands as we may not be able to actually achieve our desired image, say as a thrusting successful manager, but we can buy part of the image through using and displaying brands that we believe to have the appropriate symbolic meaning, e.g. the *Financial Times* and a Blackberry WiFi device.

Although the consumer learns and develops consumption symbols through socialization processes and exposures to mass media (e.g. advertising), it does not mean that everybody who possesses the same product bought it for the same symbolic meaning. A product may carry a varied range of meanings since the creation of meaning is not deterministic and unidirectional, and each individual may ascribe different and inconsistent cultural meanings to a product depending on the extent to which they share the collective imagination. This means that we can get the symbolism wrong, that is, we can misjudge the meaning of a brand, especially in the area of culturally significant goods where taste is an arbiter of appropriateness. For example, a gold Rolex watch may carry a potent symbolic meaning of success for one sub-cultural group or social class, but may signify significant lack of taste to another group.

Lived vs. mediated experience

The symbolic resources available to the individual for the construction of the self can be distinguished as being either lived experiences or mediated experiences. Lived experience refers to the practical activities and face-to-face encounters in our everyday lives. It is situated, immediate, and is largely non-reflexive, in that we take it for granted as 'reality'. Mediated experience is an outcome of a mass-communication culture and the consumption of media products and involves the ability to experience events which are spatially and temporally distant from the practical context of daily life. It is recontextualized experience, in that it allows the experience of events that transpire far away, and will vary widely in its relevance to the self. The individual can draw selectively on mediated experience and interlace it with lived experience to construct the self. The life history and social situation of individuals will lead to differential valorization of forms of experience, varying between those at one end of the continuum who value only lived experience and have little contact with mediated forms, and others at the opposite end of the continuum for whom mediated experience has become central to the project of the self. However, central to postmodern consumer culture is a growing range of opportunities for the use of mediated experiences in the project of the self, countless narratives of self-formation, countless visions of the world such that we may be encountering 'symbolic overload' (Thompson, 1995, p. 216). This means that the battle for mindspace is not only about levels of brand awareness but also about competing visions and narratives of identity that are offered to the market. We will discuss this further in Chapter 7.

Symbolic meaning, advertising and brands

Advertising is recognized as one of the most potent sources of valorized symbolic meanings. As a part of a cultural system, advertising is viewed as a guideline to map out all aspects of the consumer's existence; on the other hand, all aspects of the consumer's existence are also guidelines to map out advertising creativity. The relationship between advertising and the consumer is dialectical: advertising not only helps in creating, modifying, and transforming cultural meanings for the consumer (Lannon and Cooper, 1983), but also represents cultural meanings taken from the consumer's world view and invested into the advertised product. This dialectical relationship drives a cyclical flow of symbolic meanings derived from culture and transferred into the semiotic world of advertising, then interpreted and used by the consumer to construct internally her/his self-concept and externally her/his social world. 'Finally as part of the external construction of an individual's life world the meaning returns back to its original starting point, the mass of flowing meanings that represents culture' (Ritson and Elliott, 1995). Thus, advertising is both a means to transfer or create meanings into culture and a cultural product itself.

Although advertisers aim to create particular meanings for their brands in advertising, meanings interpreted by the consumer may be varied and diverse. There is growing recognition that the consumer is an active and participating audience (Mick and Buhl, 1992).

The consumer may attend only to certain messages and interpret or make sense of the meanings according to her/his personal perception and her/his social knowledge. The meaning of a particular advertisement is not given within the advertisement itself, for as Anderson and Meyer (1988) point out: 'meaning is not delivered in the communication process, rather it is constructed within it'. But the meaning that consumers construct from advertising is viscous in nature, it is not firm and finalized but liable to change, and signification through the media is likely to be much less potent than signification through actual behavioural experience (Elliott *et al.*, 1993). Certainly, there is considerable empirical evidence that attitudes formed through direct experience are stronger, more accessible, held more confidently and are more predictive of behaviour than those derived from mediated experience through advertising (e.g. Fazio and Zanna, 1978). Thus lived experience with a brand, through purchase and usage over the lifecycle, will tend to dominate the mediated experience of advertising, and both forms of experience will be validated through social interaction, particularly for brands with a social-symbolic positioning.

Identity and social-symbolic consumption

The creation of meanings does not just consist of a negotiation process between advertising text, the brand, and the consumer only during the period of exposure to the advertisement. Since advertising is a form of mass communication, its meanings also emerge in the interpersonal communication among consumers and may later become socially shared meaning: 'Shared meanings involving media content will arise among participants in the social action performances of reception and subsequent accommodation' (Anderson and Meyer, 1988, p. 47). Yet, these meanings are not solid, but remain viscous and tentative. A variety of meanings are created as outcomes of the consumer's personal interest-driven, culturally situated act of advertising interpretation (Mick and Buhl, 1992) and their brand ecology.

The issues of cultural meaning and interactive advertising can be integrated by a model of advertising literacy (Ritson and Elliott, 1995). See Fig. 3.1.

Modelled within the framework of contemporary literacy studies, advertising literacy is not only the skills to be able to understand and transfer the meanings from an advertisement but also the ability to use those meanings within the social context of the life-world. This is a practices and events model, which shows that literacy must consider the interpretive skills (practices) that the audience brings to an advertisement, but must also look at the ways in which advertising is involved in social interactions (events) and the uses to which the meanings are put in social life subsequent to the advertising exposure. Advertising literacy becomes a significant factor employed by many consumers, especially teenagers, to locate and relocate their social groups and their identities within those groups, because advertising literacy is used by group members to evaluate each other (Ritson and Elliott, 1999). The process of *discursive elaboration* involves the social consumption of advertising meanings, as they are described, discussed, argued about, laughed at. Advertisements become 'tokens in young people's system of social exchange' (Willis, 1990, p. 57); they are

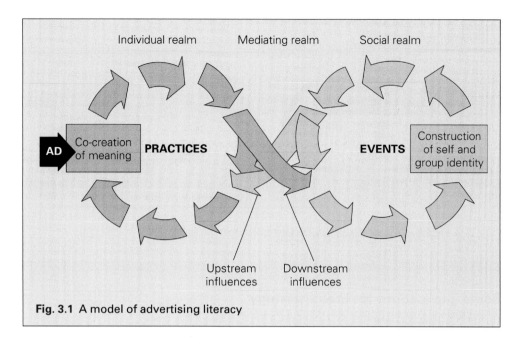

Fig. 3.1 A model of advertising literacy

a form of cultural capital for teenagers, to be invested carefully to gain dividends in terms of social status and self-esteem. Willis (1990) notes that young people are increasingly involved with advertisements and proposes that part of this increased interest in advertising stems from the ability of advertisers to utilize the latest fashions in order to make advertisements aesthetically pleasing as a product independent of the advertised item. He also describes young people deriving 'symbolic pleasure' from the advertisements and in particular they are appreciative of the 'active role' they are expected to play in understanding the advertisements.

Buttle (1991) describes several studies which show that advertising is used in some situations as a means of initiating social interactions, while O'Donohoe (1994) notes that advertisements are also used on a social level in peer relationships. Generally advertisements were seen by her respondents as being facilitators to conversation. Until meanings from mediated experiences of advertising have been subjected to discursive elaboration in a social context and interwoven with behavioural significations derived from lived experience with the brand, they remain viscous, liable to be rejected or just forgotten. Only after this discursive elaboration can symbolic meanings be fully concretized and become what Eco (1979, p. 14) calls 'realized text'.

The process of the consumption of the mediated experience of brand advertising, the lived experience of the purchase and usage of brands, and the two realms of self-symbolism and social-symbolism are illustrated in Fig. 3.2.

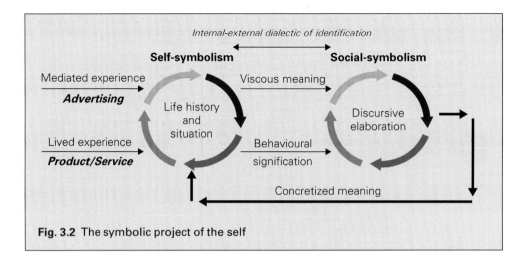

Fig. 3.2 The symbolic project of the self

Some implications for brand strategy

Brands can be used by the consumer as resources for the symbolic construction of the self, both social identity and self-identity. The symbolic consumption of brands can help establish and communicate some of the fundamental cultural categories such as social status, gender, age, and such vital cultural values as family, tradition, and authenticity. In order for the meaning of brands to become fully concrete, the mediated meaning derived from advertising and promotion must be negotiated with the lived experience of purchase and usage, and particularly for brands with social-symbolic positioning strategies these meanings must be validated through discursive elaboration in a social context: they must be authenticated by the social or peer group. But brands can also be used to counter some of the threats to the self posed by postmodernity, such as fragmentation, loss of meaning and loss of individuality.

Brands, trust and fragmentation

One of the prime features of the postmodern experience is fragmentation, where the inherited self-identity of history, from a family and traditional hierarchical postion, is no longer a stable, secure fact but requires active construction: 'A self-identity has to be created and more or less continually reordered against the backdrop of shifting experiences of day-to-day life and the fragmenting tendencies of modern institutions'. (Giddens, 1991 p. 198). This construction of self and identity is achieved partly through developing coherent narratives of the self and partly through finding opportunities for the investment of trust in institutions other than the traditional ones such as the church. Brands offer consistency in an ever-changing world and this reassurance is a vital element in their added value. As in human social relationships, from consistency over time develops predictability, then dependability and eventually trust in the brand (Gurviez, 1996). As we discussed in Chapter 2, in large part, trust in a brand evolves from the delivery of consistent benefits over time, that is from lived experience which carries behavioural signification by practical experience of using the brand. However, the viscous meaning derived from the mediated experience of advertising can enhance the consumer's experience and give a narrative coherence to it by giving words to thoughts they 'may know but can only speak of incompletely' (Polanyi, 1967). Volkswagen have captured perfectly this ability of the brand to replace other less reliable relationships: 'If only everything in life was as reliable as a Volkswagen'. We will discuss this opportunity for developing brand mythologies in Chapter 7.

Brands and deep meaning

Brands can acquire deep meaning for consumers by their involvement in the socialization process of growing up, and from then on brands can evoke profound feelings of nostalgia and provide comfort from insecurity. Olsen (1995) has explored the history of brand use, brand loyalty and intergenerational transfer in families with a recent history of emigration. She found that certain moments in our lives become powerful memories interconnecting brand, people and places and that 'family brands become part of the tool chest in strategies for survival during critical life passages'. Consumers bought brands that evoked memories of their grandparents, often through the smell which instantly returned them to the time and place of their childhood. Holbrook and Schindler (1994) have suggested that there is a 'sensitive period effect' for products, where early childhood and, particularly, adolescence are periods when we are most likely to develop preferences. Brands that we have lived experience with during sensitive periods may acquire a depth of meaning unattainable by brands at later stages in our lives. If we have frequent sensual experience, particularly olfactory experience with brands during childhood, then at later stages of our lives we may use them in nostalgic activity, and/or to restore a sense of security. Again, behavioural signification through lived experience with a brand seems by far the most potent source of meaning, but advertising can provide a narrative structure for concretizing these emotional meanings. Hovis bread and Yorkshire Tea are both masters at providing consumers with a narrative identity that encapsulates both nostalgic reverie and current life situations. We will discuss the use of nostalgia as a brand strategy in Chapter 7.

The adolescent sensitive period is captured by Levi's with their provision of both self-symbolic and social-symbolic meaning through heavy advertising support which is validated in a virtuous circle by discursive elaboration by teenagers who know and value the meanings depicted in the advertising and discuss them with their friends (Auty and Elliott, 1998).

Mass-market brands—individual meanings

The ubiquity of brands in developed capitalist societies is such that we live in a rich 'brandscape' (Sherry, 1987) from which we must select a personal 'brandspace' in which to live. In large part, the creation of personal brandspace will be achieved through the creation of deep meaning and the development of trust, but brands can also facilitate the development of personal involvement by the encouragement of the meaning transfer processes of personal ritual and social interaction. McCracken (1988) identifies four ritual activities which transfer meaning from consumer goods to the individual: exchange, possession, grooming and divestment rituals. Each ritual presents an opportunity for the individual to affirm, assign or revise the meanings derived from the mediated experience of advertising and construct an individual meaning for themselves. By suggesting brand rituals through engagement in 'brandfests', Jeep have provided their consumers with ways to make your Jeep different from other people's. We will discuss this use of brand communities as a brand strategy in Chapter 7.

At a social, sub-cultural level, Ritson and Elliott (1997) have described how the elusive audience of Generation X may be encouraged to actively interpret advertising by using deliberately 'weak' texts which encourage 'strong' reading. This openness relates to a lack of specific narrative direction and explicit meaning context. Instead these 'open' ads feature the product and simply evoke a positive general response to the ad from the consumer, by using music or imagery for example. The consumer views the deliberately 'open' ad and because it lacks any strong intended meaning is empowered to perform a very strong reading of it. As a result the consumer derives a very personal interpretation of the ad's meaning related to their own individual life situation and history. At this point, in need of the social confirmation all X'ers crave, the consumer discusses the meaning of the ad with others who share the same basic interpretation of advertising. Thus an advertising literacy event occurs and the individuals form an interpretative community, not purely by demographic or psychographic factors but by their shared interpretation of the meaning of the advertisement. The use of 'open' ads is explored further in the discussion of neo-tribes in Chapter 7.

In postmodern consumer culture individuals are engaged in a constant task of negotiating meanings from lived and mediated experience as they endeavour to construct and maintain their identity. As part of the resources for this task they utilize the symbolic meanings of consumer goods, and through an understanding of the dynamics of the process of identity construction, opportunities can be identified for brands to play an important role in the symbolic project of the self.

CHAPTER SUMMARY

In this chapter we have discussed how in postmodernity brands can become symbolic resources for the construction, communication and maintenance of identity. Brands can acquire symbolic meaning in a variety of ways, but one of the most potent sources is advertising, particularly through narrative and the construction of socially shared meanings. We have seen that the symbolic consumption of brands can help establish and communicate some of the basic cultural categories, such as social status, gender and age. Brands can acquire deep meaning through the socialization process and such brands can restore a sense of security. We suggest that mass-market brands can acquire individual meanings through ritual and personal interpretations of meaning.

DISCUSSION QUESTIONS

1 To what extent are consumers engaged in a symbolic project of the self and how might brands be involved?

2 What is the difference between self-symbolism and social-symbolism and how does it relate to brands?

3 Are we really experiencing 'symbolic overload' in consumer culture? If so, what are the implications for brand strategy?

4 How might viscous meaning created by advertising become validated and concretized?

5 How important is the lived experience of using a brand compared to the influence of advertising?

6 What are the implications of postmodern fragmentation for brand strategy?

7 How might 'weak texts' and 'strong readings' help build individual meanings for a mass-market brand?

CASE STUDY

Love over Gold—The Untold Story of TV's Greatest Romance

Gold Blend was launched by Nestlé in the mid-1960s. It used the new freeze-dried technology to provide a smoother, richer taste and was sold at a price premium to Nescafé of around 25%. It was an excellent product, outperforming its rivals in taste tests, and was very successful in its early years. It reached a peak brand share of 7.8% in 1969, but thereafter drifted away slightly until, by the mid-1980s, the share was around 6.5%.

Up to 1987, advertising had concentrated on the product itself, using the mnemonic of a gold bean to suggest product superiority. The problem was that, although Gold Blend performed well as a product and was seen as upmarket and high quality, it was not accessible for the bulk of coffee buyers. The rational product message was only interesting to a minority of upmarket coffee drinkers. The brand's appeal was therefore limited to upmarket coffee connoisseurs.

Realizing this, Nescafé decided to create advertising which, through its popular appeal, would make the brand more accessible to the mass market while still maintaining its quality, upmarket image and premium positioning. The focus of the communication therefore moved from product claims to a more emotional approach which involved the consumer more—Gold Blend would be the coffee you drank to demonstrate your sophistication. What Nescafé tried to do was to increase the accessibility of the brand without changing its positioning.

The target audience was women of any class, who saw themselves as slightly more discriminating than the norm, but who were not coffee connoisseurs. To involve the target in the world of Gold Blend where 'Classy women drink Gold Blend', there was a softer touch in tonality. A softer form of feminism portrayed a woman who was an equal in lifestyle, success and intellect, without being aggressive—a switch from material to more human values. Moreover, research found that a sophisticated romance, the romance depicted in *Moonlighting*, a very popular TV series at that time, appealed immensely to the women who were our target. This 'sophisticated romance' became the campaign theme.

To position Gold Blend as an upmarket coffee, in a class of its own, worth every penny, but which anyone could drink, the focus was to build an emotional bond between the target and the brand through the shared Gold Blend world of sophistication and romance. Hence, the emotion of sophistication and romance could broaden the appeal of the brand to new, less overtly upmarket, users.

Further inspired by popular TV series, Nescafé applied the idea of acting like a programme maker to the Gold Blend advertising campaign. Thus, each episode ended with a cliff-hanger, leaving the viewer wanting to know what happened next. And just as TV companies advertise future episodes with trailers and press ads, so did Nescafé Gold Blend. In the days before the second episode was due to appear, small-space black-and-white press ads appeared in the TV listings pages. Just as TV companies try to create added publicity and momentum for their programmes by encouraging coverage in the popular press and by creating merchandise based on the programme, so did Nescafé Gold Blend.

The media strategy complemented this approach, building on the drama of the romance rather than simply chasing cost per thousand. The bulk of the budget was spent on TV, using a burst strategy to emphasize the cliff-hanger endings. Each burst began with a brief reminder of the previous episode. In the second week the new episode was launched, buying into high-rating programmes to build cover and impact for the new episode. In the early stages of each series the story was moved on more quickly with a faster production of episodes to get people involved in the story. The first series was originally intended to run for six episodes. In the end, because it was so successful, it ran for 12 episodes over five and a half years. However, all stories must end, and in early 1993 it climaxed with the 'I love you' ad; the screening of a compilation of all 11 episodes to date; and a final commercial where the happy couple disappeared into the sunset. This first campaign drove penetration, but the bulk of this was among over-45s. In order to reach a broader audience, for the second series Nescafé determined to extend its success to younger women. A core objective of the new series therefore was to appeal to a younger target. Nescafé deliberately made the protagonists younger, with lifestyles more relevant to this target, and more lively.

In the second series, targeting a younger audience, Gold Blend had a different storyline while keeping the core property—the 'sophisticated romance'. Instead of a story about a couple brought together through the coffee but kept apart by events, it was the classic battle between romance (and Gold Blend) on the one hand and material wealth on the other, represented by two male suitors. The first commercial in the second series broke in November 1993. By early 1996 the second series had run for six episodes, and proved on all key measures—awareness, liking, involvement, brand awareness and sales—to build on the success of the previous campaign series. 'Sophisticated romance' was proved to be able to run and run.

Quantitatively people said that Gold Blend was an 'upmarket' coffee, and said it had advertising they liked. Qualitative research consistently showed that the advertising worked because it portrayed an upmarket, sophisticated image for Gold Blend. This image reflected the populist nature of the advertising that was accessible to everyone. Therefore, the advertising was aspirational for its target and, at a rational level, communicates quality: 'If people like that drink it, it must be good.' The popular appeal of the advertising meant that people accepted these messages, even though they knew the characters were advertising inventions. They seemed to be conspiring with Gold Blend to go along with the fantasy because they were enjoying it.

The campaign was also a great success in sales terms, with sales over 60% higher in terms of volume than before the campaign started. This was despite no growth in the market as a whole, and meant that Gold Blend had a sterling share of 13%, making it clearly the second-biggest brand in the market behind Nescafé granules. This sales increase comprised two clear periods. First, Gold Blend grew rapidly immediately after the start of the campaign. This growth continued thereafter but seemed to hit a plateau in 1992. Then, in 1993, the second series was introduced with a revised target. Following this, sales growth recommenced, and continued for years, despite the fact that the market declined in 1995.

On top of this, the campaign really captured the public's imagination. How many other campaigns have managed to make the front page of the *Sun*, displacing the news that Princess Anne was having a romance with Tim Lawrence to second place, and to be the feature of a *Times* editorial? How many other campaigns have had the nerve to advertise themselves in the TV listings pages, and actually get people to tune in to watch the spot? How many other campaigns are famous enough in themselves to spawn a CD and cassette compilation that went gold? The campaign spawned a book, two CD/cassettes and a video, each successful and profitable in their own right for Nestlé and, at the same time, increasing the power of the campaign. All in all, Gold Blend was a success story and continued to be so.

During the period of Gold Blend's success Nescafé as a brand performed roughly in line with the market, while some of the other new Nestlé brands, Alta Rica, Cap Colombie and Cappuccino actually increased share. Thus the growth in Gold Blend's share was all incremental for Nestlé, and was achieved without cannibalizing the other brands in the portfolio.

The Gold Blend advertising campaign was also built upon massive marketing expenses, at an average of £5 million a year in advertising. However, the increased size of the brand was worth £50 million each year in sales. A quotation from David Hudson, Communications Director of Nestlé UK, can be used to understand the balance between advertising expenses and brand growth:

> '*It is a campaign I take real pride in. Sometimes people ask me if the amount we spend on advertising is worth it. I tell them to look at the Gold Blend campaign.*'
>
> **David Hudson, Communications Director of Nestlé UK**

The Gold Blend story may be the story of a love affair, but it was also a story of success. It was advertising the public loved, but it was also advertising that resulted in sales success. It grew from a minor player to the second-biggest coffee brand and one of the country's top 50 brands. That success was no fly by night. It had been sustained over nearly ten years, with each year building on the previous one. Moreover this was not chance, but came from the aim of creating an accessible 'upmarket' brand, and the ambition to be more like the programmes between which the advertising appeared.

Source: WARC, IPA, Advertising Effectiveness Awards 1996, Love over gold—the untold story of TV's greatest romance

Edited by Hazel H. Huang

Discussion Questions

1 The focus of the symbolic meanings of Gold Blend changed from product-attribute focus (i.e. high quality) to an emotion-attribute focus (i.e. sophisticated romance). How might the change improve Gold Blend's sales?

2 How was the balance between self- and social-symbolism handled in the Gold Blend brand strategy?

3 Was it possible that Gold Blend, as a mass-market brand, could deliver individual meanings in its advertising of sophisticated romance?

4 To what extent is 'sophisticated romance' a viable brand strategy for other product categories and other cultures?

FURTHER READING

- The first major writer on marketing as a symbolic activity was Sid Levy and his collected work is a rich resource for thought: Rook, D. (ed.) (1999), *Brands, Consumers, Symbols, & Research: Sidney J. Levy on Marketing*, London: Sage.

- Helga Dittmar's excellent book extends many of the ideas in this chapter: Dittmar, H. (1992), *The Social Psychology of Material Possessions: To Have is To Be*, Hemel Hempstead: Harvester Wheatsheaf.

- Narrative and the construction of identity through cultural consumption is discussed at length in Mackay, H. (1997), *Consumption and Everyday Life*, London: Sage.

REFERENCES

Anderson, J. and Meyer, T. (1988), *Mediated Communication: A Social Action Perspective*, London: Sage.

Auty, S. and Elliott, R. (1998), 'Fashion involvement, self-monitoring and the meaning of brands', *Journal of Product and Brand Management*, 7, 2 & 3, 109–23.

Baudrillard, J. (1988), 'Consumer society', in M. Poster (ed.), *Jean Baudrillard: Selected Writings*, Cambridge: Polity.

Belk, R. (1988), 'Possessions and the extended self', *Journal of Consumer Research*, 15, 139–68.

Buttle, F. (1991), 'What people do with advertising', *International Journal of Advertising*, 10, 95–110.

Csikszentmihalyi, M. and Rochberg-Halton, E. (1981), *The Meaning of Things: Domestic Symbols and the Self*, Cambridge: Cambridge University Press.

Derrida, J. (1977), *Of Grammatology* (trans. G. Spivak), Baltimore: Johns Hopkins Press.

Dittmar, H. (1992), *The Social Psychology of Material Possessions: To Have is To Be*, Hemel Hempstead: Harvester Wheatsheaf.

Douglas, M. and Isherwood, B. (1978), *The World of Goods: Towards an Anthropology of Consumption*, London: Allen Lane.

Eco, U. (1979), *The Role of the Reader: Explorations in the Semiotics of Texts*, London: Hutchinson.

Elliott, R., Eccles, S., and Hodgson, M. (1993), 'Re-coding gender representations: women, cleaning products, and advertising's "New Man"', *International Journal of Research in Marketing*, 10, 311–24.

Fazio, R. and Zanna, M. (1978), 'On the predictive validity of attitudes: the role of direct experience and confidence', *Journal of Personality*, 46, 228–43.

Fiske, J. (1989), *Reading the Popular*, Boston: Unwin Hyman.

Giddens, A. (1991), *Modernity and Self-Identity: Self and Society in the Late Modern Age*, Cambridge: Polity Press.

Gurviez, P. (1996), 'The trust concept in the brand-consumer relationship', in J. Beracs *et al.* (eds.), *Marketing for an Expanding Europe. Proceedings of the 25th Annual Conference of the European Marketing Academy*, Budapest: Budapest University of Economic Sciences, 559–74.

Holbrook, M. and Schindler, R. (1994), 'Age, sex, and attitude towards the past as predictors of consumers' aesthetic tastes for cultural products', *Journal of Marketing Research*, 31, 412–22.

Jenkins, R. (1996), *Social Identity*, London: Routledge.

Kleine, S.S., Kleine, R.E. III, and Allen, C.T. (1995), 'How is a possession "me" or "not me"? Characterizing types and antecedent of material possession attachment', *Journal of Consumer Research*, 22, 327–43.

Lannon, J. and Cooper, P. (1983), 'Humanistic advertising: a holistic cultural perspective'. *International Journal of Advertising*, 2, 195–213.

Markus, H. and Nurius, P. (1986), 'Possible selves', *American Psychologist*, 41, 9, 954–69.

McCracken, G. (1988), *Culture and Consumption: New Approaches to The Symbolic Character of Consumer Goods and Activities*, Bloomington: Indiana University Press.

Mick, D.G. and Buhl, C. (1992), 'A meaning-based model of advertising experiences', *Journal of Consumer Research*, 19, 317–38.

O'Donohoe, S. (1994), 'Advertising uses and gratifications', *European Journal of Marketing* 28, 8/9, 52–75.

Olsen, B. (1995), 'Brand loyalty and consumption patterns: the lineage factor', in J. Sherry (ed.), *Contemporary Marketing and Consumer Behavior: An Anthropological Sourcebook*, Thousand Oaks, CA: Sage Publications.

Polanyi, M. (1967), *The Tacit Dimension*, London: Routledge and Kegan Paul.

Ricoeur, P. (1977), *The Rule of Metaphor: Multi-disciplinary Studies of the Creation of Meaning in Language*, trans. R. Czery, London: Routledge and Kegan Paul.

Ritson, M. and Elliott, R. (1995), 'A model of advertising literacy: the praxiology and co-creation of advertising meaning', in M. Bergadaa *et al.* (eds.), *Marketing Today and for the 21st Century: Proceedings of the 24th Annual Conference of the European Marketing Academy*, ESSEC, Cergy-Pontoise, France: Imprimerie Basuyau.

—— (1997), 'Marketing to generation X: strategies for communicating with "Advertising's lost generation"', *Proceedings of the AMA Special Conference: New and Evolving Paradigms: The Emerging Future of Marketing*, Dublin: AMA.

—— (1999), 'The social uses of advertising: an ethnographic study of adolescent advertising audiences', *Journal of Consumer Research*, 26, 3, 260–77.

Sherry, J.F. (1987), 'Advertising as a cultural system', in J. Umiker-Sebeok (ed.), *Marketing and Semiotics: New Directions in the Study of Signs for Sales*, Berlin: Mouton de Gruyter, pp. 441–62.

Thompson, J.B. (1995), *The Media and Modernity: A Social Theory of the Media*, Cambridge: Polity.

Wicklund, R.A. and Gollwitzer, P.M. (1982), *Symbolic Self-Completion*, Hillsdale, NJ: Lawrence Erlbaum.

Willis, P. (1990), *Common Culture: Symbolic Work at Play in the Everyday Cultures of the Young*, Milton Keynes: Open University Press.

Cultural Meaning Systems and Brands

4

Introduction

We live in a symbol-rich environment, where we must construct meaning from a plethora of images. Within this cultural space brands play an important role in the ways in which we communicate to each other the fundamental meaning categories of age, gender, social groupings and social hierarchy. It is the meaning of brands that gives them their added value and these brand meanings are partly added by the producers (McCracken, 1993). In this chapter we will explore how brands can be used as signalling systems to create and send meanings of social differentiation and social integration; but first we need to understand the basic analytical tools of semiotics, the science of signs.

Semiotics and brand meanings

A crucial distinction in the semiotic analysis of signs is between the signifier and the signified. The signifier—for instance a brand name—has no meaning in its own right, but must acquire meaning through associations with other pre-existing meanings until it comes to signify some concept or idea. The signifier is a denotative communication, a simple statement of fact, the signified is a connotative communication which can be literally any meaning that can be associated with the signifier, in most cases through advertising and packaging. What marketers need to do is to understand the systems of meaning or communication codes operative in a particular cultural situation. Codes are sets of unspoken rules and conventions that structure sign systems and link signs to meaning (Lawes, 2002). An illustration of the semiotic analysis process can be gained from a study of the advertising for beer brands (Harvey and Evans, 2001). From detailed study of TV and print ads the advertising for two major brands in the UK were analysed in terms of codes deployed, codes challenged or explicitly broken and the overall profile of codes used by each brand. The resulting semiotic analysis is illustrated in Fig. 4.1.

The researchers then went on to analyse major beer brand advertising from six major markets world-wide and identified 26 key codes which mapped into seven clusters of which three sample codes are illustrated in Fig. 4.2.

This analysis enabled the clients to feel that they had a good grasp, in an international context, of how beer advertising communicates and the underlying propositions competitor brands were conveying to consumers. This enabled them to develop new advertising propositions as part of brand strategy planning.

A different approach to semiotic analysis has been used to explore the meaning of special, irreplaceable possessions (Grayson and Shulman, 2000). Based on the principle of indexicality, a relationship can exist between a sign and an object based on a factual connection beyond just psychological perceptions and shared meanings. Consumers demonstrated a semiotic linkage between their special possessions and their personal history. The possessions served as physical evidence of a special relationship with people, places and events. This verification function underlay connections with a wide range of possessions which had been 'contaminated' by real experiences and could therefore remind people of

Carling Black Label

- Key codes
  - heritage, roots, masculinity, sports

- Brand codes
  - nationalism, tabloid attitude

- Substantiators
  - Football sponsorship, popularity

Stella Artois

- Key codes
  - parody, humour, heritage

- Brand codes
  - France/French language, music, cinematic references

- Substantiators
  - Premium price
  - 'Reassuringly expensive'

Fig. 4.1 Semiotic analysis of UK beer ads

Source: Harvey and Evans (2001).

Cosmopolitan style	Alternative humour	Totem of the tribe
Modern city life • Style bars • Bright lights, big city • Market savvy	Self-deprecating humour • Twist in the tail	Bonding focal points • Dances, music • Teams • Couples, family
Western (v. local) lifestyle • Western music • Western attitude	Irony, cynicism • Defining style clans • Sub-cultures	Nation and icons • Flags • Music • Humour • Funny foreigners
Beautiful people • Style • Confidence, self-ssurance • Narcissism	Parody • Making fun of mainstream • Humour and 'serious' genres • Reinterpreting other brands and equities	Looking alike • Uniforms • Animal allegories • Lizards, frogs

Fig. 4.2 International language of beer advertising—signifiers for three sample codes

Source: Adapted from Harvey and Evans (2001).

their past. More than 85% of the irreplaceable possessions in the study were in fact mass-produced, but none the less, consumers could invest them with a semiotic meaning of authenticity which enabled them to distinguish between objects which on the face of it looked identical.

Personal meanings

Two major approaches to the person–brand relationship have been based on metaphors: the brand-as-a-person metaphor and the brand-as-a-friend metaphor.

Brand personality: the brand-as-a-person

The idea that consumers may think of a brand as if it had some of the characteristics of a person has a long history. The basic approach is that human personality traits come to be associated with a brand directly through the real people consumers associate with a brand, such as their typical users, celebrity endorsers or a chief executive, such as Richard Branson and the Virgin brand. Personality traits can also become associated with a brand indirectly through a wide range of features such as brand name, symbol, advertising stylistics, price and distribution channel (Aaker, 1997). It has also been argued that brand personality includes demographic categories such as gender, age and class (Levy, 1959). Recent approaches have taken the route of transferring personality concepts and measurement techniques from human psychology to brands and Aaker (1997) demonstrated that five major factors summarized the traits that consumers attributed to a wide range of brands: sincerity, excitement, competence, sophistication and ruggedness.

Subsequent work has shown that personal meanings of brands are partly socially constructed and that they also vary across cultures. It has been suggested that through a process of 'linguistic sedimentation', words that describe human personality are extremely functional in the development and maintenance of social relations and they become a vital part of the vocabulary of everyday life which we learn through socialization into social and cultural groups (Caprara *et al.*, 1998). As individuals tend to perceive other people on the basis of the characteristics they display in social situations then the same argument applies to brands and their use in particular situations so that personal meanings have also to be negotiated as social meanings (Ligas and Cotte, 1999). Indeed it has been shown that there are important boundary conditions for the generalizability of Aaker's (1997) brand personality framework to individual brands and that it works best when applied to aggregated data across diverse product categories (Austin *et al.*, 2003). When applied across different cultures, the five factors of brand personality have to be revised. In Japan and Spain, only three of the factors transferred from the USA (Aaker *et al.*, 2001), and similar results were found in Russia (Supphellen and Grønhaug, 2003).

Brand relationships: the brand-as-a-friend

A more recent approach to metaphorical thinking has been the idea that a consumer can form something similar to a dyadic interpersonal relationship with brands. Fournier (1998) describes how some consumers move beyond simply ascribing human-like personality traits to brands and form meaningful human-like relationships. She suggests that brands can form viable partners in a relationship, playing a number of roles within the relationship. Consumer-brand relationships differ in their quality, and the strength of the relationship can be evaluated according to the nature and depth of the bond using a 'brand relationship quality scale'. The theory is that brand relationships which are high on such factors as intimacy, commitment and love will exhibit high degrees of enduring loyalty and the consumer will tolerate and forgive the brand for lapses. Although the concept of a human-like relationship with a brand opens up some fascinating possibilities for brand strategy which will be explored in Chapter 7, as yet there is little published evidence of the existence of relationships involving love and passion and the predicted beneficial outcomes occurring. One experimental study in Korea found that subjects scoring a brand high on relationship quality indicated that they would be more likely to accept a brand extension, but this in no way suggests that a meaningful relationship actually existed (Park *et al.*, 2002). Children used interpersonal relationship metaphors when asked to talk about the brands in their lives (Mindy, 2002), but again this does not mean that they see these relationships as the same as human relationships. Similarly, towards the other end of the age spectrum, women at the mid-life stage appear to relate brands to a number of life themes, especially comfort and security (Olsen, 1999).

Another finding which has important implications for using brand–consumer relationships in brand strategy is some experimental evidence that men and women may relate to brands in a different way. It seems possible that men distinguish brands that are close to them in terms of their own actions towards the brand, while women distinguish close versus distant brands in terms of their mutual actions, that is how the brand behaves towards them as well as their own action towards the brand (Monga, 2002).

Before leaving the brand-as-friend metaphor, it is worth remembering that it is only a metaphor. A brand is an inanimate object and cannot think and feel, and just because, when asked, a consumer can talk about brands in terms of personalities does not entail any form of reciprocal interpersonal relationship (Bengtsson, 2003). However, it does seem possible that consumers can form some kind of emotional attachment to a brand based on meanings in their life in which the brand is implicated and this can be part of building a brand over time.

Nostalgia

When a brand is associated with sensitive periods in people's lives, then enduring preferences may be formed (Holbrook and Schindler, 1994). At the heart of this form of brand relationship is the concept of nostalgia: 'a preference towards experiences associated with objects that were more common when one was younger' (Holbrook and Schindler, 2003). A key aspect of the nostalgic sentiment is that it attaches to products at certain times in the lifespan, particularly the sensitive periods of adolescence and early adulthood. At the most person-centred level, sensory experiences, smell and taste, connect people with pleasurable incidents in their past which can be recalled in great detail. But people also recall not just pleasurable incidents but more complex experiences, especially friendships and loved ones: a product can provide a material representation of human affection. The power of nostalgic bonding between a brand, a person and their past life events offers some intriguing opportunities for developing symbolic brand strategy and this will be explored later.

We shall return to consideration of semiotic codes and personal meanings and their possibilities for brand strategy in Chapter 7, but now we turn to cultural meaning systems and how they function in society.

Social differentiation and social integration

Consumption practices are involved in processes of both differentiating between social groups, for example between classes and genders, and creating new social groupings such as brand communities. These two broad categories of meaning can be utilized as the basis of alternative brand strategies and this will be discussed in Chapter 7.

Social differentiation

But let us start by considering the traditional areas of the use of goods to differentiate between people, starting with the concept of conspicuous consumption (Veblen, 1899). Veblen argued that it was a basic fact of human society that people need to display their social status, and that the consumption of goods could be used to maintain a position of social prestige. In order to demonstrate a separation between the upper and lower classes, it was necessary to accord most status to the consumption of goods that had little or no functional value, a conspicuous waste of time and money. Thus consumer goods can be seen as signifiers of advantage in a competition for social status: symbolic brands become status symbols. Conspicuous consumption is part of a process of emulation: 'Goods are able to mark status because they are part of the lifestyle of a high status group. Consequently, lower status social climbers lay claim to higher status by emulating that lifestyle, by buying those goods, consuming after the fashion of the higher orders, "aping" their manners, style, etiquette and so on' (Slater, 1997, p. 156). Importantly, the process of emulation is dynamic, as the higher-status groups attempt to maintain distinctions between themselves and the lower-status groups by changing their lifestyle and consumption patterns. This is a 'trickle-down' theory about social change and the crucial role played by fashion.

For Veblen (1899, p. 168), the very public nature of clothing makes it an ideal site for displaying status, especially by demonstrating that fashionable clothing is not actually functional: 'in an inclement climate . . . to go ill clad in order to appear well-dressed'. Fashion in clothing can be seen as expressing the tensions between oppositions of class, gender and wealth and as an essential element in the maintenance of social divisions (Davis, 1992). So branded fashions are symbolic markers of a wide range of cultural categories and are used to communicate identity among an ever-greater number of fragmented social groupings. A key issue in understanding the marketing of branded fashions is the concept of exclusivity. By carefully limiting access to the brand both by price and by supply, the value of the brand is maintained at both the status-marking level and at the identity-marking level (Park *et al.*, 1986). We shall return to how fashion can be a vital element in developing symbolic brand strategies in Chapter 7.

The theory of conspicuous consumption was based on assumptions about the relative distribution of wealth: economic capital; but a significant development more appropriate to consumer culture in developed economies is the concept of 'cultural capital' based on differences in taste and style. Bourdieu (1984) suggests that in contemporary Western societies, where there is much less strict hierarchical division between social classes and much more equality in terms of wealth, distinction between social groups is maintained through structures of taste. In the act of consumption we both exercise and display our taste or style, and taste is not an individual preference but is socially structured into hierarchies of taste (Slater, 1997). The choice of opera rather than soap opera communicates a great deal about a consumer's educational and class background, income and social aspirations. Thus brand choice, particularly for cultural products, displays an unconscious knowledge of the legitimacy of various lifestyles, and this is usually conditioned by social class. Holt (1998) showed that differences in cultural capital, based on class position, structure both patterns of taste and consumption practices in American mass culture. Thus the choice between certain brands may be seen as demonstrating relative amounts of cultural capital and thus individual choice will be partly determined by historical social background rather than recent marketing activity. The implications of cultural capital for brand strategy will be discussed in Chapter 7.

The final manifestation of social differentiation through consumption is that of gender. Gender is a major social category which we use in marking distinctions between people, and it is widely used in marketing practice, e.g. market segmentation and advertising management. Many products and services are gender-associated, and much consumption behaviour is also gendered. Basic judgement processes between brands show gender differences, and perceptions of the symbolic meaning of brands are gendered (Elliott, 1994). There is also considerable evidence that men and women interpret the same advertising executions in very different ways (Elliott *et al.*, 1995), and because gender is a cultural construct gender differentiation may be very marked in traditional cultures (Costa, 1994). But gender roles are changing rapidly, and in this developing cultural space there is potential for brands to use gender identity as a social differentiation brand strategy for women and men; and as a social integration brand strategy, especially for non-heterosexuals (Kates, 2000).

Social integration

The communication value of brands can be thought of as fundamentally integrative, in that knowledge of consumption codes and attendance at consumption events are essential to being included as part of a social group (Slater, 1997). The meanings of goods can be used within everyday consumption practices to make and maintain social relationships (Douglas and Isherwood, 1979). Brands are involved in the construction, maintenance and membership communication through brand communities, neo-tribes and sub-cultures.

Brand communities

The seminal study of Muniz and O'Guinn (2001) defined a brand community as a non-geographical community based on a set of structured relations between admirers of a brand. They demonstrated that three brands—Ford Bronco, Macintosh and Saab—had groups of consumers who shared not just ownership of the brand but three traditional markers of community: shared consciousness, rituals and traditions and a sense of moral responsibility. Shared consciousness relates to the perception that 'we sort of know one another' even if they have never actually met. This triangular relationship between a consumer, another consumer and the brand is a central facet of a brand community. There is also a sense of brand users being different from other people, and this extends into the concept of legitimacy which differentiates between true members of the community and more marginal consumers who might buy the brand but for the 'wrong' reasons. The wrong reasons are usually revealed by failing to truly appreciate the culture, history rituals and traditions of the community. At the extreme, shared consciousness involves oppositional brand loyalty, that is the community derives much of its cohesion from opposition to rival brands. For example, members of the Macintosh brand community used their overt opposition to Microsoft as a source of unity. Rituals and traditions typically centred on shared consumption experiences with the brand. For example, members of the Saab brand community would always flash their headlights or wave at other Saab drivers they encountered on the road. The sense of a shared moral responsibility involves a sense of duty to other community members and is demonstrated in integrating new members into the community and in assisting members in the 'proper' use of the brand.

A broader perspective on brand community is to focus not on a triangular relationship but on a customer-centric model which involves a customer's relationship with the actual product, and with marketing agents and institutions as well as other customers (McAlexander *et al.*, 2002). This puts the focus on the customer's experiences rather than on the brand around which that experience revolves. In particular, the attendance at 'brandfests' where customers meet at events hosted by the brand, in this case Jeep, for Jeep Jamborees and Camp Jeeps was related to the development not only of brand community but a resultant brand loyalty. Brand tracking data indicates that Jeep's community-building efforts through brandfests resulted in significantly increased repurchase rates among participants. A key implication here is that a brand owner can invest in building a community around their brand as a primary brand strategy which may result in long-term brand loyalty.

Neo-tribes

A more temporary and fragmented form of social grouping is that based on the metaphor of tribal communities arranged around consumption. Cova and Cova (2001) argue that neo-tribes are inherently unstable, small-scale and involve 'shared experience, the same emotion, a common passion', but unlike a brand community the tribe is characterized by a 'volatility of belonging' which means that homogeneity of behaviour and formal rules are eschewed. A tribe is defined as a network of heterogeneous persons, in terms of age, sex, and income who are linked by a common emotion. In fact, individuals can belong to more than one neo-tribe and can vary dramatically in the extent of their tribal affiliation. A study of in-line roller skaters demonstrated that neo-tribes are a fuzzy concept, a shifting aggregation of emotionally bonded people in an open system that use consumption as but one sign of tribal identity, which can vary from devotees, through participants at events to mere sympathisers, from skating fanatics to occasional amateurs. But whatever the depth of their affiliation with the tribe, they still consume not only branded skates but also symbolic brands such as tribal magazines and tribal T-shirts.

Sub-cultures

A more stable and structural social grouping is that of the sub-culture. Sub-cultures related to consumption are predominantly based on geography, age, ethnicity and class.

Class-based sub-cultures have traditionally been located within a framework of social resistance and reaction against dominant hierarchies of control. Historically this perspective has been used to explain the emergence of such sub-cultures as the 'Teddy Boys', Punk Rockers and Hippies. Most of the studies of sub-culture identify social class and particularly the powerlessness of the working class as the main catalyst for the developments of these sub-cultures (Goulding *et al.*, 2002).

However, increasingly, sub-cultural spaces are becoming sites of creativity and self-expression for both male and female participants from all social backgrounds. There is a plethora of sub-cultures which exhibit tendencies of style and behaviours which characterize the consumption of music, fashion, and symbolic experiences which exist in modern society. Sub-cultural activity is important for the construction and expression of identity, rather than cells of resistance against dominant orders. It is also important to recognize that sub-cultural choices are also consumer choices involving fashion, leisure and a wealth of accessories, which speak symbolically to members of the group.

Thornton (1995) draws attention to the importance of 'authenticity' in the performance of identity in what she calls 'taste cultures', where people can develop 'sub-cultural capital' through authentic displays of 'cool'. The vital role played by authentic performance was identified in Nancarrow *et al.*'s (2002) study of 'style leaders' which analysed 'cool' as requiring the bodily expression of 'ironic detachment'. In becoming members of a sub-culture we need to develop competence in the performance of appropriate cultural codes. The boundaries of a sub-cultural world are 'transgressed and rendered visible through "overperformance" of appropriate behaviour' (Horton, 2003). If an aspiring member of a sub-culture becomes aware of their inability to perform authentically, aware of their ignorance of their cultural codes, then self-consciousness and discomfort emerge.

Goffman (1969) uses a dramaturgical metaphor to discuss the performance of identity, what he calls 'face work'. The body plays a crucial part in a competent performance, constantly signalling to others and reading the signals of other sub-cultural members. Thus authentic performance is both transmission and reception of culturally appropriate actions. He maintains that the performer must believe in the action, must believe in the part being played. In order for the performance to be interpreted as authentic, the performer him/herself should believe the performance is authentic. Failure to believe in the performance is what Sartre (1956) meant by 'bad faith', using the example of a café waiter who acted the part but did not perform it authentically, a form of self-deception.

In a study of style sub-cultures and the consumption of fashion brands and music, Elliott and Davies (2005) demonstrate the importance of the performance of identity, how authenticity can be recognized and how consumers learn how 'to get it right' as they move from novices to a respected member of the sub-culture. They found that authenticity of performance played a vital role in building sub-cultural capital and facilitating membership of micro-cultures and their associated brand communities of music and fashion.

Sub-cultures and appropriation of brand meanings

The ability of brands to help sub-cultures develop and express their identities has been demonstrated in a number of studies. Holt (2002) shows how the practice of 'creative resistance' enables some postmodern consumers to act as 'citizen-artists' in adopting the brand meanings they choose in acts of personal sovereignty. Brands are used as one form of expressive culture, similar to film, TV or music, that can be used in their identity projects.

A more active sub-cultural activity is to adopt the imagery of a famous brand, and then use it to build an alternative identity to that originally associated with the brand. A study of one particular sub-culture, a radical lesbian group, focused on their use of meanings associated with the IKEA brand to create group identity (Ritson *et al.*, 1996). 'Gay Pride Marches' take place in many major cities throughout the world, including New York and London, and feature an annual procession around the city limits with all the participants converging on a central city location. The Pride Marches represent an opportunity for the gay community to demonstrate their sub-cultural identity to both themselves and the general public The group appropriated the IKEA logo and reframed it as DIKEA. They dressed in identical uniforms of hard hats and overalls imprinted with a large logo of DIKEA on the back printed in the style of IKEA thus connecting this image with that of a 'Dyke' (slang for lesbian). Several members of the group had come up with this idea together and all the informants showed a overt consciousness of this sub-cultural re-signification of the meanings of IKEA.

Aikido brands

Aikido is a Japanese martial art involving some throws and joint locks that are derived from Jujitsu and some throws and other techniques derived from Kenjutsu. Aikido focuses not

Reproduced with the kind permission of IKEA

on punching or kicking opponents, but rather on using their own energy to gain control of them or to throw them away from you. A classic Aikido brand that uses the fame and image strength of a brand against itself is Mecca Cola.

Mecca Cola was launched in France in late 2002, designed to exploit anti-American sentiment around the world. The aim is to make Mecca Cola the soft drink of choice for Muslims: 'it is about combating America's imperialism and Zionism by providing a substitute for American goods and increasing the blockade of countries boycotting American goods' (Mathlouthi, 2003). The bottles bear the slogan 'No more drinking stupid, drink with commitment' and promise that 10% of the profits go to Palestinian charities and 10% to European NGOs working for world peace. There are two similar Islamic colas: ZamZam Cola in the Middle East and Qibla Cola in the UK. Qibla Cola also promises that 10% of its profits will go to the Muslim charity Islamic Aid. The founder of Qibla Cola said: 'Muslims are increasingly questioning the role some major multinationals play in our societies. Why should the money of the oppressed go to the oppressors?' (Parveen, 2003).

We can expect that following the world-wide success of Naomi Klein's (2001) *No Logo*, the strength of global brands' awareness and image will be used against them by anti-capitalists and other sub-cultural and political groups both to build and integrate their own group identity and to exploit the market power of the brand for their own ends.

CHAPTER SUMMARY

In this chapter we have explored some of the ways in which brands can help communicate a variety of cultural meanings, and how these can be categorized as fundamentally concerned with either social differentiation or social integration. We have also suggested that powerful brands may expect to have their brand hijacked by anti-capitalists and other sub-cultural groups and their brand awareness and meanings used against them by Aikido brands.

DISCUSSION QUESTIONS

1 How can an understanding of the semiotic codes used by competing brands help in developing strategy?

2 To what extent do brand personalities transfer across cultures?

3 Can consumers really have a relationship with a brand?

4 How may brands differentiate between social classes?

5 How may brands differentiate between genders?

6 What markers of community are shared by members of a brand community?

7 What makes a neo-tribe different from traditional ideas of a tribe?

8 How does 'bad faith' relate to the consumption of brands?

9 How does an Aikido brand use a famous brand's image?

CASE STUDY

The Power of the Brand—A Best Case Look at a Brand Transformation: MasterCard's 'Priceless' Campaign

The power of the MasterCard brand, with Priceless and its transforming effects on the MasterCard franchise, shaped up to a best case study of emotionally salient and targeted advertising, coordinated and integrated on a global scale. Its durability and enduring success continued to impress advertising industry watchers as it delighted and compelled consumers, encouraging them to reach for their MasterCard cards.

Actual brand differences among cards in the payments industry are not dramatic. All competitors share a basic overall business strategy—to increase consumers' use of cards instead of cash and cheques. While cards' member banks determine the fees, rates, rewards, and benefits for their own, MasterCard relies on its portfolios to differentiate its product offering from one another. It is MasterCard who defines and communicates the brand. How the brand performs is largely dependent on its positioning and marketing.

However, when MasterCard surveyed the market place in 1997, the brand was in need of a total repositioning. At that time, the brand was farther from 'top of wallet' with the consumer than MasterCard wanted it to be. While MasterCard had always been well respected and trusted, the brand lacked a distinct brand image that could capture the hearts and minds of consumers. Although research on MasterCard's brand equity revealed positive consumer perceptions of the MasterCard card as everyday (to displace cash and cheques), practical (the card that is an enabler) and unpretentious (standing for core values), five different brand campaigns in less than a dozen years weakened its ability to become the first-choice card of consumers. Meanwhile, MasterCard was working with 15 different agency partners globally. Even though MasterCard had some consistency in taglines, it had no consistent positioning or strategy word-wide. Realising the danger the brand was facing, MasterCard put its advertising account into review in the US and its ultimate goal was to uncover an idea that would work not only in the US, but also around the world.

The development of the Priceless campaign was based on solid research. MasterCard had applied rigorous marketing research and analytical techniques to reveal shifting consumer attitudes. What consumers considered important now, in life, were the values of family and relationships. They were moving away from the materialistic. Five agencies pitched and 35 campaigns were tested. McCann-Erickson was chosen and its message, *'The best way to pay for everything that matters'* touched consumers' hearts. McCann-Erickson's campaign had immediate success with the four spots introduced in 1997.

With that success, MasterCard's challenge was to determine if it would work around the world. The strategic concept behind the campaign was tested in 15 global markets with the assumption that the things that matter the most in life are generally the same everywhere. The testing results confirmed that it was true. Following the research, MasterCard then went on a region-to-region basis to present the campaign to local markets. Each had its own campaign going on, and each local campaign was tested against Priceless. The Priceless campaign won each market and, within a year and a half, all regions applied McCann-Erickson's Priceless campaign. Priceless was the only payments brand advertising that was consistent on a global scale. It was used in over 90 countries and in over 45 languages. The Priceless theme continued to cross cultures and geography, providing a transcendent platform for all of MasterCard's payment programmes and marketing activities. It reinforced the message that MasterCard knew what was truly important in life.

MasterCard kept global integrated marketing vibrant. The quick grasp appeal of Priceless allowed it to easily adapt locally produced spots for global markets. Some spots are universal and can be used without change. The bottom line was that Priceless struck a universal chord and provided versatility that has global reach. The company gathered all the top marketing people from around the world annually to share best practices and experiences. From these meetings came a solid global platform for all MasterCard marketing activities, including many sponsorships and numerous new ideas.

MasterCard began its alliance with FIFA World Cup Soccer in 1990 as the Official Card and Official Product Licensee of Italia 1990. Furthering this successful alliance, it became an Official FIFA sponsor of a comprehensive package of tournaments played around the world and continued its involvement through the 2002 World Cup in Korea/Japan. Soccer has been the most important global sponsorship, starting with the FIFA World Cup. As the world's number one sport, soccer has more than 200 million players world-wide and more than one billion spectators. The game surpasses all others by a wide margin and touches more consumers than any other sport. From a strategic standpoint, MasterCard's alliance with FIFA was an important component of the association's overall strategy to create business-building opportunities for its member banks, as well as offer value and 'priceless' moments for millions of cardholders around the globe. The FIFA World Cup sponsorship worked perfectly as a platform to utilize the Priceless campaign for world-wide reach. It provided the perfect vehicle to reach consumers with the MasterCard brand on a truly global scale.

The Priceless platform's utility went beyond sports. MasterCard created a college intern programme, called the 'Priceless Edge', that gave global college students a chance for real-life work experience in the highly competitive music industry, while providing the brand with an opportunity to build a relationship with young consumers, which was hoped to be life long. The programme was aimed at students aged 18–25 and offered an internship experience in four music disciplines at a music industry production office in Los Angeles. Interns worked on a production of a music special that would air on MTV. In addition, a five-week business entertainment course at Belmont University and an on-line course on the music business were key components of the programme.

Even though the Priceless campaign focused on the globally consistent programmes, MasterCard provided local markets with some flexibility to best shape the essence of the programme. For example, in the US, the Priceless campaign began a long-term relationship with Major League Baseball in 1997 by signing on as an official sponsor and the official card. Furthermore, in 2002, MasterCard announced, along with Major League Baseball, the 'Memorable Moments' programme for that year's season. The programme gave fans the opportunity to vote on baseball's most memorable moment via in-stadium balloting and on MLB.com, the official website of Major League Baseball. The 'Memorable Moments' programme includes: Priceless TV ads that launched the All-Star game in July, Priceless print ads, advertising on consumer ballots, and public relations outreach, with some of the players involved in 'Memorable Moments'. At MasterCard, 150 member financial institutions and over 350,000 merchant locations participated in the programme via a variety of advertising and merchandising materials.

MasterCard continued to innovate with the Priceless theme, working to reach new market segments and adapt innovative marketing and promotional opportunities. It was the first payments company to market to the Hispanic audience via Spanish language TV, print, and an education website inaugurated in 1999. With this move, the brand garnered a 13 percentage point ad awareness in just 18 months.

With Priceless, MasterCard created a common image for the brand: '*The MasterCard you have in your pocket is the same MasterCard around the world.*' It had a common platform to develop marketing programmes, programmes that can cross into different markets: it maximized its resources by focusing efforts in a single direction; it consolidated its agency relationship globally; it increased the use of MasterCard cards. A significant result was that 24% of the gross dollar volume was attributed to the campaign—driving six times more volume than anything else the company had done before.

The Priceless campaign continued to address the question 'What matters most?' It worked to continuously refine the message to reinforce relevancy, credibility and efficiency with a goal to gain share and become the payments leader. The key to the success of Priceless is its adaptability in the global arena. The Priceless platform gave the brand a way to develop integrated marketing programmes and promotions that logically fit with the brand. This adaptability extends to international markets as well. The campaign helped MasterCard realize a 64% gain in gross dollar volume since 1997, as well as increase the number of MasterCard-branded cards by more than 52% over the same time period. Priceless was winning for MasterCard and continued to provide the versatile, global platform that enables the brand to reach consumers and build the MasterCard franchise.

Source: WARC, The Advertiser, October 2002, The Power of the Brand—A Best Case Look at a Brand Transformation: MasterCard's 'Priceless' Campaign, by Debra M. Coughlin

Edited by Hazel H. Huang

Discussion Questions

1 Why was a globally consistent brand image important to MasterCard?

2 With a consistent global brand strategy, why did MasterCard allow local offices a degree of autonomy in designing the Priceless campaign?

3 Why could the Priceless campaign communicate with its audience across country boundaries?

4 MasterCard believed that the Priceless campaign established a successful platform to reach consumers in different countries. Discuss the possible differentiation and integration facilitated by such a platform.

FURTHER READING

- An excellent introduction to the sociology of consumption is Slater, D. (1997), *Consumer Culture and Modernity*, Cambridge: Polity Press.

- Seminal contributions to the theory of consumer society are contained in Lee, M. (ed.) (2000), *The Consumer Society Reader*, Oxford: Blackwell.

- Leading-edge thinking about branding as a cultural process are in Schroeder, J. and Salzer-Morling, M. (eds.) (2005), *Brand Culture*, London: Routledge.

REFERENCES

Aaker, J. (1997), 'Dimensions of brand personality', *Journal of Marketing Research*, XXXIV, 347–56.

—— Benet-Martinez, J. and Garolera, J. (2001), 'Consumption symbols as carriers of culture: a study of Japanese and Spanish brand personality constructs', *Journal of Personality and Social Psychology*, 81, 3, 492–508.

Austin, J., Siguaw, J., and Mattila, A. (2003), 'A re-examination of the generalizability of the Aaker brand personality measurement framework', *Journal of Strategic Marketing*, 11, 2, 77–93.

Bengtsson, A. (2003), 'Towards a critique of brand relationships', *Advances in Consumer Research*, 30, 154–8.

Bourdieu, P. (1984), *Distinction: A Social Critique of the Judgement of Taste*, London: Routledge.

Caprara, G., Barbaranelli, C., and Guido, G. (1998), 'Personality as metaphor: extension of the psycholexical hypothesis and the five factor model to brand and product personality description', *European Advances in Consumer Research*, 3, 61–9.

Costa, J. (ed.) (1994), *Gender Issues and Consumer Behavior*, London: Sage.

Cova, B. and Cova, V. (2001), 'Tribal aspects of postmodern consumption: the case of French in-line roller skaters', *Journal of Consumer Behaviour*, 1, 1, 67–76.

Davis, F. (1992), *Fashion, Culture and Identity*, Chicago: University of Chicago Press.

Douglas, M. and Isherwood, B. (1979), *The World of Goods: Towards an Anthropology of Consumption*, London: Allen Lane.

Elliott, R. (1994), 'Exploring the symbolic meaning of brands', *British Journal of Management*, 5, Special Issue, 13–19.

—— and Davies, A. (2005), 'Symbolic brands and authenticity of identity performance', in J. Schroeder and M. Salzer-Morling (eds.), *Brand Culture*, London: Routledge.

—— Jones, A., Benfield, A., and Barlow, M. (1995), 'Overt sexuality in advertising: a discourse analysis of gendered responses', *Journal of Consumer Policy*, 18, 2, 71–92.

Fournier, S. (1998), 'Consumers and their brands: developing relationship theory in consumer research', *Journal of Consumer Research*, 24, 4, 343–73.

Goffman, E. (1969), *The Presentation of Self in Everyday Life*, London: Allen Lane.

Goulding, C., Shankar, A., and Elliott, R. (2002), 'Working weeks, rave weekends: identity fragmentation and the emergence of new communities', *Consumption, Markets, and Culture*, 5, 4, 261–84.

Grayson, K. and Shulman, D. (2000), 'Indexicality and the verification function of irreplaceable possessions', *Journal of Consumer Research*, 27, June, 17–30.

Harvey, M. and Evans, M. (2001), 'Decoding competitive propositions: a semiotic alternative to traditional advertising research', *International Journal of Market Research*, 43, 1, 171–87.

Holbrook, M. and Schindler, R. (1994), 'Age, sex and attitude towards the past as predictors of consumers' aesthetic tastes for cultural products', *Journal of Marketing Research*, XXXI, 412–22.

—— (2003), 'Nostalgic bonding: exploring the role of nostalgia in the consumption experience', *Journal of Consumer Behaviour*, 3, 2, 102–7.

Holt, D. (1998), 'Does cultural capital structure American consumption?' *Journal of Consumer Research*, 25, 1, 1–25.

—— (2002), 'Why do brands cause trouble? A dialectical theory of consumer culture and branding', *Journal of Consumer Research*, 29, 1, 70–90.

Horton, D. (2003), 'Green distinctions: the performance of identity among environmental activists', *The Sociological Review*, 64–77.

Kates, S. (2000), 'Out of the closet and out on the streets: gay men and their brand relationships', *Psychology and Marketing*, 17, 6, 493–504.

Klein, N. (2001), *No Logo: Taking Aim at the Brand Bullies*, London: Flamingo.

Lawes, R. (2002), 'Demystifying semiotics: some key questions answered', *International Journal of Market Research*, 44, 3, 251–64.

Levy, S. (1959), 'Symbols for sale', *Harvard Business Review*, 37, 4, 117–24.

Ligas, M. and Cotte, J. (1999), 'The process of negotiating brand meaning: a symbolic interactionist perspective', *Advances in Consumer Research*, 26, 609–14.

Mathlouthi, T. (2003), Interviewed on BBC World News/BBC News Online, 8 January 2003.

McAlexander, J., Schouten, J., and Koenig, H. (2002), 'Building brand community', *Journal of Marketing*, 66, 38–54.

McCracken, G. (1993), 'The value of the brand: an anthropological perspective', in D. Aaker and A. Biel (eds.), *Brand Equity and Advertising*, Hillsdale: Lawrence Erlbaum.

Mindy, J. (2002), 'Children's relationships with brands: "true love" or "one-night stand"?', *Psychology and Marketing*, 19, 4, 369–81.

Monga, A (2002), 'Brand as relationship partner: gender differences in perspective', *Advances in Consumer Research*, 29, 36–41.

Muniz, A. and O'Guinn, T. (2001), 'Brand communities', *Journal of Consumer Research*, 27, March, 412–32.

Nancarrow, C., Nancarrow, P., and Page, J. (2002), 'An analysis of the concept of cool and its marketing implications', *Journal of Consumer Behaviour*, 1, 4, 311–22.

Olsen, B. (1999), 'Exploring women's brand relationships and enduring themes at mid-life', *Advances in Consumer Research*, 26, 615–20.

Park, J., Kim, K., and Kim, J. (2002), 'Acceptance of brand extensions: interactive influence of product category similarity, typicality of claimed benefits, and brand relationship quality', *Advances in Consumer Research*, 29, 190–202.

Park, W., Jaworski, B., and MacInnis, D. (1986), 'Strategic brand concept-image management', *Journal of Marketing*, 50, 135–45.

Parveen, Z. (2003), Interviewed on Islam-Online.net/English/news/2003–02.

Ritson, M., Elliott, R., and Eccles, S. (1996), 'Reframing IKEA: commodity-signs, consumer creativity and the social/self dialectic', *Advances in Consumer Research*, 23, 127–31.

Sartre, J-P. (1956/2003), *Being and Nothingness: An Essay on Phenomenological Ontology*, London: Routledge.

Slater, D. (1997), *Consumer Culture and Modernity*, Cambridge: Polity.

Supphellen, M. and Grønhaug, K. (2003), 'Building foreign brand personalities in Russia: the moderating effect of consumer ethnocentrism', *International Journal of Advertising*, 22, 203–26.

Thornton, S. (1995), *Club Cultures: Music, Media and Subcultural Capital*, Cambridge: Polity Press.

Veblen, T. (1899/1979), *The Theory of the Leisure Class*, New York: Kelly.

Brand Equity

This section introduces the concept of brand equity and provides a model for its assessment, with detailed consideration of consumer research methods and tracking systems.

Brand Equity

 KEY CONCEPTS

1 Brand equity has both a financial and a consumer aspect.

2 Brand equity, from a financial perspective, considers the importance of brands in terms of asset value to a company.

3 Brand equity from a consumer perspective results from awareness of a brand leading to brand knowledge and positive attitude towards the brand, resulting in loyalty to the brand.

4 Brand attitude plays the most important role in building brand equity.

Introduction

In the last chapter, it was pointed out how brands can be used as signalling systems in order to create and send social meaning, and that it is the meaning of brands that give them added value. In this chapter we are going to take a closer look at this notion of added value. Since the late 1980s marketers have talked about this idea of added value in terms of something they called brand equity. But what is meant by the term 'brand equity' is anything but clear. Nevertheless, there is a general consensus, and we shall be exploring it, why it is important, and how to build and sustain a positive brand equity.

Name value

Before turning attention to the concept of brand equity, it would be a good idea to consider the general idea of how a particular name, and that name alone, may be associated in memory with specific value. Thinking about areas of life outside of the realm of products and services, there are many places where a 'name' makes all the difference in the world. For example, when not well, it is one thing for a friend to suggest a cure, quite another a doctor. People recognize the added credibility associated with the 'name' doctor when it comes to ailments. There is a definite added value to a doctor's recommendation.

Have you ever been in a museum or art gallery and found yourself looking at a painting with which you were not familiar? How does your opinion of that painting differ if you learn it is the work of a familiar 'great master' artist vs. if you see that it is by an unknown artist, one you have never heard of? Even when someone does not like a painting, they tend to think better of it if they learn it is by a master. In these situations, it is the name value that makes a difference. In fact, the name value in a case like this can also have very real financial value.

In 1968, a group of eminent art historians were charged with the task of examining Rembrandt's oeuvre, with the goal of compiling a definitive catalogue of his paintings. It was called the Rembrandt Research Project, and it was to go on for over 30 years. The art historians involved travelled the world to examine over 600 paintings reputed to be by the hand of Rembrandt. Many proved to be overly optimistic attributions. In their examination of 280 paintings just from the period 1625–1642, only 146, a little over half, were considered to be autograph works (i.e. actually by the hand of Rembrandt). Many of the paintings no longer attributed to him were found in the collections of many of the world's greatest museums.

The value of the paintings no longer considered to be autograph works dropped dramatically. It was not unusual for paintings that had been valued at well over £2 million to suddenly be re-valued at less than £100, 000. The point here is that the actual painting itself, the image on the canvas, did not change. It was exactly the same painting originally acquired by the collection. But the perceived value was in the *name* Rembrandt.

This idea of name value is at the heart of what is known as brand equity. There is a value to a brand over and above the intrinsic value of the product itself. Just as with the de-attributed Rembrandt, the product itself, the painting, had one value; but with the name Rembrandt attached to the painting, significant added value was created.

Defining brand equity

Marketers have always understood the idea that brand names add value to a product, but it was not until the late 1980s that this notion began to figure in the actual asset value of a company. Kapferer (1998) has suggested that this change came about during the massive wave of mergers and acquisitions among large companies with well-known brands that occurred in the 1980s. Those spearheading these transactions were looking beyond the traditional sense of asset value and net income to include 'goodwill'. They were interested in a company's brand portfolio because of the power of these brands in the market. Even if accepted accounting procedure did not permit considering the added value of a brand name on the balance sheet, it was nonetheless being factored into the net value of the firm.

Out of all this activity the term brand equity was born. Unfortunately, there were almost as many definitions of brand equity as there were people using the term. Fig. 5.1 lists just a few definitions offered by marketing executive at the time. While they each take a somewhat different specific view, they all are describing how a brand name provides added value to a product. In the end, they seem to see this added value either in financial terms, or in how consumers perceive the brand.

In Fig. 5.2 we have several definitions of brand equity that were offered by academics in 1980 at an MSI (Marketing Science Institute) conference called to address the issue. Although the language may be more 'academic', it is clear that both marketing executives

---

- Brand equity can be thought of as the additional cash flow achieved by associating a brand with the underlying product or service (Alexander Biel)[1]
- Brand equity is the difference between the value of the brand to the consumer and the value of the product without that branding (Josh McQueen)[2]
- Brand equity is the measurable financial value in transactions that accrues to a product or service from successful programs and activities related to branding (J. Walker Smith)[2]
- Brand equity to me in its simplest definition is the value of worth that resides in a particular brand name, trademark or product. It is not one single thing but a composite . . . it is all the elements created by marketing, advertising, research, and production, that over the years have made the product or service what it is in consumers' minds today (John Pagano)[3]
- One expert might say it is the residual equity that remains after you compare the blind and identified versions of the same product (Richard Chay)[3]

[1] ARF Researching the Power of Brands Workshop, 12–13 February 1992.
[2] ARF Brand Equity Workshop, 5 February 1991.
[3] ARF Brand Equity Workshop, 22–23 February 1990.

Fig. 5.1 Brand equity definitions from marketing executives

- Specific attribute beliefs and global evaluative beliefs consumers have learned to associate with the brand name (John and Loken)[1]
- Net value of brand image (i.e. mental inventory which people hold for a brand); brand image is specific associations with brand and overall attitudes toward brand in memory, as perceived by decision-makers (Aaker and Keller)[1]
- The incremental cash flows which accure to a branded product over and above the cash flows which would result from the sale of a product (Simon and Sullivan)[1]
- The **added value** with which a given brand endows a product. A product is something that offers a functional benefit (e.g. toothpaste, a life insurance policy, or a car). A brand is name, symbol design or mark that **enhances the value of a product beyond its functional purpose** (Faquhar)[2]

[1] MSI working paper presented at 1990 Marketing Science Institute Conference on brand equity.
[2] Marketing Research, 1, September, 24–33 (1989).

Fig. 5.2 Brand equity definitions from academics

---

and academics define brand equity in much the same way. Both groups see it in terms of either financial considerations or consumer perceptions of a brand.

Some people at the time defined brand equity in terms of both financial considerations *and* consumer perceptions of the brand. William Moran (1991), a marketing executive much involved with the strategic importance of brand equity in the 1990s, defined it in 1991 as: 'I believe the concept of brand equity to be that any given brand name, itself, has particular meaning and value to its consumers and to its direct customers, the distributive trade, which affects the future earning potential of the product or products which are sold under that name.' In the same year, in his book *Managing Brand Equity* (arguably the first book to deal with the subject seriously), Dave Aaker (1991) at the University of California in Berkeley defined brand equity as: 'A set of brand assets and liabilities linked to a brand, its name and symbol, that add to or subtract from the value provided by a product or service to a firm and/or to that firm's customers.'

But in looking at all these definitions of brand equity, are we really closer to *understanding* it? There have been any number of ways proposed to measure brand equity, but they are as varied as the definitions. In the early 1990s Sattler (1994) looked at forty-nine different studies of brand equity that had been conducted in Europe and the US and found in them at least twenty-six different ways of measuring it! How to measure brand equity will be discussed in the next chapter, but this incredible lack of consensus reflects the rather unsettled state of just what constituted brand equity (a situation not much changed today).

In a very real sense, understanding brand equity must come from the consumer's point of view because that is what ultimately will affect brand success. It is the consumer's sense of added value that will lead to preference for a particular brand. Financial consequences of brand equity will follow from the consumer's perception of added value. But before considering more carefully how consumers come to understand this added value for a brand, the financial consequences to a company of a positive brand equity will be addressed.

Financial perspective

Strong brands have become an important part of the asset value of a company. Prior to 1980, when large companies were acquired or merged, the ratio of the price paid to the firm's earnings were generally in the area of about eight to one. After 1980, multiples of twenty or more times earnings were not unusual (Aaker, 1991). Why was this? While there are always special circumstances in some cases, at the heart of things was an increasing realization of the importance of strong brand names to a company's long-term *financial* success.

Gone was the notion that only traditional assets in bricks and mortar, patents, or R&D had value. Brand names were increasingly seen as one of a company's most important assets. In earlier times a firm interested in acquiring a beer marketer would be thinking in terms of a brewery; now they want to acquire names like Molsen or Bass. Even if a company is not doing well financially, it could still be an attractive merger or acquisition target if it has strong brands. As Kapferer (1998) has put it so well in describing such situations: 'Balance sheets reflect bad management decisions in the past, whereas the brand is a potential source of future profits.'

For financial analysts, a key consideration when looking at companies with strong brands is that they present less risk. Strong brands generally remain strong, and this assumes the likelihood of a solid income stream. This strong income stream reflects the interaction of several factors. With a strong market share usually comes relatively higher price points, coupled with lower price elasticity relative to competitors. This leads to better margins and a higher return on investment. Poor management can be corrected; significantly increasing market share for a weak brand is much more difficult.

Well-known brands are much more likely to enjoy good distribution, which helps maintain high market share. For fmcgs (fast moving consumer goods), where the competition for shelf space is fierce, strong brands have the advantage. Because of strong consumer demand, distributors and retailers will be inclined to carry the brand. For less frequently purchased products, especially industrial products, wholesalers and distributors will again be keen to associate with a strong brand because they know it will sell.

Summarizing all this, strong brands, brands with a strong positive brand equity, are generally brands with a highly loyal core of consumers; and high market share as a result. This leads to a number of advantages in marketing the brand that help sustain its position, and contribute to its financial value. With a high degree of brand loyalty, a company can expect sales to remain stable and strong over time. Because of continuing consumer demand, a strong brand will be more attractive to the trade, leading to good levels of distribution. This in itself will help maintain higher market share.

Having high brand loyalty means a company can charge a relatively higher price for its product and maintain higher margins than its competitors in the category. It also means price elasticity is low (the brand will be less sensitive to competitive price reductions, especially competitor promotions). All this helps generate a high net profit and ROI (return on investment) for the company, as we see in Fig. 5.3.

In addition, there are many other areas where having a strong brand name will help contribute to building and maintaining higher profits. For example, a strong brand discourages new competitors from entering the market. It also means less risk when

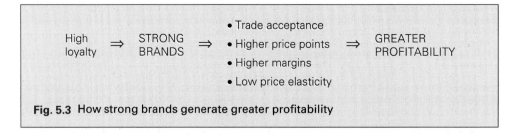

Fig. 5.3 How strong brands generate greater profitability

- High brand loyalty sustains future sales
- Greater trade cooperation and support, minimizing the need for trade incentives
- Sustainable higher price points
- Higher margins vs. competitors
- Low price elasticity
- Barrier to new competitors
- Less risk for line and product extensions

Fig. 5.4 Strong brand contributions to financial value

introducing line extensions, or extending the brand name into new product categories (areas that will be covered in Chapter 11). Additionally, a strong brand has internal resonance, and can lead to becoming an 'employer brand' and improved employee relationships (as discussed in Chapter 10). How strong brands contribute to financial value is listed in Fig. 5.4.

There is no question that the financial value of a brand reflects its brand equity, and some people even define brand equity in terms of financial value. But, we would argue that the financial value of a brand is the *result* of brand equity (among other things, of course) and not the definition of brand equity. Rather, a positive brand equity provides value to a company by enhancing such things as marketing programmes, brand loyalty, price and margins, and trade leverage, and by providing a platform for brand extensions. In our view, as mentioned above, brand equity must be considered in terms of the consumer's response to the brand, and this is reflected in their overall attitude toward the brand.

Consumer perspective

If brand equity is something that adds value to a brand, how is that reflected in consumer perceptions of the brand? In the last chapter, for example, we discussed how the perceived social meaning of brands adds value. Aaker (1991) talks about how brands bring value to the consumer by reducing risk, and offers eight functions of a brand that create value for a consumer (things like the ability to easily identify the product, an assurance of consistency, and quality). Franzen (1999) looks at a brand's value to the consumer in terms of something he calls 'mental brand equity', described in terms of awareness, perception, and attitude, and 'behavioural brand equity' that accounts for various aspects of purchase behaviour.

Aaker (1991) describes brand equity as a set of assets and liabilities that he groups into four categories: brand awareness, brand associations, perceived quality, and brand loyalty.

While the words may be different, the ideas expressed here are basically the same. What they all have in common is a sense that brand equity springs from a consumer awareness for the brand that triggers associations in memory that are linked to the brand. Over time, this positive brand attitude takes on strong emotional associations that extend well beyond simply 'liking' the brand. At its most positive, brand equity is much like what Hall (1959) has described as a 'formal system'. In people's lives, they look for rules to govern certain aspects of their behaviour so that it is not necessary to make decisions continuously about everything they do. One knows when a formal system is being challenged because there is no readily available rational response. Everyone has experienced as a child asking their parents why they can't do something, or why certain things are as they are, and received a frustrated 'because' as the answer. A formal system has been challenged. There is no ready reason, it just is not done, or just is that way.

This sounds very much like what is involved with brand equity. A loyal user of a brand just 'knows' it is better. When loyal Coke drinkers are asked why they prefer it to Pepsi, they may offer some reason like it 'tastes better'. But if it is pointed out that they failed to prefer it in a blind taste test, and are again asked why they prefer it over Pepsi when they cannot tell the difference in taste, the response is often a frustrated 'because'. They just know they like it better. The favourable brand attitude built over time by the acceptance of perceived benefits for the brand, and loyal brand behaviour, has resulted in a strong positive brand equity: a preference for the brand that goes beyond any objective consideration of the product. In fact, a fascinating neuroimagery study demonstrated just that.

A taste test between Coke and Pepsi was conducted among drinkers of both brands in order to determine preferences in various pairings of the two colas, in both blind and branded conditions. Many studies over the years have shown that even for regular drinkers of the brand, in blind taste tests preference is random. The interesting aspect of this experiment was that the tasting and preference judgements were carried out during functional magnetic imaging (fMRI). In other words, when people were tasting the colas and picking a favourite, fMRI equipment was measuring the activity occurring in the brain (McClure *et al.*, 2004).

When people did not know what they were tasting, so that preference was based solely on sensory information (the objective characteristics of the product), only the ventromedial prefrontal cortex areas of the brain were active, that area of the brain dealing with sensory evaluation (essentially sweetness in this case). But when there was brand knowledge, at least in the case of Coke, for regular drinkers of Coke the hippocampus, dorsolateral prefrontal cortex (DLPFC), and midbrain were also active. Both the hippocampus and DLPFC are known to be involved in modifying behaviour based upon emotion and affect. In fact, it has been suggested that DLPFC is necessary for employing affective information in biasing behaviour.

What this means is that when taste preferences are based solely upon sensory informa- tion, when people do not know what they are drinking, only that part of the brain that deals with sensory information is utilized. But when there is brand knowledge (at least in the case of Coke in this study), additional areas of the brain are activated, modifying the strictly objective evaluation. These additionally activated areas are those that deal with emotion and affect, and are seen to influence preference decisions. How people 'feel' about a brand does indeed bias their preference for it, leading to decisions based upon much more than the objective characteristics of a product.

Brand equity from the consumer's perspective may be summarized as follows: (1) awareness of a brand leads to (2) learning and the formation of attitudes about that brand, which will be influenced by emotional associations, which results in (3) preferences for that brand, building brand loyalty. Each of these components of brand equity from the consumer's perspective are discussed next.

Brand awareness

The first component to consider is awareness of the brand itself. It may seem obvious that people must be aware of a brand in order to prefer it, but its importance to brand equity goes beyond this. In a study among business managers, where they were asked to identify those things they believe provide a substantial competitive advantage, name recognition was the third most frequently mentioned consideration. Strong brand awareness can indeed provide a significant competitive advantage. Think of centrally positioned brands that quite literally define a product category: Xerox, Kleenex, Hoover, or Levi's (Rossiter and Percy, 1997).

The power of a strong brand awareness comes from the sense of familiarity it brings. As Schacter (1996) has pointed out, familiarity involves a primitive sense of knowing without the need for specific details. This is a real asset for a brand, because in terms of memory, when attention is divided someone is *much* less likely to recall specific details of an experience, but there is little or no effect upon a sense of familiarity. As a result, when shopping, someone is more likely to 'remember' familiar brands than, say, the details of a new brand, or to remember the details of an advert trying to persuade them to switch to another brand.

Aaker (1998) has suggested that in addition to a feeling of familiarity, strong brand awareness also suggests a 'presence, commitment, and substance for the brand'. He points out that this can be especially important for buyers of high-priced products, including expensive business-to-business purchases. In a sense, this is really the result of familiarity with the brand. If someone is aware of a brand, there must be a good reason for it. One is unlikely to be aware of 'minor' or less important brands.

In the end, brand awareness is essential for *intentional* brand purchases. If someone is buying a product and is not concerned about brands, for that person, in that product category there is no such thing as brand equity in the sense we are considering it. This is true even though the brand might be familiar to that person, and even considered a 'good' brand. If that knowledge and feeling do not inform the purchase decision, it is little use to the brand (Zajonc, 1968).

Brand awareness for a purchase may take two forms: recognition or recall (Rossiter and Percy, 1997). Recognition brand awareness reflects the ability to recognize a brand at the point-of-purchase in enough detail to facilitate purchase, something that is needed for most fmcgs. For other purchase or usage decisions, a brand name must be recalled from memory once the need for the product is recognized, such as needing to remember a specific restaurant to go to when deciding to eat out. But for either of these forms of brand awareness to facilitate purchase, the brand must be *salient*. That means it is associated in memory with the consumer's set of preferred brands to meet a particular need, and is likely to come to mind when the need for such a product occurs (Ehrenberg *et al.*, 1997).

When brand awareness is considered as an asset in terms of brand equity, it is really being considered in terms of brand salience. The brand is familiar, and linked in memory with those situations where such a product would be needed; and the more salient the brand, the more likely it will be the chosen or preferred brand when a purchase decision is made. The importance of brand salience to a brand's success has been illustrated by an analysis of an eleven-year tracking study of the effect advertising has on brand awareness, brand attitude, and market share for rental cars. What was found is that market share was primarily influenced by increasing brand salience (Miller and Berry, 1998).

Brand attitude

People who think about brands and what they mean to consumers often talk in terms of things like 'value', 'perceived quality', and 'image'. What this all comes down to is brand attitude, the associations in memory linked to the brand. In the end, this is what brand equity is all about. As already noted, with brand awareness comes the beginning of knowledge about the brand, learning occurs, and salience for the brand builds. Over time, associations are built and attitudes are formed. With a strong, positive brand attitude, key preference and loyalty for the brand results. The key here is a strong, positive brand attitude (Fig. 5.5). The nature of these brand associations that underlie brand attitude will be dealt with next.

Brand associations in memory must be strong, positive, and unique to the brand in order to build a brand attitude that leads to strong brand equity. These associations are a result of any and all communication about a brand to the consumer. This is usually thought about in terms of marketing communication (everything from the package, product placement, and event marketing to traditional advertising and promotion), but it also includes such things as word-of-mouth and experience with the product, as well as more indirect means of communication such as a brand's distribution channels, its parent company, and the environment in which it is used. Every aspect of the relationship between a brand and the consumer contributes to learning that leads to the associations in memory that constitute brand attitude.

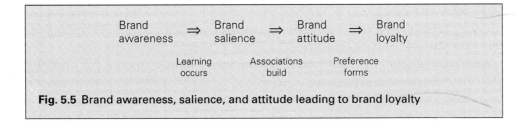

Fig. 5.5 Brand awareness, salience, and attitude leading to brand loyalty

A short review of some descriptions of these brand associations found in the brand management literature will provide a useful starting point. Keller (1998) discussed brand associations under a broader heading of Brand Image, and sees them in terms of what he calls 'attributes', 'benefits', and 'attitudes'. Before going any further, it is important to understand that different authors often use the same terms to mean slightly different things. For example, we would argue that attitudes include an assessment of benefits, which in turn could include or be built upon attributes. It is important not to become too closely focused on terms, but to consider the concepts being discussed by various scholars in the field as they look at the idea of brand associations.

When Keller talks about attributes, he makes a distinction between what he calls product-related attributes and non-product-related attributes. Product-related attributes are the objective characteristics of a brand, such as specific ingredients (e.g. '100% certified organic') or qualities such that they may be specifically measured or discussed (e.g. 'Nationwide over 150 approved installers'). This is in fact how we (Percy and Elliott, 2005) define attributes (in their role as a potential benefit). Keller's non-product-related attributes are described as things that do not directly affect product performance, such things as price, imagery, and feelings. He defines benefits as the personal value and meaning consumers attach to a brand's attributes, and are seen as either functional, symbolic, or experiential. Finally, attitudes are the consumer's overall evaluation of a brand, the typical consumer behaviour definition.

Franzen (1999) discusses what we are talking about as brand associations in terms of 'mental brand equity', one of his three components of brand equity (the others are behavioural brand equity, an area which is considered later; and financial-economic brand equity, a subject already discussed). Three of his characteristics of mental brand equity may be seen in terms of brand associations in memory: product meaning, which deals with a consumer's perceptions of the functional aspects of a product; symbolic meaning, or 'brand personality', which reflects values important to consumers and which differentiates the brand from competitors; and perceived quality.

Aaker (1998), like Keller (1998), talks about this in terms of brand associations, which he broadly defines as anything that is directly or indirectly linked to the brand in memory. He discusses product attributes and consumer brands and details such associations as: organizational, where the focus is more on corporate than product attributes; brand personality, where the brand-as-person is used as a metaphor; symbols to represent the brand; emotional benefits; and something he calls 'self-expressive' benefits, where the brand offers a way for personal expression by the consumer.

In considering these various ways of looking at brand association in memory, what conclusions might be drawn? Although these authors may appear to be describing brand associations in brand equity from different viewpoints, actually there is a reasonable similarity in their views. A careful review suggests that brand associations in memory are seen basically in terms of the objective and subjective characteristics of a product.

Brands have attributes that may be either product or non-product specific, but which are objective characteristics of the brand. This reflects a person's specific knowledge about a brand in memory, and may or may not be seen as a benefit. For example someone may know that a snack brand is 'sugar-free', or that a watch is 'Swiss-made', attributes of the product. These associations in memory form part of their knowledge about the brand. If 'sugar-free' or 'Swiss-made' is important to them when making a snack or watch brand choice, these attributes will be seen as a benefit and contribute to a positive brand attitude, which will help build a strong brand equity. If they are not important, that knowledge about the brand will not be seen as a benefit, and will not contribute to positive brand attitude.

On the other hand, brands may also be seen in a number of subjective ways, reflecting perceptions of the brand's 'personality' or symbolic meaning. These too may or may not be considered benefits by the consumer, but they constitute a person's assumptions about a brand in memory. Both knowledge and assumptions are brought to bear when a person sees or thinks about a brand, during what neuropsychologists call *top-down processing*. On the other hand, a person could see a brand in the store, recognize it, and purchase it almost reflexively without 'thinking' (along the lines of what Howard (1977) long ago talked about as 'routinized response behaviour'). This would be analogous to what neuropsychologists call *bottom-up processing*, where no real 'thinking' or cognitive activity is involved. But when you think about a brand choice, all of someone's knowledge and assumptions about the brand will become involved. Usually, this has been summarized in what is considered brand attitude, so a choice decision can be made quickly and easily.

In effect, what people like Keller, Franzen, and Aaker are doing when they detail various brand associations is to try and describe how knowledge and assumptions about brands might be organized. While useful, it does not help in understanding *how* these brand associations are likely to be involved in actually making a brand choice. Another way of looking at this objective vs. subjective distinction in brand associations is in terms of the functional vs. emotional domains introduced in Chapter 1. Recall that the functional domain deals with basic consumer benefits that reflect a brand's ability to perform as promised. This requires positive associations in memory related to product attributes, as well as with product quality. When choices are not easy and more trust in a brand is needed, emotional associations become more important. While there are emotional associations with all memories, the involvement of emotional associations with particular memories increases when these memories deal with more socially or personally relevant experiences, those with more symbolic meanings.

How does this distinction help in understanding how brand associations influence brand choice decisions better than a simple objective vs. subjective distinction? This important distinction between functional and emotional domains takes things one step further, because it better reflects how the mind deals with processing information when making brand decisions. In the early chapters of this book we looked at the emotional, social, and cultural meaning of brands, and how this reflects trust in a brand, and also helps transform how a person experiences life and projects social and cultural identities. All of this meaning is informed by non-declarative emotional memory (NDEM), which is located in the amygdala, out-of-consciousness.

What seems to happen is that when a person experiences something, a brand in this case, what is known about it (their knowledge and assumptions), is called into working memory *along with* any emotional associations with that experience. In the functional realm, brand choices are easy because of a simple trust in the brand. There are no emotional complications because the NDEM associations with that brand reflect a fundamental emotion of comfort. Someone sees a brand, 'knows' it is one they like, perhaps even remembers a benefit, and 'feels' comfortable with it.

In the emotional realm, a brand must do more, so more is involved. More will have gone into the formation of brand attitude, and potentially many NDEMs will be associated with various aspects of the brand in memory. And the more difficult the choice, the more involving, the more *emotional* associations are likely to be involved. The wider array of knowledge and assumptions stored in declarative memory (that part of memory that contains what we 'know we know', what we are conscious of), reflecting more complicated brand meaning, enter working memory when someone is confronted with a more difficult brand choice, along with NDEMs. A person imagines how they will *feel* if they choose a particular brand, what it might say about them, or perhaps simply that they need not be afraid of spending so much money on it. This process is illustrated in Fig. 5.6.

In summary then, the many different ways of looking at brand associations reflect the basic distinction between the objective and subjective characteristics of a product that go into building brand attitude. They form the foundation of one's knowledge and assumptions about brands, and are used in making brand evaluations. This is enough when dealing with easy decisions where only negative motivations are involved, the need to solve or avoid a simple problem, and where the role of emotion is relatively minor. But when brand choice involves positive motivations, where personal or social rewards are sought in using a product, or when there are serious consequences attending a bad brand choice decision, emotion is much more involved in making brand evaluations. Thinking about brand associations as reflecting objective vs. subjective product characteristics, but within either a functional or emotional domain, provides a good way of understanding the role brand associations play in forming brand attitude, leading to a strong brand equity.

As a person learns about brands, over time a summary judgement is made about the brand. They like it, hate it, love it, or don't really care much about it. This judgement is the

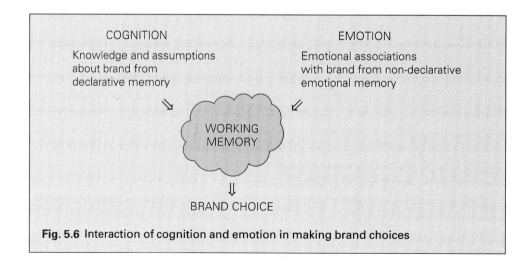

Fig. 5.6 Interaction of cognition and emotion in making brand choices

result of many things; in fact, all those things Keller, Franzen, Aaker and others talk about, and much more. It reflects a person's knowledge and assumptions about a brand, and their emotional associations with it. This summary judgment is basically what we have been talking about as brand attitude. People do not start from scratch every time they evaluate a brand, recalling everything they have learned and experienced about the brand. Rather, they rely upon already formed attitudes; attitudes that reflect *trust* in the brand.

Why? Because it reflects a person's evaluations of a brand over time. For brand loyal consumers (considered in the next section) and for simple brand choice decisions, an overall brand attitude is enough to make a decision. But for more involved choices in the emotional realm, other aspects of a brand's meaning will also be involved in working memory as a brand choice decision is made. But overall brand attitude will still *frame* the decision. Changing brand attitude is very difficult because of everything that goes into forming it in the first place; and in the end, this is why a favourable brand attitude is at the core of a strong brand equity.

Brand loyalty

A strong positive brand equity is also marked by strong loyalty to the brand. In effect, it is a *consequence* of the brand equity, just as was noted for financial value. The building of a strong positive brand attitude generally leads to a preference for the brand, and over time a loyalty towards it. Basically, brand loyal consumers have a reluctance to switch brands. As Franzen (1999) has put it, loyal brand users have a 'high degree of bonding with the brand and do not show much of an urge to switch'.

This 'bonding' he speaks of is a part of brand equity. But brand loyalty does not necessarily need to be a *function* of brand equity, even if it contributes to it. Brand loyalty may simply be out of habit; or it may be that the cost of switching to another brand is too high. Sometimes, it is simply not worth the effort. But when loyalty to a brand results from a genuine preference for it, it contributes to brand equity; and when it transcends rational preference (as seen, for example, in the cola taste test discussed earlier in the chapter), it becomes sustained by brand equity.

Let us consider this issue of brand loyalty from a management perspective, and how to determine whether or not loyal brand behaviour may be accounted as part of the brand's asset value. If brand loyalty is the result of habituation, it may or may not be a sustainable asset. Such purchases will usually fall into the functional realm because the brand choice is easy and there is general satisfaction with the product. The brand manager's job is to see that satisfaction is maintained, in terms of product performance as well as perception. To the extent that satisfaction is maintained and switching minimized, habitual brand purchase may be factored into the asset value of the brand, and hence a part of brand equity. But care must be taken to maintain satisfaction.

The role of perceived risk in switching when looking at brand loyalty is illustrated by Percy and Elliot (2005) in their Loyalty Model (Fig. 5.7). As shown, even though someone regularly purchases or uses a brand, their loyalty is not assured. Only when a consumer is very satisfied and there is high perceived risk in switching can their loyalty be assured. Even someone very satisfied could be lured away if the barriers to switching are low.

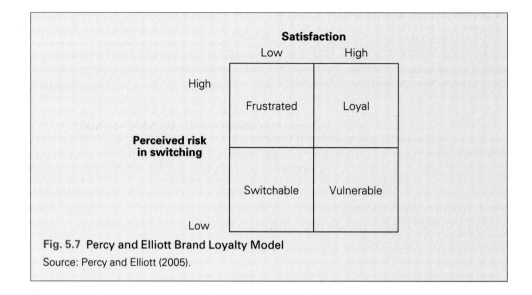

Fig. 5.7 Percy and Elliott Brand Loyalty Model
Source: Percy and Elliott (2005).

This is especially true for low-involvement purchase decisions, as is the case with most fmcgs. Think about a snack brand you really like, and buy all the time. What if you learned about a new brand entering the market that was very similar to your favourite, and when shopping you saw a special display for the new brand? It is being offered at a special introductory price that was about half the price of your favourite brand. Would you be tempted to try it? There is almost no risk involved in buying. It is very inexpensive, and if you don't like it as well as your favourite, you are not out very much.

What this example illustrates is that even very satisfied consumers may be vulnerable if the cost of switching is low. In this case, the brand manager for your favourite snack might want to run a promotion of some kind just prior to the introduction of the new brand to encourage loyal customers to 'stock up'. This is something called a *loading promotion*, and in effect takes people out of the market during the new brand's introduction, minimizing the likelihood of customers trying the new brand at its lower, introductory price.

Another model that takes into account the fact that brand loyalty involves more than just purchase behaviour is the so-called Conversion Model suggested by Hofmeyr (1990). It recognizes, as does the Percy and Elliot Loyalty Model, that it is the attitudinal component of brand loyalty that is the key to its role in a brand's equity. The Conversion Model looks at brand loyalty in terms of commitment to the brand in the case of users, and availability (i.e. openness to trying) among non-users (see Fig. 5.8). Users are seen as either 'secure' or 'vulnerable', and non-users are either open to possible trial or unavailable. Within the context of brand equity, secure users are a part of a brand's assets, but vulnerable users are unlikely to attach positive equity to the brand. Non-users open to a brand will have at least a positive brand attitude, even if not strong, and thus the potential for building brand equity. Those 'unavailable' are not likely to hold attitudes toward the brand that offer any potential for building brand equity.

In an interesting study using the Conversion Model to segment category users, people who are more committed to a brand reflecting a positive brand equity respond to advertising

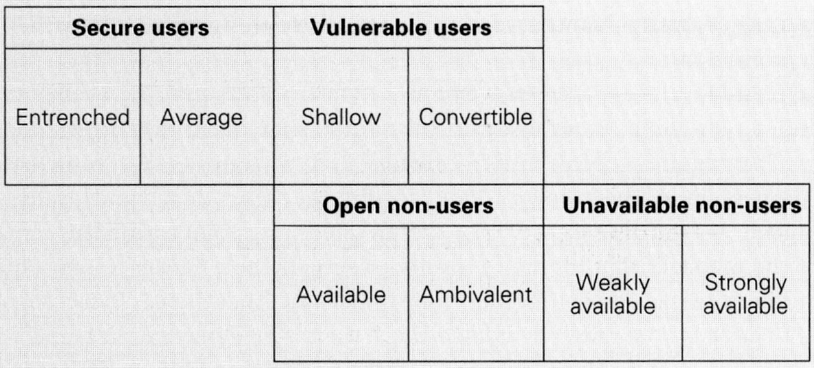

Secure users		Vulnerable users			
Entrenched	Average	Shallow	Convertible		

		Open non-users		Unavailable non-users	
		Available	Ambivalent	Weakly available	Strongly available

Fig. 5.8 Hofmeyr conversion model for mature fmcg markets

for the brand in a significantly more positive way. The results of the study are important for any product where the purchase decision is driven by positive motives, and in the emotional realm, where 'liking' advertising is critical to its effectiveness. It was found that those committed to a brand are 2–3 times more likely to 'like' a brand's advertising vs. those classified as vulnerable. Additionally, non-users open to a brand are significantly more likely to find the brand's advertising 'likable' than those unavailable (Rice and Bennett, 1998).

The management implications for building brand equity are clear. Among 'vulnerable' brand users, the task of building positive brand attitude will be difficult. Their general lack of commitment to the brand seems to lead to less interest in and 'liking' of marketing communication aimed at building positive brand attitude. This is certainly what might be expected from the results of neuropsychological studies. Without being able to communicate effectively with less committed consumers, it will be difficult to build a positive brand attitude, at least for those brand purchase decisions involving positive motivations within the emotional realm. And this, as already discussed, will make it unlikely that brand equity will develop.

This is another example of why it is so important to understand the *attitudes* of consumers, not simply whether they are regular purchasers of a brand. In this case, those not committed to a brand, even though they are users, will not perceive much equity in the brand, and will be less inclined to be positively influenced. This does not mean, of course, that it is impossible to build positive brand attitude and equity, and with it increased commitment to the brand, only that it will not be easy. Again the important thing is to realize that it is the brand equity that leads to brand loyalty; and just because someone regularly uses a brand does not mean that their behaviour is sustained by a positive brand equity.

When strong positive brand equity leads to brand loyalty it results in significant competitive advantages; and these advantages tend to last over time because of that loyalty. Perhaps the most important competitive advantage is that when a brand enjoys a large core of loyal consumers it significantly reduces marketing costs. Sustaining positive brand attitude is much easier, and less costly, than building brand attitude. Repeat purchase objectives are less costly than trial objectives. And, with strong brand loyalty there is less need for promotion.

Strong brand loyalty can also form a barrier to new brands entering a category. To be successful, a new competitor must gain substantial share from existing brands in the category. This requires getting current category users to consider switching (or at least trying) the new brand. The stronger a brand's equity, the higher their brand loyalty and the more difficult this will be. Aaker (1998) makes an interesting point within this context. He reminds the manager that for brand loyalty to actually be a barrier to new entry in a category, the potential competitor must fully understand that there is in fact high brand loyalty, not just behaviourally, but *attitudinally*. If there is a feeling that the brand loyalty is soft, that users are vulnerable in terms of satisfaction or commitment, it will not be seen as much of a barrier. Aaker suggests that a brand with substantial strong brand loyalty makes certain the market knows it.

Finally, strong brand loyalty leads to better leverage with the trade. When distributors and retailers know that a brand enjoys strong customer loyalty, they know the product will move out of their warehouses and off their shelves. They will also understand that there is a strong consumer demand for the brand, and that if they do not handle it, they will lose customers.

Model of Brand Equity Synthesis

In the previous sections a number of components of brand equity were discussed. These components may be synthesized into a model, as shown in Fig. 5.9. This Model of Brand Equity Synthesis illustrates the importance of brand attitude in driving brand equity, as well as the roles of other significant components. No single component may be used to define brand equity, although brand attitude does *approximate* brand equity because in the end it is the target market's attitude towards a brand that will determine its success. This is why brand attitude is shown as an umbrella, covering all aspects of brand equity. Although a brand may have high awareness without a positive brand attitude (e.g. a brand that has suffered from bad publicity), without a favourable brand attitude a brand is unlikely to enjoy positive emotional associations in memory, brand loyalty, or the resulting financial value that attends a strong positive equity.

In looking at the model, the major components of brand attitude are outlined at the top. Here are the major distinctions between objective and subjective characteristics of a brand and how they lead to knowledge and assumptions about the brand. This reflects the target market's cognitive understanding of a brand, and may be further understood in terms of the functional vs. emotional realm that define the social psychology of brands. While objective characteristics dominate considerations in the functional realm and subjective characteristics in the emotional realm, they are by no means discrete. Each will in some way also influence the other.

The other major components of brand equity are brand awareness, emotional associations, brand loyalty, and financial value. Brand awareness is an obvious, but also critical

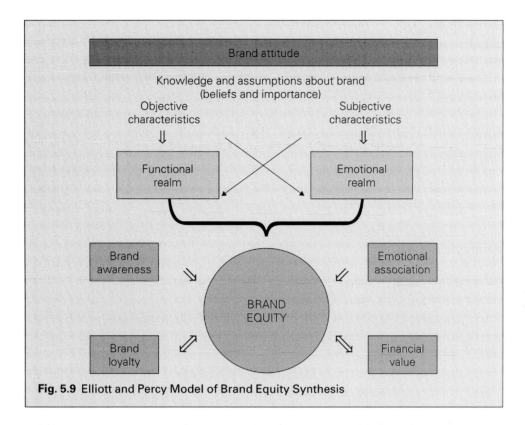

Fig. 5.9 Elliott and Percy Model of Brand Equity Synthesis

component of brand equity. It is not enough to simply think that one must be aware of a brand before anything else. It is important to realize that strong brand equity *reflects* high brand awareness. Many studies have shown a strong correlation between a strong brand equity and high levels of brand awareness. In fact, some people even use brand salience (or first brand to come to mind with a category cue) as a rough measure of brand equity.

Emotion is important because there are emotional associations in memory with all brands with which someone is aware. These emotional associations will be active in any consideration of a brand, interacting with knowledge and assumptions, and mediating brand equity. Brand loyalty, that is true *attitudinal* brand loyalty, is a contributor to as well as a consequence of brand equity, hence the two-way arrow in the model. As favourable brand attitude builds, leading to increases in brand equity, the target market becomes more loyal to the brand, and as the brand is more regularly purchased and used, that behaviour in itself reinforces and helps build brand equity. Financial value too enjoys a two-way relationship with brand equity. A strong brand equity will lead to significant financial advantage for a brand in its market, as we have seen. At the same time, because of the leverage available as a result of a strong brand equity (e.g. in terms of higher price points and elasticity, and better distribution), marketing strength is available to sustain and build brand equity.

The Elliot and Percy Model of Brand Equity Synthesis provides a good summary of the indicators and consequences of brand equity.

CHAPTER SUMMARY

In this chapter the rather amorphous idea of brand equity has been explored. We began by looking at how a name has the ability to provide value beyond the objective characteristics of an object, and noted that this concept is at the heart of brand equity. It was seen that there are many definitions of brand equity, all of which address this notion of 'added value', some in terms of financial considerations, but most from a consumer's perspective. These consumer-oriented definitions all seem to have in common the idea that brand equity is the result of awareness for a brand triggering associations in memory linked to it, leading to a strong brand attitude with positive emotional associations that go beyond merely 'liking' the brand. A Model of Brand Equity Synthesis was introduced, which highlights the key components of brand equity and emphasizes the critical role of brand attitude.

DISCUSSION QUESTIONS

1 Contrast the role of brand equity from a financial vs. consumer perspective.

2 How does brand equity 'add value' to a brand?

3 Discuss what you see as the most critical component of a strong brand equity.

4 What do the various definitions of brand equity offered by Aaker, Frazen, and Keller have in common; and how are they different?

5 How important are the differences between these definitions?

6 Discuss the relationship between and among the components of brand equity that make up the Model of Brand Equity Synthesis.

CASE STUDY

Evergood Coffee

Norway is a country of few brands. One of the main exceptions to this rule is Evergood coffee, which can look back on 36 years of steadily rising popularity and market share, and always at a profit. In the course of these years there have been Cannes Lions and several Clio golds. Most important though: to be part of Norwegian marketing history.

- Over the past 32 years, Evergood Coffee has invested NOK 138 million in advertising, to create a revenue stream exceeding NOK 5 billion.

- In the past five years alone, the profit on this investment has been NOK 195 million, building a 'hidden value' of NOK 300 million in brand equity along the way.

- The brand is by far the most preferred in the market as a whole, but also amongst the customers in the two chains that never even carried the brand.

The Norwegian market for ground coffee

The Scandinavians are indeed heavy drinkers of coffee. The most common type of coffee by far is ground roast, constituting more than 90% of coffee consumed. With such a high consumption there should be no surprise that this market is hotly contested with several nationally distributed brands that all invest heavily in marketing and distribution. Approximately 34,000 tons of coffee is sold annually in Norway. 85% of this volume is sold through grocery stores.

In our case, Evergood is distributed in only half of the Norwegian grocery stores, the reason being that Joh. Johannson, the owner of the brand, has since 1991 also been the majority shareholder in Norgesgruppen. Therefore, the three competing groups (Rema, ICA and Coop) are reluctant to sell a brand that is owned by their biggest grocery competitor. Only the ICA group sells some Evergood due to the strong preference that the brand enjoys, but has upped the price since 1992, and as a result given it 'less favourable' placement in the shops to milk its popularity. Altogether Evergood has a market coverage of 57%.

The marketing strategy for Evergood

Right from the start it was decided that the strategy of being 'slightly more expensive because taste matters' should be the guiding star for all marketing actions. Evergood was never intended to be a big brand. Instead it was meant to be a small and profitable brand. This resulted in a brand with an unusual consistency—never discount—always the same strategy.

1. The product: The blend was a quality selection, including a small percentage of the most exclusive quality offered on the commodities exchange, the Kenya Blue Mountain quality. Extra care was taken so that the taste should not differ from season to season, or year to year (thus the name Evergood). This made it the first brand with a consistent product strategy.

2. The price: Evergood should be 'slightly more expensive'; it was never to be discounted. Even though consumers will find 'specials' on the marque, this is only because the trade has cut their margins to attract more customers. From the coffee house of Joh. Johannson the product has never been discounted! (UK readers should note that coupons are forbidden in Norway, so price reductions are given in store and available to everyone when offered.)

3. The distribution: Being the first to aim for a national brand, Evergood rapidly increased distribution to a point where it peaked at 60%. Owing to the integration of the retail trade over the past years it has fallen out of grace with major chains that would rather sell other brands or even own brands, so market coverage has taken a slight dip down.

4. The promotion: This is what makes this case especially interesting: without coupons and with very limited use of other promotions, the Evergood brand has been the product of good old-fashioned mass communication such as commercials and print advertising. This combined with the fact that the mass communication has had a national reach, but only 62% market coverage, has created an ideal testing ground for a 'split run' situation to control the effect of the advertising.

In 1976, Evergood started below Friele—its main competitor—in preference but passed it after a couple of years, and has maintained a steady lead. It is an interesting fact that every time Evergood has been facing stiffer competition, the consumer response has been new levels of preference, and as a result it has remained the most popular coffee brand even amongst customers of chains that never carried the brand.

The owners of Evergood believe in advertising and have been outspending their competitors up till 2002. It seems very likely that this is the main explanation for Evergood's remarkable ability to hold on to its preference in the population being under hard attack from both Friele and $\frac{3}{4}$ of the distribution. However, in the last year Friele has for the first time been the best selling brand probably due to increasing advertising spending and better market coverage.

What kind of values has the Evergood advertising created?

In addition to market share and profits there has been a substantial build-up of 'hidden values' in brand equity for Evergood coffee. There are several ways to estimate brand equity. None of the methods can claim superiority, and the fact is that when a brand is up for sale one can usually apply several methods. The most common methods seem to be:

Estimated net value of the communications investment corrected for inflation: This method is characterized by overestimating the value of young brands with heavy advertising investments. In Evergood's case it is the opposite that is true having been advertised for more than 30 years. With this method the value is estimated at NOK 300 million.

The conversion model: This method is characterized by trying to convert a given budget to results in the form of awareness, trial, penetration, frequency, market share. The calculations are done backwards from market share to awareness, that is: how much must you gain at every level to obtain a certain market share? To achieve results at Evergood's level we can estimate the cost and thus the value at NOK 140 million. To this an insurance premium must be deducted in case one doesn't achieve sufficient distribution or fails the positioning. In total a sum of NOK 250 million seems realistic. The insurance premium constitutes the brand's estimated result over three years.

Indirect value assessment: This is more of an economist's method. One estimates the brand's contribution to the profits over the years the brand is expected to 'live' (normally restricted to 10 years). This is discounted to a cash flow analysis corrected for the risk in these years. The sum of the cash flow plus the estimated value of the brand at the end of the period will be the value of the brand. With this method we estimate the value of Evergood to NOK 240 million.

The royalty method: This method is based on estimating a royalty fee had the corporation leased the brand to a competitor for say a 10-year period. The royalty fee is mostly estimated from a percentage of turnover and is calculated for the period the leasing runs (normally 10 years). With this method we arrived at NOK 350 million.

From these estimates one could argue that the brand equity value of Evergood is close to NOK 300 million, which translates to £300 million since the UK has 16 times more inhabitants than Norway.

Conclusion

Brand equity is an estimation of the 'hidden value' in brands that consists of two dimensions: the qualitative element of psychological values and the quantitative dimension consisting of economical values.

We think we have proved beyond reasonable doubt that the main influence in creating these values has been in this case the advertising since:

- Evergood has almost the same high preference amongst its loyal consumers as the consumers in chains that never stocked Evergood. Hence one cannot argue that this preference is a result of seeing the brand in store or experiencing it.

- Evergood sustains its market growth even though it has suffered significantly in distribution and priority vs. its main competitor Friele, due to its continuous investment in advertising.

Source: WARC, IPA, Effectiveness Awards 2004, Evergood Coffee—The Norwegian coffee that has been slightly more expensive for 36 years.

Edited by Natalia Yannopoulou

Discussion Questions

1   Critically evaluate the three brand equity approaches discussed in the case.

2   Would you characterize Evergood as a brand trusted by the consumers and why?

3   How could Evergood—the most preferred brand—become the best selling coffee brand again?

4   How could Evergood capitalize on its brand equity in order to plan its future brand strategy?

FURTHER READING

- Although the words brand equity do not appear in the book's index or table of contents, Leslie De Chernatony's discussion of strategically building brands in his book *From Brand Vision to Brand Evaluation*, Oxford: Butterworth (2001) nevertheless reflects what brand equity is all about.

- Two books on companies as brands that provide a good overview of how those working in the areas of corporate image, identity, and reputation deal with many of the same issues related to product brand equity are: Dowling, G. (2001), *Creating Corporate Reputations*, Oxford: Oxford University Press; and Jackson, K.T. (2004), *Building Reputational Capital*, Oxford: Oxford University Press.

- The significant role played by brand attitude is discussed in Aaker, D.A. and Jacobson, B. (2001), 'The value relevance of brand attitude in high technology markets', *Journal of Marketing Research*, November, 485–93.

- Kalafut, P., Lau, J., and Robinson, J. (1997) offer insight into a number of financial brand equity issues in their book *Measures that Matter*, New York: Ernst & Young.

REFERENCES

Aaker, D.A. (1991), *Managing Brand Equity*, New York: Free Press.

Aaker, D.A. (1998), *Strategic Market Management*, 5th edn, New York: John Wiley & Sons.

Aaker, D.A. and Keller, K. (1990), 'Extending brand equity: the impact of fit and multiple extensions on perceptions of the brand and future extensions', *MSI Working Paper*.

Biel, A.L. (1992), 'How brand image drives brand equity', *ARF Researching the Power of Brands Workshop*, 12–13 February.

Chay, R.F. (1990), 'Managing brand equity for a product consumers can't buy', *ARF Brand Equity Workshop*, 22–23 February.

Ehrenberg, A., Barnard, N., and Scriver, J. (1997), 'Differentiation salience', *Journal of Advertising Research*, November/December, 7–14.

Farquhar, P. (1989), 'Managing brand equity', *Marketing Research*, 1, September, 24–33.

Franzen, G. (1999), *Brands and Advertising: How Advertising Effectiveness Influences Brand Equity*, Henley-on-Thames, UK: Admap Publications.

Hall, E.T. (1959), *The Silent Language*, New York: Doubleday & Co.

Hofmeyr, J. (1990), 'Conversion model—a new foundation for strategic planning in marketing', 3rd EMAC/ESOMAR Symposium, New Ways in Marketing Research, Athens.

Howard, J.A. (1977), *Consumer Behaviour: Application of Theory*, New York: McGraw-Hill.

John, D. and Loken, B. (1990), 'Diluting brand equity: the negative impact of brand extensions', *MSI Working Paper*.

Kapferer, J.N. (1998), *Strategic Brand Management*, 2nd edn, London: Kogan Page.

Keller, K.L. (1998), *Strategic Brand Management*, Upper Saddle River, NJ: Prentice-Hall.

McClure, S.M., Li, J., Tomlin, D., Cypert, K.S., Montague, L.M., and Montague, P.R. (2004), 'Neural correlates of behavioural preference for culturally familiar drinks', *Neuron*, 44, 379–87.

McQueen, J. (1991), 'Leveraging the power of emotion in building brand equity', *ARF Brand Equity Workshop*, 5 February.

Miller, S. and Berry, L. (1998), 'Brand salience versus brand image: two theories of advertising effectiveness', *Journal of Advertising Research*, September/October, 77–82.

Moran. W.T. (1991), 'The search for the golden fleece: actionable brand equity measurement', *ARF 3rd Annual Advertising and Promotion Workshop*, 5–6 February.

Pagano, J. (1990), 'Definition of brand equity: trademark, product, or both?', *ARF Brand Equity Workshop*, 22 February.

Percy, L. and Elliott, R. (2005), *Strategic Advertising Management*, 2nd edn, Oxford: Oxford University Press.

Rice, B. and Bennett, R. (1998), 'The relationship between brand usage and advertising tracking measurements: international findings', *Journal of Advertising Research*, May/June, 58–66.

Rossiter, J.R. and Percy, L. (1997), *Advertising Communication and Promotion Management*, New York: McGraw-Hill.

Sattler, H. (1994), 'Der Wert von Marken', Research Paper No 341, Institut für Betriebswirtschaftslehre, Kiel University.

Schacter, D.L. (2001), *The Seven Sins of Memory*, New York: Houghton Mifflin.

Simon, C. and Sullivan, M. (1990), 'The measurement and determinants of brand equity: a financial approach', *MSI Working Paper*.

Smith, J.W. (1991), 'Thinking about brand equity and the analysis of customer satisfaction,' *ARF Brand Equity Workshop*, 5–6 February.

Zajonc, R.B. (1968), 'Attitudinal effects of mere exposure', *Journal of Personality and Social Psychology Monographs*, 9 (2, part 2), 1–27.

6

Auditing and Measuring Brand Equity

⟶ **KEY CONCEPTS**

1 There is an important difference between the strength and the nature of brand equity.

2 To effectively measure brand equity one must understand how it is built and developed.

3 A brand equity audit helps uncover the elements of a brand and its market likely to affect its equity.

4 Both qualitative and quantitative methods for measuring brand equity are necessary.

5 The effective measurement of brand equity leads to a better understanding of its nature and how to manage it.

Introduction

While 'brand equity' as such is a relatively recent addition to the marketing vocabulary, the idea of brand equity as discussed in the last chapter dates back to much earlier times. In fact, over a century ago Karl Marx is quoted as saying that 'the mystical value of commodities does not originate in their value'. This sounds very much like the idea of brand equity.

Given this long history, it is surprising that it was really not until about twenty years ago that people began in earnest to develop methods for measuring brand equity. It was in about 1990 that the Marketing Science Institute (MSI) in the US began to seriously address the issue of measuring brand equity. They remarked at the time that the response to their call for proposals had exceeded anything they could remember. They awarded six grants in two categories: two for studies in the financial area and four in what they called the 'behavioural and psychological area'. Interestingly, three of the four 'behavioural and psychological' studies looked at brand equity only in terms of brand extension. The fourth utilized supermarket scanner data in an attempt to model the residual utility of a brand after objective characteristics are accounted for, such as specific product attributes and store environment (things like price and promotion).

This chapter is concerned with the 'behavioural and psychological' nature of brand equity, not the financial dimension, and it will be discussed in terms of the *strength* of a brand's equity and its *nature*. In the management of a brand, the building, strengthening, and nurturing of its equity will lead to a more positive contribution to market value for the company. *Fortune* magazine reported on a study of the market value of 3,500 US companies that showed that the relationship of goodwill vs. book value increased from 3% in 1978 to 72% in 1998 (2001). There is no question that this reflects a recognition on the part of the financial community of the value of a brand name—a brand's equity. But from a strategic brand *management* standpoint, one is concerned with measures that will help better manage that equity. If successful, the financial value of a brand name will take care of itself.

In order to successfully manage a brand's equity, one must understand how it is built, and where it is likely to lead. It is necessary to assess the strength of the brand and to understand its nature. And because brand equity is dynamic, and subject to change, its impact over time (along with that of competitive brands) must be tracked. Too often managers are content with only assessing the strength of their brand in the market. While it is important to know where you stand, without also understanding a brand's *nature* and its equity it is impossible to develop an effective long-term strategy for the brand.

Assessing the strength of a brand's equity and understanding its nature are clearly complementary processes, and require addressing a number of important questions, such as:

- Which brands are seen by consumers as the most competitive?

- How prominent or salient is a brand in the consumer's mind relative to other competing brands?

- What are the key dimensions of a brand's identity and how do consumers single it out from competitors?

- How high a value do consumers place on a brand, and on the basis of what benefits (product attributes, subjective considerations, emotions) do they discriminate in the brand's favour?
- What is the level of commitment to a brand?
- To what extent is loyalty to a brand dependent upon the situation in which the product is used?
- What is the relative price sensitivity of a brand versus competitors?
- How extendable is a brand, and in what areas?

A variety of research techniques will be discussed that are available to help answer these questions. But the very first step in addressing these issues for a manager is to review everything currently known about a brand, something called a brand equity audit.

Conducting a brand equity audit

The first step in conducting a brand equity audit, before any new research is contemplated, is to carefully examine all the information currently available. What is known about the brand? One of the problems with brand research is that it is all too frequently conducted to address a particular issue, and never really looked at in relation to other research that is being, or has been, conducted for the brand. On at least an annual basis it is important to look at reports that have previously been done for the brand, or even done for other brands in the company's product portfolio. When reviewing different research findings, from different sources, together for the first time, the result may offer significant new insights (Robinson, 1992).

In this review of available information about a brand, the primary objective is to generate hypotheses concerning the key 'assets' of the brand that are likely to mediate its equity. These hypotheses will help guide and frame the measures of brand equity that should be used in any research that is conducted. Also, depending upon the brand's marketing strategy, a manager may also want to consider the information under review in light of other potentially related issues, for example possible line or brand extensions.

The real benefit of conducting a brand equity review on a regular basis is that it helps provide a look at the current state of knowledge about a brand's equity as well as providing a fresh understanding of the brand. It will also provide the manager with a better understanding of what role advertising and other marketing communication has played and can play in maintaining the brand.

What should be reviewed? In a word, *everything*. At least, everything that is reasonably available and likely to be relevant to the brand. Obviously, this will include any recent research that has been conducted for the brand, but also studies of general market trends and other information about the category, distribution channels, competitive activity, etc. How far back to go in looking at this information must be determined specifically for each brand. But, for whatever period is appropriate, everything available should be reviewed.

It is critical that this 'everything' looks at all the marketing communication that surrounds the brand. A brand really only exists in and by the marketing communication about it and its competitors. It is essential, therefore, in a brand equity audit to review the marketing communication for a brand and its key competitors. An advertising content analysis should be completed for the entire category, in terms of both underlying communication strategy and the claims each brand makes; and this analysis should reach back in time.

Even though most (if not all) of the information included in a brand equity audit will have been available and studied by the manager before, the benefit comes from looking at everything *together*, at one time. In this way themes can be detected that may not have been obvious when each report was being considered in the light of a specific issue. The brand equity review is an opportunity for a complete and comprehensive look at a number of elements likely to affect a brand's equity. Generally speaking, it should be summarized in a written report that presents what is currently known about a brand in three areas: the overall market, competitive strategies, and insights into brand equity.

The overall market   Given that a brand's equity is relative, that it only makes sense within a particular marketing and competitive context, it is important to understand what is known about the existing state of things in the market where the brand competes. What the manager should be particularly interested in are any external factors likely to affect a brand's equity. This will provide the context necessary for understanding brand equity in the category.

Competitive strategies   The second area should provide a clear summary of current marketing and communication strategies and tactics for your brand and key competitors. It will be in this section that an analysis of the current advertising and other marketing communications will be summarized in relation to brand equity.

Insights into brand equity   Here is where the report summarizes what has been learned about the brand that helps to evaluate its strengths or weaknesses. This is where the manager should speculate on the current strength and nature of the brand's equity, and what must be done to sustain, nurture, and protect it.

With this report in hand, the manager is in a position to look into what new measures of brand equity should be considered. This decision will be guided by gaps in the current understanding of the brand (or of key competitors, especially if they have changed), as well as key ongoing measures and measures necessary for new strategic considerations.

Measuring brand equity

The brand equity audit makes use of existing research and other already available information. Building upon that base of understanding, research to measure current brand equity is needed. This type of research is known as *primary* research, and is conducted among members of the brand's target market (as opposed to *secondary* research, which is published research that is generally available from various other sources).

There are two fundamental ways of conducting primary research: using qualitative methods and using quantitative methods. *Qualitative* research is done either with focus groups, where 8–10 members of a target population are led by a group moderator in a discussion of a topic, or with one-to-one individual in-depth interviews. *Quantitative* research is conducted among a larger sample of the target population (usually 100 to 1,000, depending upon the complexity of the target market and the degree of reliability desired), utilizing a structured questionnaire.

Qualitative research

The number of focus groups or in-depth interviews conducted will be a function of any number of market considerations. How many important market segments are involved? Are brand attitudes or behaviours expected to differ among particular demographic or geographic populations? If so, it is important to ensure adequate representation in the research design.

While occasionally it may only be necessary to conduct in-depth interviews, rarely will only conducting focus groups be sufficient. More often both in-depth interviews *and* focus groups will be needed. When each are conducted, both the social and individual considerations involved in decision-making will be accounted for. Many aspects of people's responses to brands are mediated by their interaction with others, and focus groups permit this interaction to be explored. But a great deal of what *motivates* how people think and react is deeply personal, and this requires in-depth interviews, one-to-one, to explore these issues.

Too often when thinking about qualitative research, especially focus groups, managers do not see it as part of a systematic or purposeful plan. Focus groups are looked upon as a (relatively) inexpensive and easily interpreted means of gathering information about an issue, one where answers are readily and quickly forthcoming. But in point of fact, there are no 'findings' from focus groups, only *learning*. Focus groups do not provide answers. What they do is help focus our thinking by treating reality as it is understood by people, and relating it to the everyday experiences of people. This is not easy, and requires a moderator well versed in the psychology of consumer behaviour, and a moderator's guide that reflects this same understanding.

One of the important inputs from using qualitative methods as a first step toward measuring brand equity (remember there are no results as such) is the identification of the key aspects of the equity: what many people think of as emotional vs. functional aspects. In reality, these terms can be misleading, because they are not necessarily independent. Brands and their equity are better understood in terms of perceived benefits, and these benefits may be either specific attributes, subjective characteristics, or emotions associated with the brand or its use (Percy and Elliott, 2005). This will be dealt with in more detail.

There are many, many techniques that skilled moderators and interviewers may use in qualitative research, more than can be dealt with here. But in terms of laying the foundation for measuring brand equity, there are two key areas that must be covered: motivation and benefit structure. Some of the techniques used to address these two areas are discussed next.

Motivation

Understanding the underlying motivation that drives behaviour in a product class is critical. Without that knowledge, it is impossible to set strategy because brand attitude is related to that motivation. In fact, back in the early days of qualitative research, it was known as 'motivation research', pioneered by the psychologist Ernest Dichter (1964). Motivation can be explored with either focus groups or in-depth interviews. But because consumers are really not introspective about their behaviour, skilled probing is necessary to ensure that you get 'under the surface' and to the real nature of the motives involved. Some useful probes for getting at motivation include questions like:

- How does thinking about the brand make you feel?
- What is the significance of the product in your life?
- How do you use the brand?
- How do you feel when you use the brand?
- What else makes you feel that way?
- What is your first memory of the product?
- What would your life be like without products like this?

Careful analysis of a series of probes such as this will provide insight into motivation. Do not simply ask: 'Why do you buy this brand?'

Another popular way is to use what are known as projective techniques. These can be especially useful in situations where someone may be reluctant to talk about personal feelings, or where the actual motives involved are ambiguous. In such cases one might ask a question like: 'Why do your friends buy these products?' There are a wide variety of projective techniques available (Semeonoff, 1976). Some popular projective techniques include using cartoon characters in various brand purchase or usage situations and asking people to fill in what they are saying in the 'balloons' over their heads, or asking people to 'become the brand' and talk about themselves. Projective techniques can provide important insight into people's motives (Levy, 1985).

What one is looking for is a sense of whether the underlying motivation is either positive or negative. Does the brand make you happy? Does it solve or avoid a problem for you? One thing to look for is to see if the responses people give are brand-focused or people-focused. Brand-focused responses tend to reflect negatively oriented motivations (the more 'functional' aspect of brand equity); people-focused responses tend to reflect positively oriented motivations (the more 'emotional' aspect of brand equity). This is not an absolute, but does generally hold.

Benefit structure

To really understand a brand's equity it is necessary to understand how it is constructed. It is this understanding that ensures an effective positioning for the brand, and the ability to adjust that positioning over time as needed to continue building and sustaining positive brand equity. This is where a brand's image or 'personality' comes from. Think about brands you know. Sometimes that image is well-formed, while in other cases it may be less well defined. For example, what one word comes to mind when you think about Volvo? Most people would say 'safety'. What comes to mind when you think about Ford? Different people are likely to come with different thoughts here because Ford does not have a well-defined and focused image like Volvo. Does this mean that Ford's brand equity is not as strong as Volvo's? Not necessarily, only that Ford's equity is not so easily defined. They could both be equally positive.

The point here is that to fully understand a brand's equity it is necessary to understand the *benefit structure* that supports it. What this means is knowing what people know or feel about a brand, and how important these things are to them. One of the most important functions of qualitative research is to uncover what constitutes this benefit structure (Bong *et al.*, 1999). Note that it is important to understand the benefit structure of a brand as well as the benefit structure of its competitors. This means that in the qualitative phase of research the benefits associated with the *product category* are explored as well as individual brands. With quantitative research the benefit structure of specific brands will be assessed, as discussed later.

There are a number of qualitative techniques that help in identifying the components of a brand's image or personality, and its benefit structure. One way is to use projective techniques such as those already discussed in the section on motivation. Another way is to ask for cognitive associations (Krishnan, 1996), the first thing that comes to mind when a person thinks of the category or brand (as illustrated in the example earlier with Volvo and Ford). This technique can then be enhanced by 'laddering' the responses, asking what that word brings to mind, and then what that response brings to mind (something called means-end analysis) (Rossiter and Percy, 2001).

Laddering is a good way of getting at benefit structure. Consider this example for a building society. When asked for the first thing that comes to mind when someone thinks about saving (cognitive responses), they might respond with comments like 'security', 'children', 'retirement', or 'money'. In itself, this is important information. But with laddering, it is possible to learn even more. If someone initially said 'security' when asked for the first thing that came to mind when thinking about saving, they would then be asked: 'And what does security make you think of?' They might respond, 'family'. Then they would be asked: 'And what does family make you think of?' The answer might be 'the future'. This laddering exercise has uncovered a series of associations in the person's mind related to the product category. Fig. 6.1 shows the results of an actual laddering exercise for 'saving'.

security	→	family	→	future
future	→	security	→	preparation
or				
future	→	retirement	→	fear
children	→	future	→	preparation
retirement	→	no children	→	freedom
money	→	security	→	retirement

Fig. 6.1 Means-end laddering analysis of 'savings'

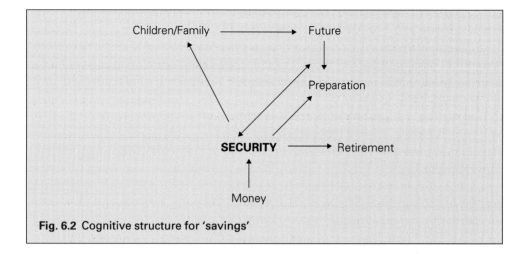

Fig. 6.2 Cognitive structure for 'savings'

What is really important in looking at these responses is that they are all strongly *inter-related* in people's minds. This suggests a tightly associated benefit for the category. Each of the key benefits initially associated with the category is likely to stimulate one of the other benefits. A careful analysis of this laddering exercise suggests that at the heart of saving in people's minds is the benefit of security. How a building society rates in terms of perceived security will go a long way towards determining the strength of its brand equity; and this will depend upon associations in the target market's perception of the brand in terms of the other key benefits. These interrelationships are illustrated in Fig. 6.2, and reflect something known as cognitive structure.

When strong interrelationships among key benefits are found, it generally means that the brand equity for all brands in the category will be constructed in basically the same manner, since the perception of one key benefit is strongly related to the other important benefits. But this is the exception rather than the rule. More often, when laddering, all the associations are not interrelated. When this occurs, it means that individual brand equities may be equally strong, but constructed in different ways, built upon different key benefits.

Consider a second example, this time fruit drinks. When asked for cognitive associations with their favourite fruit drink people might respond with things like 'great taste', 'gives me energy', 'real fruit flavour', and 'lots of vitamins'. It is highly unlikely that when thinking of 'great taste' one of the other benefits mentioned would come to mind, or that any of these benefits would be likely to trigger another. This would mean that the equity for some brands might be built upon taste benefits, others on more health-oriented benefits. Each could have positive brand equities, but those equities would be built upon quite different benefit structures. Exactly what benefit structure defines a brand's equity must be measured in the quantitative research, as discussed in the section later on Brand Attitude. But the manager will have learned quite a bit about how brand equity in the category is constructed from qualitative research.

Before leaving this subject, there is something else to be learned from these examples. The nature of the benefit structure can also help better understand motivation. Looking back at the benefit structure for savings it is clear that it is very *functional*, suggesting the likelihood of negatively originating motives for saving. The fruit drink category is less well defined. Benefits such as 'taste' or 'flavour' suggest a more emotional association, and hence positively originating motives; benefits such as 'energy' or 'vitamins' could suggest more negatively originating motives. But remember, this is *qualitative* research, and we are not looking for answers, but direction. The answers, the actual *measures* of brand equity, will follow from the quantitative research discussed next.

Ethnography

While not normally thought about when thinking of measuring brand equity, because of its ability to help gain insights into consumer behaviour, the use of ethnographic research can be useful. Beyond the generally understood use of ethnographic research in observing behaviour, good ethnographic research will also include extensive personal interviews. While similar to traditional in-depth interviewing, it is characterized by questioning that is much less focused. As Hammersley and Atkinson (1983) have put it, ethnographic interviews should be used as triggers to help stimulate the respondent into telling about a particularly broad area.

At the heart of ethnographic interviewing is a very informal approach where the interviewer does not use a structured set of questions, but a series of question-asking strategies. A strategy is picked according to the direction the discussion takes. Also, the interview itself may take place anywhere: while the subject is cooking a meal, on a shopping trip, or sharing a drink. In other words, the aim is for casual conversation where the person being interviewed is in control (Geertz, 1973). For a review of the role of ethnographic research in consumer behaviour, see Elliott and Jankel-Elliott (2003).

Quantitative research

At the beginning of this chapter, it was pointed out that in auditing brand equity it is necessary to assess the strength as well as understand the nature of a brand's equity relative to competitive brands, and to track it over time. This is the job of quantitative research. Up to this point the discussion has centred on those things it is necessary to understand before actually measuring brand equity. Everything currently known about a brand has been reviewed and the manager has conducted qualitative research to help understand the motivations driving category and brand behaviour, and to identify the benefit structure involved. Now it is time to choose appropriate measures of brand equity. First a number of techniques that may be used to assess the strength of brand equity will be considered, and then other techniques that should be used to gain an understanding of its nature. For a more detailed look at the text available for quantitative research, see any good marketing research text (such as Churchill and Brown, 2006).

Assessing the strength of brand equity

The most common measures of brand equity involve measuring its strength. While this is important, such measures are really only addressing the *results* or consequences of brand equity. Managers do need to know about awareness and preference, who is buying the brand, and the effects of price. These are the practical measures that 'describe' a brand and its users, and where it stands in the market relative to competitors. But we must remember that this does *not* tell the manager *why*, or what can be done to positively effect brand equity. That will require more than descriptive measures. Nevertheless, the measures described in this section are essential because they provide managers with an assessment of their brand's performance in the market.

Brand awareness and salience

Brand awareness reflects the extent to which people can either remember or recognize a brand (Sroll, 1984). When people think about brands in a product category, those that come to mind represent *recall* brand awareness; they are recalled based only upon a category cue. If someone is shown a list of brand names or pictures of packages, those that can be identified represent *recognition* brand awareness. Generally, recognition awareness is easier to achieve than recall awareness, but whether recall or recognition awareness is more important is a function of how people make purchase decisions in the category (Percy and Elliott, 2005).

The idea of brand salience goes beyond simple measures of brand awareness. Brand salience depends upon awareness, but it also reflects the relative *strength* of that awareness in relation to the target market's awareness of other brands in the category. This relationship will be reflected in the relative relationship between what is known as 'top-of-mind' awareness and all the other brands in the category of which someone is aware.

To measure brand salience one asks a representative sample of a brand's target market for 'all the brands that come to mind' in the category, and record the order in which they are mentioned. Then, take these responses and plot the number of first mentions for each brand vs. the total number of mentions. Once this has been plotted, fit an exponential curve to the data, as seen in Fig. 6.3 . These are awareness figures for brands of mineral water in France, and the plot is typical of what one usually finds. Most brands fall along the curve, indicating the relationship between total mentions and top-of-mind is proportional.

Evian is clearly the strongest brand, most likely to come to mind first and recalled by almost everyone. But what is of more interest are the results for Contrex, Volvic, and Badoit. Volvic and Badoit have proportionately greater top-of-mind awareness compared with total awareness, suggesting they are 'niche' brands with high brand salience. If one is aware of Volvic or Badoit it is likely to be mentioned first, ahead of any other brand; otherwise they are much less likely to be mentioned. This suggests that only a small segment of the market is aware of them, but that those who are buy them. Contrex, on the other hand, is likely to be mentioned by most people, but relatively unlikely to be on the top of their mind. This suggests a low brand salience even though it has high overall brand awareness. Brand salience is important because brands that come to mind first are usually the brands we buy most often.

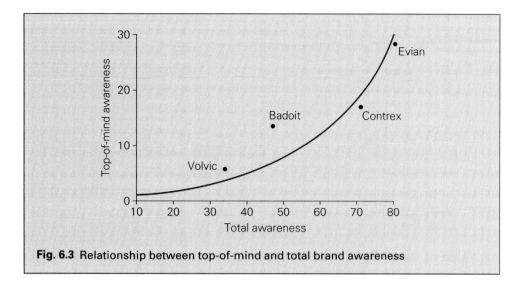

Fig. 6.3 Relationship between top-of-mind and total brand awareness

Table 6.1 Contingency table of brand awareness

Brands aware	Brand mentioned top-of-mind		
	Evian	Volvic	Contrex
Evian	—	75%	49%
Volvic	28%	—	62%
Contrex	55%	60%	—

Another aspect of brand salience that provides insight into brand equity is the relationship between first brands mentioned and other brands mentioned by the same people. Since the first brand mentioned is a good indicator of current usage (and in fact correlates highly with brand share), and other brands mentioned by the same person are potentially in their considered set for switching, comparing this relationship between brands provides a useful insight into brand equity. This can be done with a simple cross-tabulation of the awareness data gathered, as seen in the contingency table in Table 6.1.

Looking at this example, there is an asymmetrical relationship between Volvic and Evian. It suggests that it is not unusual to find that those who mention Volvic first are aware of Evian, the brand with the greatest awareness (or with Contrex, given its overall high awareness), and that those who mention Evian first are unlikely to mention Volvic because it appears to be a niche brand. On the other hand, Contrex is clearly symmetrical in structure to both Volvic and Evian. What is surprising here is that those likely to be using Contrex are well aware of Volvic, a brand not otherwise well known. Such a finding should alert the manager to look into what is going on here. Perhaps Contrex users actually prefer

Volvic, but have trouble finding it. Whatever the case, the brand manager for either Volvic or Contrex will want to get to the bottom of this.

Brand preference

Brand preference, like brand salience, can be an indicator of the strength of brand equity. Obviously, brands that are preferred are likely to enjoy greater equity than those that are not. But this is not always a straightforward relationship. It has already been shown that looking only at the level of overall brand awareness will not provide a good understanding of the strength of niche brands (which will have strong awareness only within their own segment of the market). This will also hold when looking at overall brand performance in a category. Preference for a niche brand may be high in its market segment, but relatively low in the market as a whole.

In addition, there is another aspect of overall brand preference that can be misleading, and that is the issue of perceived substitutability. Brands that are seen as having few likely substitutes are brands that are likely to have strong brand equity regardless of their share (assuming, of course, brand attitude is positive). Table 6.2 illustrates an asymmetric table of potential brand switching for washing powders. What it shows are perceived alternatives to their preferred brand, mentioned by people who use Ariel, Persil, and Skip. In this example, it is clear that people who say they prefer Skip see both Ariel and Persil as good alternatives if their regular brand was not available. Those who prefer Ariel, on the other hand, do not see either Persil or Skip as an alternative. If a Skip user could not find their brand on the shelf, they would be happy to buy either Ariel or Persil; if an Ariel user could not find their brand, it would not be an easy choice to find a substitute. From these data it would be fair to assume that Ariel enjoys a strong brand equity while Skip's is rather weak.

The result for Ariel and Persil is less dramatic, but it shows basically the same situation. Persil users are more open to alternatives than are Ariel users. But suppose market shares for Ariel and Persil are roughly the same. What does this say about the relationship between brand preference and brand equity? Clearly, brand share would not be a good measure of likely equity. Ariel would surely enjoy a stronger brand equity because users of Ariel (in this example) are much less likely to feel that another brand would be a good alternative.

Looking at brand preference is useful, but it is important to go beyond overall preference and examine likely switching behaviour. Questions of preference and switching are bound up with issues of brand loyalty, which will be discussed in the next section.

Table 6.2 Asymmetric table of potential brand switching

Alternative brands considered	Brand preferred		
	Ariel	Persil	Skip
Ariel	—	60	80
Persil	25	—	60
Skip	5	30	—

The Procter and Gamble Company

Brand users

One of the primary functions of quantitative research is to gain an understanding of category users, and specifically users of a brand vs. users of competitive brands. How similar are category users to the general population? In what ways are users of a brand similar to or different from users of competitive brands? How committed are users of each brand in the category? Who are the brand's loyal users, and how do they differ from loyal users of other brands? There are two basic types of measures that are used in answering these questions. First is a measure of 'loyalty', which is a combination of brand purchase behaviour and brand attitude. Then, based upon this, one is able to 'profile' various user segments.

Core loyalty

Traditionally, researchers look at purchase behaviour and infer loyalty. They measure how often people buy a brand, repeat purchase behaviour, or share of occasions. But these measures do not go far enough. Brand loyalty is a function of people's *attitude* toward both brands and the category, and measures must take this into account. This means using more attitudinally based questions such as having people choose one of the following to indicate their brand behaviour:

> 'I prefer this brand over others in the category.'
> 'I buy a number of brands in the category and don't feel strongly about any of them.'
> 'Although this is my favourite brand, I will buy others that I like if they are on sale.'

Questions like this get at the attitudes that underlie category purchase behaviour, and help identify people who are willing to switch among brands in the category.

In the last section it was pointed out how the extent to which users of a brand see other brands as an acceptable alternative can provide an indication of the strength of a brand's equity. What one is trying to do in measuring brand loyalty is identify the extent of a brand's core commitment. All brands have users with various degrees of commitment. The stronger the commitment, generally speaking, the stronger the brand equity. The stronger the perceived brand equity, the less willing a user is to switch. Because the brand is seen as providing 'more' of what they want, purchase is more likely to continue, even in the face of things like competitive price-off promotions.

While it is important to identify and understand these loyal users, in reality there will be more 'switchers', those users who buy the brand but also buy competitor brands as well. From the manager's perspective, *strategically* these brand switchers are more important because that is where the brand's growth is most likely come from, always remembering that brand loyals will usually provide the foundation of a brand franchise, and must never be taken for granted. As a result, marketing communication will be aimed at attracting increased usage from switchers while reinforcing positive attitudes among brand loyals. The key here is brand attitude. In order to successfully target switchers and retain brand loyals it is critical to understand what drives brand attitude, the foundation of a brand's equity for its users.

This issue will be addressed later in the chapter, in the section on measuring the nature of brand equity. But in addition to the attitudes of a brand's users, it is also useful to have profiles of just whom they are, and how they compare with the users of competitor brands.

Profiling brand users

Determining the profile of brand users is perhaps the most common use of quantitative research. Profile measures are useful to managers because they provide an idea of who it is that uses their brand, and can be especially useful when developing marketing communication. The most common measures for profiling brand users reflect what Gerrit Antonides and W. Fred van Raaij (1998) have described in their book on consumer behaviour as *general level* characteristics of a market: demographics (e.g. age, income, geographic area), lifestyle (e.g. active in sports, like to travel), and psychographics (e.g. outgoing, conservative). Like all the assessments of brand equity strength discussed so far, profile measures reflect the *results* of brand equity. Some brands are seen as 'young', some as 'old', and the demographic profile of their users is likely to reflect this. Some brands are thought of as 'cutting edge' while others in a category are more 'traditional', and this is likely to be reflected in the psychographic profile of their users.

In effect, these profiles are user *images*. In the main, the image of a brand's user will reflect the profile of actual users, because the image embodies the characteristics associated with the brand. If actual user profiles do not reflect the image of the user, one of two things may be happening. Either there is a misperception of who uses the brand (unlikely) or there are strong aspirational considerations involved. In either case, such differences will reflect brand equity. A brand may be seen as used only by upscale consumers, or perhaps by those engaged in a vigorous outdoor lifestyle, when in fact the brand is used by a broad spectrum of people. There may be a segment of the middle class who use a brand precisely because it is known to be the brand of choice among the rich; or football fans may use a brand because it is known to be used by athletes. In each case this will be a function of the *image* of the brand. Understanding the user image profile is as instructive as knowing the actual profile of brand users (and often more instructive).

Another important aspect of profiling brand users is an understanding of *how* the brand is used. What are the actual usage occasions? Are some brands in a category seen by users as more or less appropriate for specific occasions? Think of chocolate. While Cadbury would make a good snack, Perugino is more likely to be considered only for special occasions. Some cleaners are seen as generally for everyday use, others for really tough jobs; some brands of whisky you order at a pub, others at a fine restaurant. Why a brand is purchased and how it is used reflects brand user's image of usage occasion, part of its brand equity.

Price elasticity

Another important indicator of the strength of a brand's equity is price elasticity. To what extent is a consumer willing to accept a price increase without switching? Clearly one would expect a brand's core loyalty segment to be less price sensitive than switchers. But by their very nature, a brand's switchers use other brands, and price will be a key determinant of a switcher's choice. Usually this will be the result of a price promotion. But looking at price elasticity the concern is with regular pricing policy. If a brand's price is raised relative to a switcher's brand set, how long will that brand remain in their set? This will be a function of the strength of the brand's equity.

One of the better ways of looking at price elasticity in terms of brand equity was offered some time ago by Moran (1978). He talked about a *dual* concept of upside and downside price elasticity. Upside elasticity is measured by looking at how much sales go up when the price is lowered, and downside elasticity by looking at how much sales go down when prices are increased. It is important to understand that upside and downside elasticity are *independent*. Just because sales do not drop significantly with a price increase does not guarantee (or even suggest) that sales will not raise with a price cut. The extent to which sales do or do not go up or down with a corresponding decrease or increase in price is entirely independent, they are not related.

The *relationship* between upside and downside elasticity, however, does provide a measure of brand equity strength. What one wants is a greater upside elasticity relative to downside elasticity; and the greater that difference, or the smaller the downside elasticity, the stronger the brand equity. This is because a strong upside elasticity, a significant increase in sales when prices go down, suggests increased perceived value for the brand; and weak downside elasticity, where sales do not fall off much when prices are increased, suggests a strong positive brand equity and reluctance to switch.

Choice and brand equity

A valuable (but often misused) technique that can be used to measure the strength of brand equity relative to specific product or marketing considerations likely to influence choice is a multivariate procedure called conjoint analysis (Green and Srinivasau, 1990; Lattin *et al.*, 2003). Conjoint analysis assumes that people make direct trade-offs among a set of product characteristics (e.g. package design, available flavours, promotions, etc.) when choosing among brands, and that the pattern of those trade-offs will 'predict' their preference. When a competitive set of brands is included as one of the variables, conjoint analysis will measure the extent to which brand name is a factor in choice relative to other considerations, reflecting not only the impact of brand name on choice, but also the strength of the individual brand equities.

The results of a conjoint analysis provide a summary of the importance of each variable studied to choice, as well as the 'part worth' of each level within the variables studied. An example should help make clear what is meant. In the pasta category, what is the effect of brand name, price, and promotion considerations (a coupon or free recipe book) on the choice of pasta? The results of a study looking at this found that brand name is very important. People seem willing to stick with the brand Mueller's even if Skinner is offering *both* a price-off coupon and a free recipe book (assuming both brands are at regular price). No amount of marketing would give store brands an advantage over Mueller's without a price cut. The reason one can draw this conclusion is that conjoint analysis is what is called an 'additive' model. This means that by combining the part-worth values for any combination of variables one is able to 'predict' what the choice will be. Table 6.3 contains the part-worth values and shows, for example, that Mueller's at 0.98 is greater than Skinner with a 20¢ off coupon and free recipe book at 0.94 (0.26 + 0.34 + 0.34).

Consider another example. Suppose the brand manager for an airline wishes to measure the impact of a brand equity relative to a number of specific operational considerations: schedule, on-time performance, and ticket price. In other words, would people would still prefer to fly with an airline even if it did not have the most convenient schedule, best on-time performance, or lowest price. Fig. 6.4 shows the results of a conjoint analysis that addressed this issue.

What it shows is that in this example brand name has *no effect* on airline choice relative to schedule (the most important consideration), price (the second most important consideration), or on-time performance. In this case, any positive brand equity associated with a specific airline is not enough to overcome scheduling or price considerations. This does *not*, however, mean that airline brand equity plays no role at all in choice. If schedule,

Table 6.3 Part-worth values for pasta choice

Brand		Price		Coupon		Incentive	
Mueller's	0.98	20¢ off	0.96	20¢	0.34	Free Recipe Book	0.34
Skinner	0.26	10¢ off	−0.08	15¢	−0.34	No Incentive	−0.34
Store Brand	−1.20	Regular Price	−0.88				

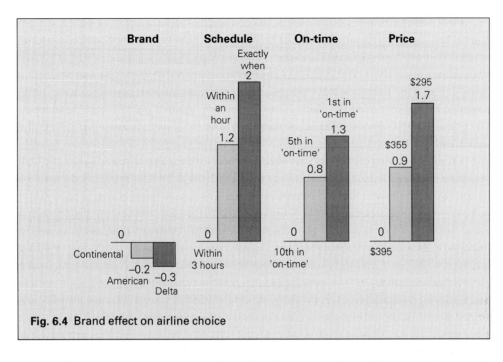

Fig. 6.4 Brand effect on airline choice

price, and on-time performance are all roughly the same, individual brand equities would then be likely to influence choice.

It is important to remember when using conjoint analysis that it is an additive model, assuming that people make direct trade-offs among alternative variables, but most actual decisions are not, strictly speaking, linear. So while conjoint analysis can be a useful measure of the relative extent to which brand equity may be influencing choices in a category, actual prediction of behaviour using conjoint models (unless they are non-linear) will be subject to the extent that people actually do make linear trade-offs in their decision-making among the product or marketing considerations studied.

Understanding the nature of brand equity

Up until this point the discussion has been about measures of brand equity strength. In this section measures of brand equity that provide insight into understanding its nature are considered. Specifically, the questions of brand image and brand attitude.

Brand image ownership

Brand images are created by benefit claims that are made about a brand, usually through marketing communication. Benefits, which are discussed in more detail in the next section, are either attributes (e.g. low in fat), subjective considerations (e.g. healthy), or emotions (e.g. look great), that are associated with a brand. Benefit *claims* are how these benefits are presented to the consumer.

In positioning a brand, benefits are selected that are important to the brand's target market and that they feel the brand can deliver (and ideally uniquely associated with the brand). They are then presented in marketing communication as a visual or verbal benefit *claim* (Percy and Elliott, 2005). For example, through research it may be learned that a brand is perceived to taste better than most of its competitors. This benefit of 'great taste' might be turned into a benefit claim along the lines of 'so good you will want to share it'. The type of benefit selected will suggest the orientation of the benefit claim, which may be looked at in terms of rational, emotional, relational, or value considerations. As Rossiter and Percy (1997) have pointed out, benefit claims should be designed to elicit an emotional response that will help motivate the consumer to consider the brand, and create or reinforce positive beliefs about the brand.

An important key to *understanding* brand equity is to identify those claims that 'signal' a brand's image. These 'signals' are those aspects of the brand that are most likely to come to mind or be associated with the brand. As already mentioned, benefit claims may be either visual or verbal, so brand signals too may be either visual or verbal. A good example of a visual brand signal is the one associated with Andrex toilet tissue in the UK. If you are familiar with the brand, what are you now thinking about? If you are like most people, you will be thinking about the Labrador retriever that was introduced into their advertising way back in 1972 and was a part of their advertising for over three decades. The retriever puppy 'signals' Andrex, and helps drive the brand's image.

In measuring a brand image, and more particularly its image relative to competitors, one is looking for something that might be thought of as 'image ownership'. This is measured by asking questions about what brands are linked to what claims, and what benefits are related to those claims. A general idea about what benefits and claims are associated with the category will come from qualitative research. What is

® Registered Trademark of Kimberly-Clark Worldwide, Inc., or its affiliates.

measured quantitatively is specifically what brand or brands people associate with each benefit and claim.

Based upon what is learned from the quantitative measures of the importance of the benefits and claims, and their association with a brand, it is possible to paint a good picture of how the market 'sees' or understands the image of specific brands in a category; and with that, an understanding of brand equity. A particularly good way of looking at this is to plot the strength of claim associations in a category with the number of brands associated with each claim, as shown in Fig. 6.5. This relationship helps to clarify image ownership, and underscores the desirability of coming up with a believable claim, appropriate to the category, but unique to the brand.

This helps the manager understand brand equity in the following way. Assuming only claims that are based upon benefits important to the target market are considered, if it is found that only one brand in the category is strongly associated in people's minds with a claim, in effect that brand 'owns' the image suggested by that claim. If people in the target market are asked which brand or brands of tea are '. . . a lovely cup of tea' and almost everyone says Yorkshire Tea, this suggests a strong and unique brand image for it built upon the benefit claim of 'a lovely cup of tea'. Suppose people in the market are asked for the name of an automobile which is 'for life', and while a few people mention Volvo, most people do not associate the claim with any automotive name plate. Since only one brand is associated with the claim, and only among a small segment of the market, this benefit helps define an important market *niche*. This would suggest that for that particular segment of the market, the claim 'for life' helps define the brand equity of Volvo.

On the other hand, if the target market for private banking is asked what bank or banks 'challenge us, we'll find the solution' and a high association with the claim is found for Lloyds TSB, UBS Private Banking, Invertec and others, it would suggest that the claim is not 'owned' by any one bank, but is seen more as a *category* benefit, describing a number of private bankers. This would mean that UBS Private Banking (which used the claim) is

	Strength of association with category	
	Weak	Strong
High	Claim associated with many brands but not the category in general	Claim associated with many brands and the category
Low	Claim not associated with many brands or the category	Claim associated with category but 'owned' by one brand

Number of brands associated with claim

Fig. 6.5 Relative brand image ownership

getting *no differential advantage* from the benefit claim in building its own brand image and equity. If this same target market was asked which bank or banks are 'Out of the Ordinary', we might find that almost no one associates the claim with any bank. This would mean that the benefit implied by the claim 'Out of the Ordinary', while important to the target market (only benefit claims found to be important to the market are being measured), is not perceived as being a part of the image for any bank in the category. This means that while Invertec (which used the claim) had correctly positioned itself on an important benefit, it did not link that benefit to the brand, and as a result it is not contributing to the brand's image and equity.

There are many other ways of measuring brand image. Perhaps the most common is to simply develop a 'profile' of the brand by measuring how many people feel each of a number of attributes or benefits associated with the category describes a brand. In a sense, that is what is going on here, but the important difference is that one is also looking at what benefit *claims* 'signal' a brand's image, not just the attributes and benefits that are related to the brand. This enables a fuller understanding of image ownership, which in its turn leads to a better *understanding* of brand equity.

Brand attitude

Most marketers would agree that brand equity is that 'something' attached to a brand that adds value over and above the objective characteristics of the product or service, as discussed in the last chapter. Whatever that 'something' is, it is embodied in people's attitudes towards that brand. It is dynamic, and subject to change over time. It attaches itself to the brand name, providing a current summary of people's feelings, knowledge and experience with that product or service. Brand equity is a result of brand attitude, and this is what provides the key to its understanding. In many ways, building and ensuring a continuing positive brand attitude is what strategic brand management is all about, because it leads to strong brand equity.

What is needed to really *understand* the nature of brand equity is a measure of the *components* that lead to it, and this means measures of how the market forms current attitudes towards the brand. To really understand a brand's equity, it is necessary to understand how it is constructed. It is this understanding that ensures an effective positioning, and the ability to adjust that positioning over time as needed to continue building and sustaining positive brand equity.

One of the best ways to measure brand attitude is by using an expectancy-value model (considered by most researchers in consumer behaviour to be the best model of attitude). Mathematically, this is expressed as:

$$A_o = \sum_{i=1}^{n} a_i b_i$$

Where A_o = attitude toward an object

a_i = importance of belief, and

b_i = belief about the object

Basically, this model states that an attitude towards an object, a brand or product in our case, is the sum of everything we know about it weighted by how important those beliefs are to us (Fishbein and Ajzen, 1975). Obviously, it is impossible to study 'everything' about a brand or product, but one can and should consider everything critical to the *benefit positioning* of the brand. This will be known from the benefit structure uncovered in the qualitative research.

At its most general, a brand position is a 'supercommunication' effect that tells the buyer what the brand is, who it is for, and what it offers. This reflects the relationship between brand positioning and the two core communication effects of brand awareness and brand attitude. It is easy to understand that strong awareness is necessary if a brand is to be considered when the 'need' (however the *consumer* defines it) occurs; and awareness is necessary for strong brand equity. Brand attitude, however, is not quite so easy to deal with. Who exactly *is* the target? Is everyone looking for the same thing; or the same things all the time? What is important, and to whom? How are existing brands seen to deliver on the things important to the target market? Answers to these questions are critical.

The role of benefits in effective positioning is of course essential (cf. Percy and Elliott, 2005). But benefits must be considered in relationship to brand attitude, which in its turn is the link to purchase motive. Consumers hold what might be thought of as an overall summary judgement about a brand, reflecting its brand equity. 'Clarks makes great shoes' is an *attitude* about Clarks that connects the brand in the consumer's mind with what is the likely purchase motive, sensory gratification (i.e. they buy Clarks shoes to *enjoy* them). This brand attitude, however, does not just spring from nowhere, but is the result of one or more beliefs about the *specific benefits* the brand offers in support of that overall attitude. This is why understanding what that belief structure is, and how it builds brand attitude, is so important.

The overall positioning of a brand will reflect a particular benefit emphasis and focus. It is important to remember that purchase motive is really the *underlying* basis of the benefits associated with a brand. Purchase motives are, after all, the fundamental 'energizers' of buyer behaviour. These same motives also energize the usage of products. Motive-based positioning requires a *correct* answer to the question of why buyers in the category are *really* buying particular *brands*. Again, this is why it is so important to explore this issue in the qualitative research. Unfortunately, most benefits tend to be motivationally ambiguous.

We must also be careful to distinguish between motives that drive product category decisions rather than *brand* decisions. Continuing our Clarks example, people may buy casual footwear because it is comfortable (a negative motive), but buy particular brands for more 'style'-related reasons (a positive motive). This is an absolutely critical distinction. Benefits like comfort or low price relate to negative motives, and are unlikely to drive *specific brand* purchases, and as a result will be less relevant to brand equity. Yes, someone may be looking for a good price in the category, but *not* at the expense of 'style'. The reason this is such an important point is that positive motives suggest marketing communication where the execution itself actually becomes the product benefit. In such cases more than ever a truly unique execution is required where the brand owns the 'feeling' and image created for the brand, as we discussed in the last section. You can't 'prove' you have a more 'stylish' or popular shoe, but you can make people *believe* you do.

What we are looking to include in measuring brand attitude are those benefits associated with the category and the benefit claims for the brands in it that define the positioning of those brands; and especially those related to the underlying motives driving behaviour in the category. Table 6.4 lists a number of benefits and benefit claims associated with hard candy. While in reality there may be as many as fifteen or twenty benefits associated with a category and its brands, these (which came from an actual study) will serve to illustrate how an expectancy-value model is used to measure brand attitude and help understand brand equity.

In a quantitative survey of the target market, people are first asked how *important* each of the benefits and benefit claims are to them when considering buying hard candy. Importance may be measured using a 3-point scale where if the benefit is essential to them it is weighted a '3', if the benefit is desirable but not essential it is weighted a '1', and if it is not all that important it is weighted '0'. Then, for the brand under study and each of its major competitors people are asked how well that brand *delivers* the benefit. Here again, a 3-point scale may be used where if the brand is thought to definitely deliver the benefit it is weighted a '3', if it is thought to only do an okay job in delivering the benefit it is weighted a '1', and if it is not perceived to deliver the benefit it is weighted a '0'.

After conducting a study among hard candy consumers, suppose the results shown in Table 6.4 are found. What understanding does this provide about the equity of Taverner's Drops and Cavendish and Harvey? Overall, people's attitudes toward the two brands are the same (the expectancy-value weighted sum of importance times benefit delivery is the same for each). But the real insight is that the *equity* for each brand is different, even though they are both seen as equally good. Taverner's equity is built upon a perception in the market that it has a good fruit taste while Cavendish and Harvey's equity is a function of the fact that it is perceived to last a long time and offers many flavours.

Table 6.4 Comparative expectancy-value model of attitude for hard candy

	Importance weight (a_i)	Belief (b_i)	
		Taverner's Drops	Cavendish and Harvey
Lasts a long time	3	1	3
Real fruit flavour	3	3	1
Burst of fruity flavour	1	3	1
So good to share	1	1	1
Wakes up taste buds	0	1	0
All familiar flavours	1	1	3
$A_o = \sum_{i=1}^{6} (a_i)(b_i)$		17	17

Because people's attitude toward these two brands is positive and equally strong, measures of their brand equity strength are also likely to be positive and roughly the same. If the only measures available are of brand equity strength there would be no *understanding* that while both are strong brands, their positive brand equity is a result of quite different perceptions of each brand.

This understanding is important for the *managing* of a brand. What could the marketing manager for Taverner's Drops do to increase its brand equity and create an advantage over Cavendish and Harvey? At least three strategies are options, based upon an understanding of the market as revealed by the research. They could attack Cavendish and Harvey's strength along the 'lasts a long time' benefit, or introduce more 'favourite' flavours. Creating the perception that the brand really delivers on the 'lasts a long time' benefit, not just does an okay job, makes the most sense because it is more important to people, and they would not need to change their flavour line. If the brand could convince the market that Taverner's Drops do indeed last a long time, overall attitude toward the brand would increase significantly (applying the expectancy-value model, going from the current level of 17 to 23).

Another option open to them would be to try and raise the importance of 'burst of fruity refreshment' in people's consideration of hard candy from desirable to essential because the brand already enjoys an advantage over Cavendish and Harvey on that benefit. If successful, it would again significantly increase favourable brand attitude, and hence brand equity.

CHAPTER SUMMARY

The importance of *understanding* the nature of brand equity should now be clear. While it is important to measure brand equity in order to know where a brand stands relative to others in the market, to successfully *manage* a brand, understanding brand equity is critical. In the final analysis, there is no one measure of brand equity. Rather, as we have seen, it is important to use measures of both strength and understanding.

DISCUSSION QUESTIONS

1   What is a benefit structure, and why is it so important to the measurement of brand equity?

2   Conduct a laddering exercise for two competing brands, and discuss what the results tell you about the image and positioning of the two brands.

3   What are the essential measures of a brand's equity strength and how does each contribute to a better understanding of the brand equity?

4   What is the benefit of profiling a brand's users?

5   Discuss how price elasticity can indicate the strength of a brand's equity.

6   What does it mean to 'own' an image, and how does that help build strong brand equity?

7   Discuss how the expectancy-value model is used to uncover brand attitude, and what that means for understanding the nature of brand equity.

CASE STUDY

B&Q—'You can do it'

B&Q had been Britain's foremost home improvement retailer employing over 36,000 people in over 320 stores in the UK since Richard Block and David Quayle opened their first shop in Southampton in March 1969. Its growth had been startlingly impressive in recent years. Between 1997 and 2003 B&Q's turnover increased by 140%, over three times the rate of the DIY market and nearly five times the rate of all retail sectors.

The main focus for this B&Q case is on the period between 1999 and 2003, when B&Q adopted a consistent and creative media strategy which demonstrates advertising's contribution to B&Q's business. Advertising played an important role in B&Q's growth. Unlike High Street stores, which benefit from browsers and passing foot traffic, visits to B&Q's out-of-town locations are almost entirely planned. Advertising is B&Q's shop window. Its most proud and successful advertising was the 'Staffer' campaign. Although the B&Q 'Staffer' campaign began in the mid-90s, a media test in 1997 subsequently led to the decision to significantly increase investment in TV advertising in 1999.

The 'Staffer' campaign was originated from the characteristics of DIY-ers. DIY-ers are amateur enthusiasts. Making mistakes and learning from experience are part and parcel of being an amateur enthusiast. Regardless of experience, they can often feel quite intimidated by the specialist knowledge of tradesmen. Through the years consumer market research revealed a common experience:

> *'I'm laying that laminate flooring in the kitchen and it's a right bastard. I've right bogged it up and had to start again.'*

> **The Nursery, 2003**

As a result, the major emotional barrier to consumers taking on more DIY projects more often was lack of confidence. The emphasis for the advertising campaign was, therefore, to build consumer confidence in tackling DIY projects in order that they would tackle more projects. Celebrity gloss, 'addy' jokes and trickery would not help B&Q at all. B&Q, instead, wanted to show that DIY is not glamorous and it's easy work.

A number of the staff at B&Q Warehouses were experienced tradespeople. Their age and experience gave consumers reassurance that they were getting the right advice, tools and materials for their project, and they seemed to enjoy a degree of status with customers. It seemed that the staff were already giving customers the messages they needed.

So the creative idea was to make B&Q staff the spokespeople in the advertising. The ads may not impress directors or win awards, but they were the equivalent of a conversation with the bloke behind the counter at a hardware store who knows what he's doing and can help you. Put in the role of presenters, the staff were seen as approachable and their lack of pretentiousness put them firmly on consumer's side. They could give advice, information and highlight the great product offers to consumers with authority and integrity. They would encourage consumers to believe that '*You can do it*'.

The 'Staffer' campaign set out in the mid-90s. In 1997 a media test conducted in Scotland demonstrated that investment in television advertising paid back at a far greater level than press advertising. As a result, in 1999 the advertising spend on the 'Staffer' campaign on TV increased substantially. Following the increase in exposure of the 'Staffer' campaign on TV, B&Q experienced phenomenal growth between 1999 and 2003.

The 'Staffer' campaign achieved high levels of advertising awareness. Consumers credited B&Q with being innovators when it came to featuring members of staff so prominently in advertising. Qualitative research showed that the 'Staffer' was clearly a strong advertising property and branding device for B&Q.

> 'Staff are a major communications strength for the brand. B&Q are credited with innovating in this area whereas other companies (e.g. Halifax) are seen to be copying B&Q.'
>
> **Direct Dialogue, November 2002**

Moreover, B&Q's tracking study measured the prompted takeout of key messages since 1997. Using prompted questioning means the scores are generally recorded at high levels. Since the introduction of the 'Staffer' campaign, the scores of consumers recalling the key strategic messages of product range, low prices and knowledgeable staff had been reaching high levels. The scores peaked with the increased investment of the campaign on TV in 1999 and all key messages experienced further increases since. As a result, the annual Marketing Adwatch survey had the 'Staffer' campaign as the most strongly recalled campaign in the UK in 2000, 2001, 2002 and 2003.

While the 'Staffer' campaign increased B&Q's awareness and delivered the messages it wanted, B&Q examined its brand image in order to further confirm that the advertising's contribution was in line with its brand strategy. Several brand responses were investigated. However, it is important to eliminate as far as possible the effect of store location on brand image. These brand response results were then based on respondents who had both B&Q and Homebase or Wickes in their local area since Homebase and Wickes were identified as B&Q's primary competitors.

First, consumer confidence in B&Q was tested. Giving consumers confidence is central to encouraging them to take on more projects and was the principal goal for the 'Staffer' campaign. B&Q became the leader on the attribute of 'gives you confidence to tackle more DIY projects'. By 2003 this confidence association rating increased from 39% to 54%. B&Q was synonymous with the phrase 'You can do it', which acted to inspire confidence in consumers.

> 'For both men and women, "You can do it" is often the precise response: confidence to tackle a particular project using a product or technique discovered at B&Q.'
>
> **The Nursery, November 2003**

Second, the perceptions of price level and product range were tested. In 1997 consumers believed that B&Q offered lower than average prices. By 2003 consumers perceived that B&Q offered the best prices in the DIY market and the difference between its nearest competitor (Wickes) on this attribute increased dramatically. Meanwhile, B&Q was seen as a retailer with a wide range of products. 78% of people felt B&Q had a 'wide range of products' in 1997; this percentage increased to 86% by 2003.

Third, the brand values and personality were explored. As well as serving as an immediate, strong branding device, the 'Staffer' campaign was found to help build an emotional relationship between the brand and consumers.

> 'Staff personalize the message—"Their staff are now their corporate identity—when you think of B&Q that's what you think of". They come across as real, not false, genuine folk of us and like us.'
>
> **Direct Dialogue, November 2002**

The staff encapsulated the brand's core values. Research indicated that consumers responded to the humanity inherent in the advertising.

> *'These are real people, doing a real job in the stores, with an enthusiasm for the company and the products. In this sense they are the antithesis of "stick-on celebs" (Homebase) or disembodied voiceover.'*

Direct Dialogue, November 2002

Furthermore, indicative of the strength of relationship consumers hold with the brand is a *Reader's Digest* survey published in 2004 which ranked B&Q amongst the most trusted brands in the UK.

In addition to qualitative consumer insights, B&Q's overall aim was greater volume. All figures confirmed that B&Q improved dramatically. The indexes B&Q used included frequency of visiting B&Q, the number of transactions per annum, the average spent per trip (average transaction value), and market share. They had all increased over the life of the 'Staffer' campaign.

B&Q has been an incredible retailing success over the last decade, even though at a superficial level the 'Staffer' campaign might appear creatively simple and straightforward, almost naïve. Dig a little deeper and you would find an advertising campaign single-mindedly and deliberately planned around the core consumer need in the market. In fact, this campaign had been a driving force behind an expansion programme that helped to power Kingfisher, B&Q's parent company, to the position of third largest DIY retailer in the world.

Source: WARC, IPA Effectiveness Awards 2004, B&Q—'You can do it', by Frank Bethel

Edited by Hazel H. Huang

Discussion Questions

1 What were the indexes that B&Q applied to measure its brand equity over the life of the 'Staffer' campaign? Why were those indexes important to brand equity?

2 In addition to the sales-related figures, why was it necessary to explore consumer insights when measuring the effectiveness of the advertising campaign?

3 When assessing the brand image, B&Q used the results based on the respondents who had both B&Q and Homebase or Wickes in their local areas. It said that 'it is important to eliminate as far as possible the effect of store location on brand image'. Why is it so?

4 This case emphasizes the importance of advertising to branding. Advertising is important to brand development; however, in order to build a successful brand, what other elements do we need to take into account? Discuss the possible elements in the case of B&Q.

FURTHER READING

- For a good general text on research methods for marketing, see Aaker, D., Koman, V., and Day, G. (2004), *Marketing Research*, New York: John Wiley & Sons; and for a good overview of qualitative methods, see Lenzin, N.K. and Lincoln, Y. (2005), *The Sage Handbook of Qualitative Research*, Thousand Oaks, CA: Sage Publishers, Inc.

- Cleland, A. and Brune, A. (1990) offer insights into measurement issues related to more financial brand equity considerations in their book *The Market Value Process: Bridging Customer and Shareholder Value*, San Francisco: Jossey-Bass.

- In their book *Advertising and the Mind of the Consumer* (2000) St Leonards, Australia: Allen & Unwin, Max Sutherland and A.K. Sylvester cover a wide range of issues related to brand equity, supported by empirical results from continuous tracking studies.

- While there are still some concerns, much research today is conducted via the Internet, and this method is discussed in Wilson, A. and Laskey, N. (2003), 'Internet-based marketing research: a serious alternative to traditional research methods', *Marketing Intelligence & Planning*, 21,2, 79–84.

REFERENCES

Antonides, G. and van Raaij, W.F. (1998), *Consumer Behaviour: A European Perspective*, Chichester, England: John Wiley & Sons.

Bong, N.W., Marshall, R., and Keller, K.L. (1999), 'Measuring brand power validating a model for optimizing brand equity', *Journal of Product and Brand Management,* 8, 3, 170–84.

Churchill, G. and Brown, T.J. (2006), *Basic Marketing Research*, Mason, OH: Thomson, South Western Publishing.

Dichter, E. (1964), *Handbook of Consumer Motivation*, New York: McGraw-Hill.

Elliott, R. and Jankel-Elliott, N. (2003), 'Using ethnography in strategic consumer research', *Qualitative Market Research,* 6, 4, 215–23.

Fishbein, M. and Ajzen, I. (1975), *Belief, Attitude, Intention, and Behaviour*, Reading, MA: Addison-Wesley Publishing Co.

Fortune Magazine (2001), 16 April.

Geertz, C. (1973), *The Interpretation of Culture*, London: Fountain Press.

Green, P.E. and Srinivasau, V. (1990), 'Conjoint analysis in marketing: new developments with implications for research and practice', *Journal of Marketing*, 54, 3–19.

Hammersley, M. and Atkinson, P. (1983), *Ethnography: Principles and Practices,* London: Routledge.

Krishnan, H.S. (1996), 'Characteristics of memory associations: a consumer-based brand equity perspective', *International Journal of Research in Marketing*, October, 389–405.

Lattin, J.M., Green, P.E., and Carroll, D. (2003), *Analyzing Multivariate Data*, Pacific Grove, CA: Thomson Brooks/Cole.

Levy, S.J. (1985), 'Dreams, fairy tales, animals, and cars', *Psychology and Marketing,* 2, 2, 67–81.

Moran, W.T. (1978), 'The advertising-promotion balance', paper presented at the Association of National Advertisers' Workshop, New York.

Percy, L. and Elliott, R. (2005), *Strategic Advertising Management*, Oxford: Oxford University Press.

Robinson, I. (1992), 'Brand strength means more than market share', *ARF Fourth Annual Advertising and Promotion Workshop.*

Rossiter, J.R. and Percy, L. (1997), *Advertising Communication and Promotion Management*, New York: McGraw-Hill.

Rossiter, J.R. and Percy, L. (2001), 'The a-b-e model of benefit focus in advertising,' in T.J. Reynolds and J.C. Olsen (eds.), *Understanding Consumer Decision Making: The Means-End Approach to Marketing and Advertising Strategy*, Mahwah, New Jersey: Lawrence Erlbaum Associates Publishers.

Semeonoff, B. (1976), *Projective Technique*, London: John Wiley & Sons.

Sroll, T.K. (1984), 'Methodological techniques for the study of person memory and social cognition', in R.S. Wizer and T.K. Sroll (eds.), *Handbook of Social Cognition*, Hillside, NJ: Lawrence Erlbaum, pp. 1–72.

Managing Brands

This section uses a combination of consumer involvement and symbolic meaning to differentiate between two approaches to brand strategy, symbolic brands and functional brands.

Brand Strategies 1 —Symbolic Brands

KEY CONCEPTS

1 An integrative model of brand-building in mindspace.

2 Advertising builds strong and profitable brands.

3 Brand strategies based on personal meanings.

4 Brand strategies based on social differentiation.

5 Brand strategies based on social integration.

6 The importance of understanding brand ecology.

7 Innovation and strategic cannibalization.

Introduction

In this and the following chapter we bring together the concepts and models discussed in earlier chapters and derive actionable insights as to how managers might develop strategic plans for brands. In Chapter 1 we separated the functional realm from the emotional realm as requiring differing brand attributes and consumer benefits (see Fig. 1.1). Additionally, we will now use the two dimensions of consumer involvement and cognition-emotion to identify two basic strategic alternatives, as illustrated in Fig. 7.1.

Managing brand strategies in mindspace

In constructing a model of how brands can be built in the market place we can turn to two large-scale commercial projects which have used data from hundreds of brands across many markets over many years to derive some essential insights into how brands develop. The BrandAsset Valuator (Young and Rubicam Group, 2003) model has involved over 350,000 consumer interviews conducted around the world measuring more than 55 different consumer perceptions with regard to over 20,000 brands. The model is based on consumer perceptions and thus explores the mindspace of the market and how it develops over time as the brand builds a relationship with its customers. The BrandDynamics model (Dyson *et al.*, 1996) is also derived empirically, from brand tracking data collected by Millward Brown covering 3,500 brands across major world markets. We have melded these findings into a model of how a brand can be built in mindspace (see Fig. 7.2).

The starting point for all brands is developing brand awareness. For all markets awareness is a necessary requirement, first because it reduces perceptions of purchase risk, but also in many low-involvement markets it may be sufficient for purchase to ensue. It is also necessary that consumers develop perceptions about the quality of the brand's

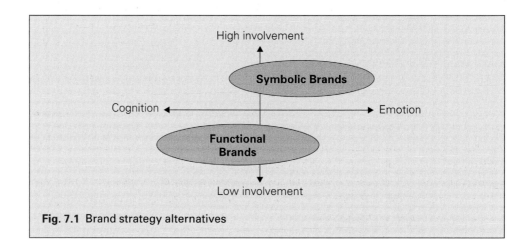

Fig. 7.1 Brand strategy alternatives

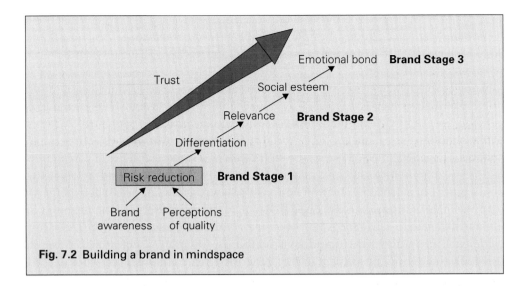

Fig. 7.2 Building a brand in mindspace

performance, and these perceptions are conditioned by the product's category and the standards set by the competition. It is about a generic perception of the product acceptability (Dyson *et al.*, 1996). Together these two perceptions reduce the consumer's perceived risk of purchase and we can say that a brand that achieves reasonable levels of both factors has reached Brand Stage 1. Millward Brown's data suggests that for many brands a substantial proportion of customers do not develop a relationship beyond this point.

In order for a brand to progress to Brand Stage 2, two vital elements are required, perceptions of differentiation and of personal relevance. To be perceived by consumers as truly differentiated from the competition, three beliefs must be developed, that the brand is different from other brands (either positively or negatively), that this point of difference is unique to the brand, and distinctive in that it is worth paying more for. Young and Rubicam's huge dataset points to differentiation being critical for brand success, not just in building the brand in the first place, but also it continues to be vital as a fall in perceptions of difference is often the first sign that a mature successful brand is starting to decline. So a key insight for managing a mature brand is to ensure that it maintains perceptions of differentiation.

Relevance reflects perceptions that the brand has something that is personally relevant or appropriate to the consumer. Data shows that relevance is the key to household penetration and the size of franchise and is thus about the market segment or segments that the brand has connected with. Successful new brands on a growth trajectory show higher differentiation than relevance, indicating that consumers see the brand as standing out from the competition so the first objective is to be noticed. However, this then has to be turned into promising a benefit that is relevant to the consumer's particular lifestyle. Young and Rubicam's data shows that relevance is not a natural outgrowth of differentiation: in the USA there is almost zero correlation between the two factors. Niche brands may often achieve high differentiation but low levels of relevance amongst the general population, but very high levels amongst a specific segment. Young and Rubicam's data suggests that these niche brands tend to be among the most profitable in the market place. So, reaching Brand Stage 2 can mean a sustainable and profitable brand, and it is likely that most brands do not progress beyond this point.

In order to reach Brand Stage 3 two further perceptions have to be developed in the mind of the market place: social esteem and emotional bond. Social esteem involves perceptions of how other people view the brand and is a socio-cultural factor as described in Chapter 4 as implying either social integration or social differentiation. So as we have both personal and social experience with a brand, the wide range of possible subtleties of perceptions become rich areas for study and management action. Emotional bond involves the development of a consumer-brand relationship based largely on personal experience with the brand and has been discussed in detail as aspects of the personal meanings of a brand in Chapter 4. As a brand is built over time, consumers gradually develop familiarity, confidence and trust in the brand, as described in Chapter 2, such that if through personal experience and perceptions of other people's opinions of the brand they develop an emotional bond with the brand we would expect that will they eventually also invest high levels of trust in the brand. Note that before trust can be developed consumers need repeated experiences with the brand so as to build beliefs about its predictability and dependability. Thus consistency in all aspects of the brand are essential in any brand strategy.

The role of advertising and promotion in brand strategy

It is clear from many studies using the PIMS database that there is a direct relationship between relative advertising expenditure against the competition and share of market. Businesses that spend a much smaller proportion of their sales on advertising versus their competitors achieved a much lower share of market than those businesses which spend relatively more and also achieve lower rates of Return on Investment (ROI) (Biel, 1990). This relationship appears to be driven partly by relative perceived quality of the goods or services. See Table 7.1.

There is evidence that companies that emphasize sales promotion in their advertising promotion mix achieve lower rates of ROI than those that emphasize advertising. See Table 7.2.

The implication is clear: advertising not only builds strong brands, it contributes to company profitability. The way in which advertising and promotion work to build strong brands will be discussed in detail in Chapter 11.

Symbolic brand strategies

Now we will concentrate on how a symbolic brand can offer to transform the consumer's experience of the world and how the social language of the brand can help a consumer enhance their perceptions and communication of self, and manage their social

Table 7.1 Advertising to sales ratio

A/S Ratio versus direct competitors	Average share of market %	Perceived Quality %	Average ROI %
Much less	14	44	17
Less	20	50	22
Equal	25	56	22
More	26	60	25
Much more	32	69	32

Source: Biel (1990)

Table 7.2 Advertising/sales promotion and ROI

Advertising/Promotion Mix	Average ROI %
Advertising Emphasis	30
Mixed Strategy	22
Promotion Emphasis	18

Source: Biel (1990)

positioning. In most cases, brand strategy will involve advertising as the primary conveyor of meaning, although in some instances, particularly in the areas of neo-tribes and sub-cultures, word-of-mouth may be the primary communication channel. Fifteen approaches to brand strategy are discussed below, organised into three categories. They build on the symbolic meaning of brands discussed in Chapter 3 and cultural meaning systems discussed in Chapter 4.

Strategies based on personal meanings:

• brand-as-a-person;

• brand-as-a-friend;

• brands and romance;

• nostalgia;

• instant heritage;

- experience brand;
- brand as underdog.

Strategies based on social differentiation:

- fashionization;
- cool and cultural capital;
- strategic cannibalization;
- gender identity.

Strategies based on social integration:

- brand community;
- neo-tribes;
- sub-cultures;
- brand mythologies.

Personal meaning strategies

Brand-as-a-person

The core idea is to create a personality for the brand so that it takes on human characteristics in the perceptions of the consumer. The personality traits that appear to be most robust across developed cultures are those of sincerity, excitement and sophistication, so these are the basic building blocks of a brand's personality. These perceptions can be built into the brand through its communications strategy. For example, Northern Foods launched the Rocky brand of chocolate biscuits aimed at households with children and

Reproduced with the kind permission of Fox's Biscuits

developed a brand personality which was rooted in the product (a big, chunky, grown-up eat with loads of chocolate) in the form of tough-talking Rocky Robin (a cartoon bird) designed to epitomize the product and its core audience:

I'm Rocky Robin.

I'm hard. My first baby bootees were DMs. My voice broke when I was 2½. I wrestle worms semi-professionally. Big 'uns an'all.

My heros are Elvis, Mick McManus and the bloke who invented Trill.

But my overriding obsession, grail and top-notch snack requisite is the Rocky bar.

Stand between me and my Rocky, disturb my indulgence or bad-mouth my biscuit and you're in bigtime jeopardy.

My collar is up.

A £20 million plus brand was built which grew faster than any other countline brand, outperforming Cadbury's Time Out brand (IPA, 1995).

But consumers also draw inferences about the personality of the brand through its market place actions. For example, a brand that is highly visible and advertises frequently has the inferred personality trait of being friendly and popular, a brand that is repositioned and changes its marketing programme constantly is seen as flighty and schizophrenic, while a brand sold through selective outlets at a high price is seen as snobbish and sophisticated (Fournier, 1998).

Brand-as-a-friend

The core idea is to build an emotional attachment to a brand through implicating the brand in important areas of consumers' lives and to offer a degree of comfort and security similar to that people find in their human relationships. An example of this strategy is that used by Nestlé to revitalise its troubled confectionary brand, Rolo, whose 'Do you love anyone enough to give them your last Rolo?' was becoming tired. Contemporary portrayals of friendship in popular culture (TV soaps, films, comedies) showed that friendship could encompass conflict as well as solidarity: friends could squabble, friends could be more brutally honest with each other than mere acquaintances. A gesture of generosity in this context could be small but meaningful. Rolo was repositioned as 'Rolo: the ultimate test of friendship'. The results were astonishing. The Rolo brand showed double-digit year-on-year volume sales growth with no increase in investment (Harman, 1999).

An example from the financial services area shows how effective the communication of reassurance can be. Standard Life, Europe's largest mutual life assurance company founded in 1825, was lacking awareness and meaning in a changing and competitive market and developed a new positioning strategy of 'With Standard Life, You are in Safe Hands'. The tone of voice was designed to be 'Finance made easy and likeble' and was delivered through advertising's first 'Talking baby' (rather than one whose thoughts you can hear) using the latest production techniques to make the lip movements possible. Spontaneous brand awareness soared from 3% to 20% and image research demonstrated communication of the positioning strategy to target consumers: 'Safe, reliable, established' (IPA, 2001). This campaign was released in the past and is no longer running.

A key focus in developing strategies to connect with consumers is on understanding the *brand ecology* (Percy and Elliott, 2005), that is, to consider not just the attitudinal, emotional and behavioural aspects of brand consumption, but to explore how this brand-related behaviour integrates with wider social and cultural experience in the life-world of the active consumer and in particular their media consumption. In an era of money-rich but time-poor people working ever-longer hours, media consumption often involves active choice behaviour between competing alternatives, and this choice behaviour is itself driven by attitudes and emotions to the various media and how its consumption integrates with other individual and social activity.

Consumers have media imperatives, such as a 'must-view' appointment with an episode of a soap opera, or a 'must-read' appointment with a heavyweight Sunday newspaper. Increasingly the same consumer can consume a paradoxical range of media, often in a different mind-set at different times of the day or week. One TV consumer may switch from low-involvement consumption of US comedies, to high-involvement consumption of a high-brow arts programme to high-involvement consumption of a football match, all on the same evening. In order to match our brand attitude strategy with media consumption we need to know how and why they are consuming the media, not just that they are in the same room as the TV. The *who* question of media consumption has a very complex answer once we recognize the variety of consumption modes within the same person's media architecture. Some media are often consumed alone, print media for example, while some depend on company for satisfying experience, for example TV comedies. But consuming media in a social setting may itself vary greatly depending on the composition of the group and the social rules and expectations that apply. The relationship with a medium may involve high levels of trust, respect, affection, personal and family history. Alternatively it may involve distrust, lack of respect, an absence of any emotional connection and little history. The close relationship between a consumer and his/her personal media architecture is at least as important as any brand-consumer relationship, because it is from our trusted media that we construct our view of the world, gain enjoyment and entertainment, stimulation and information. By understanding and leveraging the brand ecology we can build into the brand communications the key attribute of *intimacy*, and support it by customer intimacy actions in the market place (Hansen, 2003).

It should be noted that it is possible that gender makes an important difference in how people relate to brands-as-friends: men identify brands that are close to them in terms of their own actions towards the brand, while women distinguish close versus distant brands in terms of their mutual actions, that is, how the brand behaves towards them as well as their own action towards the brand. This implies that brand-building strategies must also distinguish between genders and plan interactions accordingly.

Brands and romance

Romantic love is widely used in brand communications reflecting its universality and importance in consumers' lives, as evidenced by the world-wide consumption of romantic novels and other forms of popular culture. Although it is often subsumed under sexual appeal, there is evidence that non-sexual forms of love may be very powerful motivators. In particular, spiritual companionate love has a separate influence on consumer attitudes than sexual passionate love, particularly for adult consumers when compared to teenagers (Huang, 2004). This implies that brand communications emphasizing romantic love may be more effective if they depict love as part of a meaningful relationship rather than one based primarily on sexual attraction. This has been demonstrated by the outstanding success on both sides of the Atlantic of a romantic love brand strategy for Nescafé Gold Blend in the UK (Taster's Choice in the USA) which depicts a companionate relationship developing through a shared use of a brand of instant coffee (IPA, 1987). The power of romance is also demonstrated in entrepreneurial exploitation of the Rolo brand strategy discussed above. Memorisethis.com suggest 'Show your love with a hall-marked gold-plated Rolo in a beautiful branded gift box finished with a silky red ribbon.'

Nostalgia

The evidence suggests that for some people nostalgia for early experience can determine consumer preferences later in life via a process of nostalgic bonding. This seems to occur primarily for products for which a preference is formed at age 16–20, and when it is accompanied by intense positive emotional experiences. The nostalgia effect seems to apply particularly to aesthetic preferences or styles. The implications of this are that brands may utilize designs and styles for which consumers formed an emotional preference in their teenage years in order to motivate brand preferences later in life. For example, the success of the New Beetle and the Chrysler PT demonstrates that 'nostalgia can sell cars'. The Bacardi-Hatuey beer brand was very successful amongst people of Cuban descent residing in the USA by using nostalgic imagery based on the famous Hatuey logo which was one of the icons of pre-Castro Cuba before he closed down operations of the famous Bacardi Brewery (Marmol and Brohan, 1997).

Instant heritage

However, it is possible for brands to construct their own historical connections or 'bolt-on provenance' with outstanding success in the market place. The launch of Caffrey's Irish Ale was a deliberate use of semiotics to build a new brand of high-tech nitrogen-flushed beer 'through the cunning use of our own symbolism, language and imagery' Vallance (1995). 'In assembling Caffrey's personality we were faced with an embarrassment of riches, such is the power of Irish provenance . . . old Ireland stood for lyricism, softness and tranquillity, new Ireland stood for a tougher, harder, more gritty reality.' The result was the positioning of Caffrey's as an expression of the two natures of Ireland captured in the end-line 'Strong Words Softly Spoken' wrapped in such beguiling and seductive imagery, no one for moment questioned the product's claim to greatness or its status as a nitrogenated keg beer. The semiotic alibi was complete. The results were astounding as Caffrey's grew from nothing to 500,000 barrels in

DB03 60243

Courtesy of Volkswagen

32 months, maintained a price premium against established opposition and became the UK brand leader.

Experience brand

It has been argued that we are moving into a new economic era based on experience, where competition is less about product or service but about how well companies can stage experiences (Pine and Gilmore, 1998). This represents a move from tangible products through intangible services to memorable experiences, and a brand plays a key role in promising an experience. The creation and staging of a compelling personal memorable experience that can be a major part of the brand strategy can be guided by five experience design principles. *Theme the experience*, to make it cohesive and easily remembered. *Imbue the experience with impressions*, which are 'takeways' that affirm the nature of the experience. *Eliminate all negative cues*, even minor negatives can spoil the experience. *Mix in memorabilia*; as discussed in Chapters 3 and 4, special possessions play a major role in helping people construct their identity through the memories they symbolize. *Engage all five senses*; the more senses an experience engages the more memorable it will be.

An unusual example of the creation of an experience brand is offered by Saatchi and Saatchi's success in attracting seven million customers to the Millennium Dome in London's dockland (McCann, 2001). Faced by media cynicism and overwhelming national apathy, they decided not to concentrate just on attracting visitors to the dome but to develop the Millennium Experience brand first, 'to capture the significance of the millennium and create a tide of excitement and optimism'. The positioning was based on the consumer insight that the end of a year is a time for reflection, to take stock and look forward, and was captured as 'Time to make a difference', promising that the end of a one thousand-year era and the start of another thousand years could be a time when the nation could come together to build a better future, using the millennium as a catalyst for change.

Brand as underdog

When faced with a very large and powerful competitor, there is an opportunity to position a brand as a valiant underdog, using their very strength to harness support from consumers, a version of the Aikido brands discussed in Chapter 4. This strategy has been used very successfully by Richard Branson, first by positioning Virgin Atlantic against the monolithic British Airways, and then by positioning Virgin Money against the huge, grey financial services establishment. In both cases, 'against the big institutions' carries the very valuable connotation of 'being on the side of the small guy', and takes advantage of the common feeling that somehow we are being exploited by big business.

Social differentiation strategies

Fashionization

Nokia took the mobile phone market by storm when it repositioned its phones as fashion items with a huge range of alternative covers, rather than as functional products. Similarly, no matter how much the company keeps denying it, Nike's key promise is one of fashion leadership rather than function (Goldman and Papson, 1998). Even teeth braces are now fashion items:

'Braces are becoming a girl's best friend. What was once a teenage turnoff has turned into a high fashion accessory. Rather than hide the tramlines designed to straighten their teeth, Scots youngsters are demanding multi-colours on their molars.'

Glasgow Evening Times

Car manufacturers are also replacing a traditional focus on function with an emphasis on fashion and style. For example, the launch of the Ford Ka was a deliberate decision to by-pass investment in new engineering and instead design a fashionable body. It has been a great success in many parts of the world: 'Ka owners rate aesthetics above mechanics . . . it's not a car, it's a consumer durable, it's much more like a Walkman than it is a Ferrari' (BBC News online). A key part of the Ford Ka marketing strategy was to target opinion leaders whose aesthetic tastes might be followed by others and this has been found to be viable in many fashion markets, following the trickle-down theory. There is evidence that opinion leaders can be identified and targeted through subtle use of media with whom they have a special relationship (Vernette, 2004), and that this can then lead to word-of-mouth spreading to fashion followers. But in considering fashionization as a brand

Reproduced with the kind permission of Ford

strategy it is vital to remember Oscar Wilde's warning: 'Nothing is so dangerous as being too modern; one is apt to grow old-fashioned quite suddenly.'

Cool and cultural capital

Closely linked to fashionization is the concept of cool, the leading edge of fashion usually appealing to the youth market; it includes terms like 'street', 'hip' 'authentic' and 'real'. Research by Superbrands (2002) identified Ducati as the UK's coolest brand, followed by Alexander McQueen, Bang & Olufsen, Agent Provocateur and the Tate Gallery. What they seem to have in common is a mix of aesthetics and attitude that capture the spirit of the moment ahead of the mass of brands. An important finding of the Superbrands study is that 40% of the 18–30-year-olds interviewed said that they were prepared to pay more for a cool brand. The findings established that 72% of respondents believe the personality of the brand is the most vital factor when determining if that brand is cool. 44% of respondents believe that their friends' opinion or use of a brand has an influence on their decision on whether that brand is cool, whilst only 11% take into account a celebrity's use or opinion of a brand. 31% deemed press coverage to be an influencing factor: 'The nature of cool is always a fickle thing but it fascinates us all. It is difficult to manage people's perception of cool but it can make the difference between success or failure for many brands, people and places.'

An important concept in using cool as a strategy is that of the *Sacrifice Group*. In order to be perceived as authentically cool by one group, a brand has to be rejected or at least not be liked by the majority. In deciding who the brand wants, it also needs to decide who it does not want, who are the group it will sacrifice in order to maintain the interest of its targets.

Rather than manage perceptions of cool, many marketers seek out leading-edge consumers by using specialist research agencies as 'cool hunters' in order to identify style leaders who are 12–18 months ahead of the mainstream. Nancarrow *et al.* (2002) demonstrate that it is possible to identify and interview 'cultural intermediaries' whose occupations involve symbolic goods and services and who interpret what they see and hear at work and what they read in the 'hip' media, both adopting and adapting the innovations of others. They devote considerable time and effort to acquiring cultural capital, seeking out the new and then moving on, ever fearful of being caught up by the mainstream. This study led to a realization of the importance of black culture to cool and resulted in a very successful campaign for Morgan's Spiced Rum, featuring black artists, writers, actors and musicians, groups who were identified as particularly cool and crucially relevant to the Caribbean roots of the product. 'The connection was a natural one, not forced, and there-fore the advertising itself was considered "Authentic"; it was cool.'

Strategic cannibalization

As more and more markets become driven by fashion, style and aesthetics, the demand for innovation becomes ever more intense. But rather than view this trend as a problem it can be turned into a successful strategy of deliberately limiting supply and replacing products well before their sales decline. Zara, the Spanish clothing retailer, has developed a supply chain revolution that enables it to design, produce and deliver a garment in fifteen days. Zara produces 10,000 new designs annually, but each one in only a limited supply; this drives the consumer perception 'If I don't buy it now, I'll lose my chance'. This strategy of strategic cannibalization with limited supplies of new designs available for only a short space of time has led to brand-specific buyer behaviour, as in central London, consumers visit the average clothing store four times per annum but they visit Zara seventeen times a year. This creates word-of-mouth communications that allow Zara to spend 0.3% of sales on advertising versus the 4% spent by its competitors (Ferdows *et al.*, 2004).

The importance of stimulating a sense of excitement in a market defined by low degrees of consumer loyalty is recognized by The Sanctuary brand of mass-market body care products in the UK. Management has recognized that constant new product launches are the key to keeping the brand 'talked about' and to keeping consumer promiscuity 'within the brand' (Edwards, 2004).

Gender identity

Women make or influence the purchase of as much as 80% of all consumer goods and there are a number of factors that must be borne in mind if they are to be targeted as a brand strategy. Women's roles in society have changed dramatically over the last 50 years as more and more women go out to work regardless of whether they are married or have children, and women for whom work is a career versus those for whom it is 'just a job' exhibit attitudes, buying motivations and buying behaviour which differ markedly. Along with the move into work has come the progressive breakdown of the traditional family with rising divorce rates and children born outside marriage, so women are not only juggling home and work responsibilities but also increasingly having to raise children alone (White, 2002). Compared with men, women are more sensitive to details of relevant information and tend to favour objective over subjective claims, but are better able to integrate emotional and rational factors; women take a broader view of life, bringing more factors into play when making decisions (Evans *et al.*, 2000). Learned (2004) offers some valuable insights into how brands can connect with women through developing an accessible human face. Emotional connections are built through elements like stories and testimonials from customers; visual images of employees and customers add a human face to the brand; social cause partnerships can also help humanize the brand.

An example of a brand which demonstrates successful gender identity strategy is Kellogg's Special K breakfast cereal. After forty years of success the brand was beginning to falter as it failed to gain penetration amongst younger women for whom it lacked relevance as eating habits changed along with women's value systems. Its core users were aged 55+. Research showed that although women continue to want to appeal to, and be desired by, men, they also want the man–woman bond to be based on more than looks alone. More importantly, although they love to be appreciated for their looks, especially by a man, they hate anyone to think that they're deliberately trying to please him (Chebib, 1999). The brand was repositioned as putting the woman in control and helping her be slim and attractive, but for the right reasons, for herself, not for her man. The woman is portrayed 'as able to have it all, a single figure and married status'. As a result the brand's consumption profile changed radically, penetration among women 35–54 years increasing by 22%.

Contrary to many men's self-perceptions, men are more likely to make emotional buying decisions based on partially digested evidence than women, and are less well disposed to pictures as opposed to words. There is also some suggestion that they are likely to be more brand loyal than women (Evans *et al.*, 2000). As women's roles in society have become broader, men have begun to experience role turmoil and to resent that women are in control of many areas of men's lives (Langer and Carroll, 1998). Men remain characterized by competitiveness, aggression and the desire to be, and to be seen to be, in control. Young men are highly susceptible to anything that can be seen to offer an adrenaline rush. This is seen partly as an attempt to escape the pressures of modern life. Men at all life stages tend to see life as linear; the drive to be moving forward, progressing, building is a strong one. Status anxiety is prevalent and 'offers fertile ground for brands to provide men with reassurance' (Conway, 2004).

The Hugo Boss brand of men's clothing is a classic example of adapting as male gender identity moved from the overt materialism of the 1980s towards understatement and subtlety in the 1990s. Based on the functional foundation that the clothes were very high quality, they were positioned as 'working clothes for the professional working man', and based on the portrayal of real people, not models, engaged in a broad range of professions. Using reportage photographers rather than fashion photographers the brand was depicted being worn in normal working situations by successful or up-and-coming people with a certain reputation in their field. Unusual professions were chosen rather than business men: choreographer, DJ, video games inventor, first class football manager. The result was 'emotionally charged, rich in aspiration, territory which was true to the brand's past, and yet of relevance to its future' (Robson, 1995).

An interesting example of a brand which repositioned itself from children to adult men is the Nintendo Game Boy. The problem was how to make a toy acceptable to adults, and research indicated that there was a group of men whose lives were very different, but who shared a need for entertainment that absorbed and stimulated them. The key to making Game Boy relevant was to provide permission to buy a toy because it was mental stimulation or a way to exercise the mind: 'If your mind is being challenged you are not wasting your time' (Bioletti, 1995). The play element was vital, but as a support, not the main platform; the position that 'Game Boy taxes your brain' managed to banish childish associations.

Some brands which have attempted to use both genders in a brand positioning strategy have used an approach of 'gender rancour', which appears to signal contemporary relationships in which 'women give as good as they get', for example, Smirnoff Ice. Research indicates that where the relationship between genders is depicted as playful and interactive then the response is positive; if it involves deceit, especially where a woman is showing the worst (masculine) behaviour, responses are negative for all but the youngest female respondents (Fuller and Sommerville, 2002). What seems to be most successful is a tone of celebration, males and females enjoying themselves together, which conveys a relaxed, positive brand.

Social integration strategies

Brand community

The major issue here is the extent to which marketers can construct and manage brand community and thereby enhance brand loyalty. The DaimlerChrysler Jeep brand is an exciting example of how through marketer-organized 'brandfests', including Jeep Jamborees, Camp Jeep and Jeep 101, the characteristics of a consumer-led brand community were consciously fostered by sponsorship of 2–3-day events (McAlexander *et al.*, 2002). Participation in brandfests led to a more positive relationship with the Jeep brand and with other Jeep owners and these relationships proved to be long-lasting and to prolong brand loyalty by erecting social exit barriers. Community-integrated customers serve as brand missionaries, carrying the marketing message into other communities. A key point is the importance of designing events with a focus on socializing new and intending brand owners while offering special recognition to those who are already most integrated into the brand community.

Neo-tribes

The essence of *tribal marketing* is not to follow tribes but to inspire them and earn their respect by understanding their values and standing back and letting them make most of the running (McDonald, 2001). Sony PlayStation used the time-honoured premise that to children in the target audience anything forbidden becomes immediately attractive. TV commercials run throughout Europe featured a spoof society, SAPS (Society Against PlayStation), and later moved on to more enigmatic communications derived from studies of skateboarders about competition, self-actualisation and mastery. Using the concept of the sacrifice group, Sony PlayStation positioning is all about only the tribe really understanding what the brand communications actually mean.

Red Bull energy drink also uses elements of tribal marketing. Its communications are also enigmatic, but it puts much more effort into creating and supporting 'brand evangelists', students who are recruited to be 'student brand managers' and then provided with free drinks to distribute on campus and to educate users about the product and its benefits. This grass-roots effect is enhanced by the organization of free extreme sports events and 'consumer educators' who drive Red Bull jeeps and distribute free cans.

An unusual product category to target neo-tribes is that of pain relievers. Tylenol is attempting to form 'pain partner' relationships by funding events such as skateboarding, breakdancing and snowboarding; items in an event goodie bag carry the word 'Ouch!'. 'In this target market pain is cool, they wear it as a badge' (Grapentine, 2004).

Reproduced with the kind permission of Red Bull

Sub-cultures

An opportunity for co-creation of brand meanings using gender as a sub-cultural brand strategy lies with the gay market. Recently described as an untapped goldmine (Burnett, 2000), a handful of brands have achieved legitimacy with this group through gay-friendly actions like supporting Lesbian and Gay Pride days and advertising in gay media (Kates, 2004). However, a potential problem is that homosexual consumers dislike and distrust advertising, and thus direct marketing attempts to court them may be doomed to failure (Burnett, 2000).

Brand mythologies

The concept of developing a brand mythology is based on a brand representing an idea or set of ideas that people can live by, and embody and legitimize a new way of living in a rapidly changing society (Grant, 1999). For example Calvin Klein with CK One celebrated androgyny; Clarks shoes re-defined adult shoes as things to romp around in: 'Act your shoe size not your age'. Opportunities to develop brand mythologies are legion, but many reside in social changes such as attitudes to gender, to old age and maturity, to friends versus family, to not having children, to class mobility, to the nature of relationships. Many of these themes are at the core of popular cultural forms such as the global success of *Friends*, and brands can play a role in showing people possible ways to live.

CHAPTER SUMMARY

In this chapter we have proposed a basic model of how brands are built in mindspace over time. The evidence suggests that advertising plays a key role in the process. We have discussed brand strategies based on personal meanings, on social differentiation and on social integration. We have emphasised that the social language of the brand (see Chapter 1) can provide a wide range of benefits to the consumer and help transform their experience of the brand.

DISCUSSION QUESTIONS

1 Can brand strategies be divided into just two alternatives or are there other possible approaches?

2 Why is brand awareness the starting point for building a brand?

3 What is the role of perceptions of differentiation and relevance?

4 What is the relationship between relative advertising expenditure and share of market?

5 Is it more profitable to emphasize sales promotion or advertising in the communications mix?

6 When might word-of-mouth be the primary communication channel?

7 Why is knowledge of the target market's media consumption an important factor in building a brand?

8 What are the five design principles for building an experience brand?

The Pursuit Of Luxury—Bling-Bling Vs. Savoir Faire

The business challenge

The overall consumption volume of Cognac is decreasing year on year across Europe. Fewer young people are entering the Cognac category with reduced affinity towards the Hennessy brand, which has traditionally been considered as a luxurious one. Hence, a business and marketing strategy was required which was to have a direct impact on this scenario, in order to create a situation where Hennessy becomes an active part of younger consumers' drinks repertoire.

The project challenge

The decreasing volume of Cognac is partly symptomatic of a much larger trend. At its core is a central re-definition of what luxury is for young European consumers. With the gradual but steady erosion of the traditional class system, values and perspectives have changed. The definition of luxury is also beginning to change, as common everyday products can now be a luxury. The research had therefore to define what young European consumers perceived premium and luxury in the spirits market to be, identifying emerging attitudes and values. The overall aim was to find how Cognac could be presented in a way that made the category and Hennessy brand relevant and appealing to them.

Designing the project: the bricolage approach

The project had to be designed to provide Hennessy with actionable output which could act as decision fuel to take on the challenge of inspiring younger consumers in a relevant and meaningful way. The first challenge was to understand the dynamic and ever-changing trends in the European spirits market. The second was to provide a future perspective to the output. Three European cities were targeted as key cultural and social centres where emerging and upcoming trends could be evaluated: London, Paris and Barcelona. By focusing on modern, trendy and stylish bars we could identify key trendsetters and the new movements that define fashions and ultimately filter through to the mainstream. To give us a broad view we used a bricolage approach, applying a combination of methodologies—ethnography, semiotics, artefact collection, in-depths with barmen, creative workshops—to provide us with the perspectives we needed. We also engaged opinion and trend effecters to help us anticipate and understand upcoming trends with relation to the overall cultural context.

Interim findings: the emerging picture

What emerged was that many of the new emerging spirit brands were succeeding for very different reasons. Although from a marketing point of view they seemed to represent a unified 'super-premium' category, from a consumer point of view the brands could be very different and not related in any single way to each other. From a marketing point of view, the category was defined by price but price was now only one of many different aspects that constituted modern luxury for young European consumers.

Interim findings: the broader context

Perceptions of what constitutes luxury have shifted over recent history. For many, the 'old world' definitions of luxury centred on the pursuit of exceptional quality. Then, luxury values began to shift from essential quality to more socially laden values such as opulence. The emphasis shifted from having the knowledge and the means to find luxury goods to being able to afford the price. What you knew about the essential truth behind a product became over-shadowed by a consumer's ability to afford it. This was epitomized by the 1980s yuppie culture. Conspicuous consumption of expensive luxury goods became part of the process of social climbing. This shift had wider-reaching implications. If price was the main focus, the marketers could influence perceptions of luxury with relevant imagery. Luxury was defined by what appeared to be luxury.

However, now in the increasingly meritocratic European youth economy, another shift is afoot. Luxury related to pure fictional imagery and price alone is increasingly rejected in favour of a search for more authentic brands. In other words, the emphasis of luxury moves from prestige to authenticity, and luxury is about credibility and increasingly credibility cannot simply be bought.

The impact on the brand challenge

For many young European consumers what constitutes 'luxury' in spirits is also changing. Within the sector, there are two perceptions of what luxury is: on the one side, opulent luxury exists in the form of sophisticated crystal decanters and strong prestigious, sophisticated brand imagery; while on the other, luxury is associated with the perceived authenticity of brands with credible quality that appear to be the 'real thing' but somehow remained undiscovered by the mainstream.

The brands on the sophisticated side have been there for a very long time: Hennessy, Dom Perignon, Laphroaig, Moët. On the other side, many new brands are emerging such as Zubrowka, Potocki, Grey Goose, and Bombay Sapphire. Brands in both categories can command very high prices, but their appeal and route to success are very different. The key aspect of this emerging dichotomy of luxury with regard to the business challenge is that demographics are split along certain lines. There is overlap, but as a whole, young European consumers are responding to the new emerging sense of luxury, based on discovery and knowledge rather than traditional prestige.

Thus, the interim findings had challenged the initial hypotheses we entered into the project with. The emerging picture highlighted a very different consumer landscape made up of new values and attitudes, and increasingly, new brands. Our challenge now was essentially to re-define how Hennessy could approach these consumers in terms of product, imagery and communications.

Bricolage: the value of the different methodologies

The ethnographic observations were particularly useful in allowing us to explore the dynamics of groups and between individuals and the barmen. Semiotics helped sensitize us to the effect of often contradictory semiotic codes on perceptions and imagery associated with different brands. Barman in-depth interviews proved invaluable, not only for highlighting how consumers' desires were changing, but also showing how interaction with the barmen influenced choice. They also helped us identify how trends changed according to time, occasion and season. Opinion effecter in-depth interviews gave us insights into where youth culture was going and indicated how this was being translated into the style bar environment and specifically the spirit category. Lastly, the creative workshops gave us meaningful brand directions.

Project output and findings

The key to making this a successful project was the use of innovative methodologies to under-stand a complex and fast-moving market. The research allowed us to:

- paint a picture of the youth market place;
- map existing successful brands within;

- identify the codes, styles and values that were making these brands succeed;
- re-define what prestige and luxury meant for young European consumers;
- create criteria and brand propositions that would have relevance and value for this segment;
- provide a strategic basis from which robust decisions could be made.

Analysis of the brands that were currently succeeding with young European consumers showed there are many different possible routes to success—from style, to purity, to authenticity, to age and to individuality—all equally viable if combined in the right, attractive, plausible and authentic way. The potential is there. Cognac as a category has many positive values (originality, naturalness, authenticity, history) that can be communicated. The issue is one of positioning and the way the category and brands within it are perceived by young people. They do not truly understand the category before rejecting it. The perceived values such as sophistication, status, prestige and ostentation are of limited relevance or appeal to most young European consumers, and in themselves create a distance between the consumer and the category.

Source: WARC, ESOMAR, World Association of Research Professionals, 2003, The Pursuit of Luxury—Bling-Bling Vs. Savoir Faire, Understanding the changing nature of luxury

Edited by Natalia Yannopoulou

Discussion Questions

1 The key to overall project success was the research design using a bricolage approach. What did this entail and why was it so important?

2 What are the most important factors in building a successful symbolic brand?

3 What brand strategy would you recommend for Hennessy?

4 Could the model of trust-building be applied in the case of Hennessy?

FURTHER READING

- A thoughtful approach to brand strategy which integrates theory with practice is taken in Edwards, H. and Day, D. (2005), *Passionbrands*, London: Kogan Page.

- A practitioner approach is taken in Gobe, M. (2001), *Emotional Branding*, Oxford: Windsor Books.

- An historical US approach to brand myths is Holt, D. (2004*), How Brands Become Icons*, Cambridge: Harvard Business School Press.

REFERENCES

Biel, A. (1990), 'Strong brand, high spend', *Admap*, November 35–40.

Bioletti, F. (1995), *Creative Planning Awards: Big Boys' Toys—Making Game Boy Something to do with your Brain*, London: Account Planning Group.

Burnett, J. (2000), 'Gays: feelings about advertising and media used'. *Journal of Advertising Research*, 40, 1/2, 75–85.

Chebib, J. (1999), *Creative Planning Awards: Special K: How Exploiting Men Revived a Women's Brand*, London: Account Planning Group.

Conway, J. (2004), 'Men: what are they really thinking?', *Admap*, 455, November, 12–17.

Dyson, P., Farr, A. and Hollis, N. (1996), 'Understanding, measuring, and using brand equity', *Journal of Advertising Research*, Nov/Dec, 9–21.

Edwards, H. (2004), Presentation to the MBA *Brand Strategy* elective, Saïd Business School, University of Oxford, 8 May.

Evans, M., Nairn, A., and Maltby, A. (2000), 'The hidden sex life of the male (& female) shot', *International Journal of Advertising*, 19,1, 32–41.

Ferdows, K., Lewis, M., and Machuca, J. (2004), 'Rapid-fire fulfillment', *Harvard Business Review*, 82, 11.

Fournier, S. (1998), 'Consumers and their brands: developing relationship theory in consumer research', *Journal of Consumer Research*, 24, 4, 343–73.

Fuller, K. and Sommerville, A. (2002), 'Trouble in paradise: getting to grips with the gender game', *Admap*, January, 15–23.

Goldman, R. and Papson, S. (1998), *Nike Culture*, London: Sage Publications.

Grant, J. (1999), *The New Marketing Manifesto*, London: Orion.

Grapentine, T. (2004), 'No pain, no pain reliever', *Marketing Research*, Winter, 16, 4.

Hansen, H. (2003), 'Antecedents to consumers' disclosing intimacy with service employees', *Journal of Services Marketing*, 17, 6/7, 573–89.

Harman, J. (1999), *Creative Planning Awards: How Friendship Rescued Rolo*, London: Account Planning Group.

Huang, M. (2004), 'Romantic love and sex: their relationship and impacts on ad attitudes', *Psychology and Marketing*, 21, 1, 53–73.

Institute of Practitioners in Advertising (1987), *Advertising Works 4*, London: Cassell Educational.

Institute of Practitioners in Advertising (1995), *Advertising Effectiveness Awards*, London: IPA.

Institute of Practitioners in Advertising (2001), *Advertising Effectiveness Awards*, London: IPA.

Kates, S. (2004), 'The dynamics of brand legitimacy: an interpretive study in the gay men's community', *Journal of Consumer Research*, 31, 2, 455–65.

Langer, J. and Carroll, T. (1998), *Mantrack: a case study in qualitative trend detection*, ARF Workshop, New York: Advertising Research Foundation.

Learned, A. (2004), 'How to market to women by humanising your brand', *Admap*, 456, December, 31–7.

Marmol, R. and Brohan, L. (1997), *The Legend of Hatuey*, New York: Direct Marketing Association.

McAlexander, J., Schouten, J. and Koenig, H. (2002), 'Building brand community', *Journal of Marketing*, 66, 38–54.

McCann, B. (2001), *Creative Planning Awards: Turning a Moment in Time into a Turning Point in History*, London: Account Planning Group.

McDonald, N. (2001), 'Tribe talking—tribal trends in post-cool Britannia', *Admap*, April 17–19.

Nancarrow, C., Nancarrow, P., and Page, J. (2002), 'An analysis of the concept of cool and its marketing implications', *Journal of Consumer Behaviour*, 1, 4, 311–22.

Percy, L. and Elliott, R. (2005), *Strategic Advertising Management*, 2nd edn, Oxford: Oxford University Press.

Pine, J. and Gilmore, J. (1998), 'Welcome to the experience economy', *Harvard Business Review*, July–August, 97–105.

Robson, D. (1995), *Creative Planning Awards: How to Avoid being a Fashion Victim: Hugo Boss*, London: Account Planning Group.

Superbrands (2002), *Cool Brand Leaders*, London: The Superbrands Organisation.

Vallance, C. (1995), *Creative Planning Awards: Caffrey's: Re-Inventing Keg Beer*, London: Account Planning Group.

Vernette, E. (2004), 'Targeting women's clothing fashion opinion leaders in media planning: an application for magazines', *Journal of Advertising Research*, 44, 1.

White, R. (2002) 'Best practice: advertising to women', *Admap*, 433, November, 23–28.

Young and Rubicam Group (2003), 'BrandAsset Valuator', Young & Rubicam Inc.

8

Brand Strategies 2 —Functional Brands

→ KEY CONCEPTS

1 Top-of-mind brand awareness and brand salience are critical to a brand's success.

2 Pre-conscious processes of mere exposure and classical conditioning work well where there are no salient competitors.

3 Building brand associations through all elements of communication over time and laying down somatic markers.

4 The implications of consumers buying within brand repertoires.

5 Deciding between an emphasis on increasing penetration or purchase frequency.

6 Managing consumer perceptions over time.

7 Managing choice situations in-store.

8 Building brand loyalty through loyalty programmes and consumer involvement.

Introduction

As discussed in Chapter 1, the cognitive choice processes for these functional low-involvement brands varies from very low levels of pre-conscious processing and habit, to a combination of minimal cognitive processes using a range of heuristics. Brand salience is a key objective of strategy as it drives much purchase behaviour and we will examine a number of approaches to building awareness and salience. It is also important to understand the buying behaviour tendencies of different market segments and we will consider how market segmentation by customer buying behaviour can be the focus of brand strategy and how various models of brand loyalty can be utilized for planning. We will then review approaches to managing consumer perceptions and influencing consumer purchasing behaviour.

Brand awareness and brand salience

Brand salience, often called top-of-mind awareness (i.e. first brand mentioned in response to a spontaneous awareness question), is probably the most important characteristic any low-involvement brand can possess. Ehrenberg *et al.* (2002) argue that salience also includes how many people have it in their active brand repertoire or in their consideration set, and maintain that it represents the 'size' of the brand in consumers' mindspace. From work on the double jeopardy effect in static fmcg markets, where brands with small market shares attract fewer customers but also experience less customer loyalty than more popular brands, Ehrenberg *et al.* (1997) claim that empirically there is very little difference between what brand users feel about their brands. However, the number of people for whom a brand is salient does differ greatly from brand to brand it is salience that divides big brands from little brands and this effect is related to market dominance, as we have seen when we discussed brand equity in Chapter 5. Big brands have much greater levels of salience than do small brands because salience increases exponentially in relation to total spontaneous awareness, that is, if a brand that is twice as big as the next two brands, its salience will be four times as great (Morgan, 1999).

Building and maintaining brand salience

Salience is a consequence as well as a cause of many aspects of brand strategy. A salient brand is likely to have wider distribution, more shelf-space and display, more promotions, more advertising, more word-of-mouth and more media mentions (Ehrenberg *et al.*, 1997). This is why one of the critical steps in positioning a brand is to establish the link between a category need and the brand, as we shall see in Chapter 11. We want the brand to be immediately associated with the need for the product when that need occurs.

For brands purchased largely out of habit, what John Howard (1977), one of the fathers of consumer behaviour theory, has called routinized response behaviour, Ehrenberg and his colleagues (1997) have suggested that brand salience can be built effectively by 'Here I am' advertising that focuses largely on the brand name and package and which leaves long-term memory traces for the brand, but does not try to communicate a persuasive message to change attitudes. This assumes that, for whatever reason, a positive brand attitude already exists, and needs only to be nurtured by reminding the user of the brand. The benefits associated with the brand are already in memory, even if these 'feelings' are consciously a result of the notion that 'I use it therefore I like it' (Ehrenberg *et al.*, 1997).

How brand salience is built is critical. It must take into account the way in which the link between the category need and the brand is triggered at the time a purchase decision is made. That is when the brand must be 'salient', and this may be triggered either by *recognizing* the package at the point-of-purchase, or *recalling* the brand name when the need to make a choice occurs. In the first case, marketing communication must feature the package as it will be seen at the point-of-purchase. The user sees the package, it triggers a need, and is purchased. On the other hand, when a choice is made prior to purchase (e.g. where to go for lunch) or at the point-of-purchase, but where packages are not visible (e.g. when a waiter asks you what beer you would like), the brand must be recalled. Marketing communication here must actively seek to connect the need with the brand. This will be discussed in more detail in Chapter 11.

Brand salience is critical to a brand's success, but it is not enough. Without the formation of a positive brand attitude, as discussed in Chapter 5, the development of strong brand equity is unlikely. Some researchers have suggested that because brand awareness seems to be highly correlated with market share, it should be the primary strategic concern of advertising. In one study, up to 70% of advertising's measured effect on market share was accounted for by awareness (Miller and Berry, 1998). However, this is not quite so straight-forward as it may seem. As we discussed in Chapter 6, brand awareness is a good indicator of brand equity. It is not surprising, then, that brand salience correlates well with market share, because strong brands are likely to have high levels of awareness. One must build positive brand attitude as well as brand awareness. Romaniuk (2003) has even gone so far as to suggest that since many brands seem to compete on the same basic attribute, the key seems to be to go for quantity rather than quality of associations, concentrating on linking the brand to a wide range of attributes and thus to 'obtain a wide mental distribution' for the brand. But the mind does not work like that. It makes much more sense to position a brand on one or two benefits the target market believes (or can be persuaded to believe) the brand can deliver; and ideally, can deliver better than competitors (Percy and Elliott, 2005). This too will be covered in more detail in Chapter 11.

Brands and pre-conscious processes

Mere exposure

A host of experimental studies have demonstrated that low levels of preference can be obtained by merely exposing people to a stimulus a number of times, without their conscious awareness being necessary. This 'exposure effect' has been called mere exposure, and results from the unconscious priming of a stimulus (a brand in our case). In these studies, there is no effect upon recall of the stimulus. People do not remember seeing the stimulus, but they will be more likely to 'prefer' it to other unknown stimuli to which they have not been exposed. In terms of brand marketing, however, one must be careful here. While there is no question that a preference for a brand can be created outside of awareness, that preference will only occur in the *absence* of brands with which someone is already familiar. So, while there can be pre-conscious priming of brand names at some level, and this will create an unconscious familiarity with a brand that will lead to a preference from among a set of unfamiliar brands, this is a special case. The goal of brand management is to positively affect higher-order cognitive processing, while encouraging unconscious positive emotional congruence with the brand. Repetition of a brand name or logo will aid this process.

Classical conditioning

This approach requires not just exposure of the brand or logo but also pairing with a pleasant emotional stimulus, and eventually the brand alone will automatically evoke the pleasant emotional response as the link is established in non-declarative emotional memory. An example is Direct Line's practice of pairing their red telephone with frequent repetition of a musical car horn; over time the two become fixed in memory.

Both these approaches seem to work well when there is low involvement and no salient competitors, as pointed out above. A recent study shows that mere exposure can be as successful as classical conditioning and is easier to execute, but will not be successful against known, well-established competitors (Baker, 1999). The key strategy is to maximize

The Direct Line brand is a registered trade mark of Direct Line Insurance plc. Direct Line has given permission for the use of its brand in this publication.

the prominence of both brand name and package in communications to take advantage of any potential pre-conscious processing that will positively influence choice among unknown competitors.

Minimal cognitive processes

Shallow processing

A large proportion of our daily activities operate at semi-conscious levels of awareness, which leads to implicit rather than active learning of information. Unfortunately, with the exception of emotion, implicit memory is not likely to have any impact upon the evaluation or choice of brands (Percy, 2005). But emotional brand associations are certainly important, as we discussed in Chapter 2. Damasio (1994) has talked about the ability of secondary emotion to aid in decision-making in terms of something he calls *somatic markers*. He defined somatic markers as 'a special instance of feelings generated from secondary emotions', and stated that these emotions and feelings have been 'connected, by training, to predicted future outcomes of certain scenarios'. As he put it, somatic markers do not deliberate for us, but assist the deliberation.

The key here is to build associations through repetition of all elements of communications, not just advertising, and over time to build up connections between a brand and positive feelings, through the laying down of somatic markers, which can be triggered by a choice situation and give us simple guides to action without much, or indeed any, thought being necessary for purchase to ensue. We can plan to lay down as many somatic markers as possible by using a combination of associations and meanings to differentiate the product in some way.

Building brand associations and meanings

Taste, shape and texture

The taste of Marmite, the shape of Toilet Duck, the feel of Dove soap, and the texture of Cadbury's Flake are unique associations which define the brand for many consumers (Heath, 2001).

Colours

Red means Coke, blue means Pepsi, green means ecologically friendly, purple means luxury, and all can be learned without any conscious effort being required. But a manager must be certain the colour associated with the brand in memory is consistent with the desired *long-term* positioning of the brand. For example, colours toward the red end of the spectrum (as well as more intense colours) tend to increase arousal (Osgood *et al.*, 1957). This makes sense for Coke, but it would not make sense for a brand that wanted to be associated with a sense of calm and serenity.

In an interesting study of the synesthesic effects (i.e. where one sense evokes another) of colour on taste, Percy (1973) found that the colour of a sauce (condiments such as ketchup, steak sauce, and salad dressing) is directly and consistently related to the colour spectrum. Running from orange through dark brown to black, it was found that people perceived orange sauces to be milder than red, and so forth through dark brown and black, which were perceived to be the spiciest. This can have important implications for condiment brands.

At the time of this study, both Heinz 57 Sauce and A-1 Sauce (steak sauce brands) were basically the same reddish-brown colour. But Heinz 57 Sauce was packaged in a clear bottle while A-1 Sauce was packaged in a black-tinted bottle. Because people could see the reddish-brown colouring of Heinz 57 Sauce, they perceived it to have a milder taste than A-1 Sauce, which was perceived as spicier because of the dark bottle. Unfortunately, 'spiciness' was the most important attribute of a steak sauce.

Music

We can add additional associations to the brand through adding sound to visual elements so doubling the modalities of association, e.g. Hamlet cigars and Bach, British Airways and Delibes, Intel and their reassuring four notes.

There are three main variables that mediate the effect of music on brand purchase behaviour: tempo, type, and how it is presented (Rossiter and Percy, 1997). Tempo seems to operate emotionally. Slow music has been found to have a positive effect upon sales. In Milliman's (1982) primary study of tempo, he found that when slower instrumental music was played in a retail store, customers spent 17% more time shopping and 35% more money as compared with when faster music was played (60 beats per minute vs. 108 beats per minute).

The type of music heard appears to operate more upon cognitive processes. In a study of musical types Areni and Kim (1993) found that when classical background music was played in a wine store vs. Top 40 pop music, the amount of money customers spent was three times greater (US $7.43 vs. US $2.18). In another study conducted in the wine section of a UK supermarket, it was found that when French music was played, French wine was four times more likely to be purchased than German wine. But when German music was played, German wines outsold French wines two-to-one (North et al., 1999).

Also likely to be operating upon cognitive interpretation is how music is presented. In an experiment where music was played on a clearly visible tape player in a shopping setting, younger customers were likely to spend significantly more than if the music was played in the background as part of the store's audio system. With older adults, it was just the opposite. With background music, significantly more was spent than with music played in the foreground. These results were not related to either a person's mood at the time, or whether they liked the music being played or not (Yalch and Spangenburg, 1993).

Brand name suggestiveness

Research has shown that a brand name that explicitly conveys a product benefit leads to higher recall of advertising than a non-suggestive name and thus builds positive associations more effectively (Keller et al., 1998). A brand name that explicitly conveys a product benefit (e.g. PicturePerfect televisions) leads to higher recall of an advertised benefit claim compared with non-suggestive brand names (e.g. Emporium televisions).

Celebrities

A short-cut to associating meaning with a brand is to use the ready-made meanings of a celebrity endorser, e.g. David Beckham and Gillette, Virgin and Richard Branson. The influence of sports celebrities is particularly strong on teenagers of both genders, increasing

Gillette

both positive word-of-mouth and brand loyalty (Bush *et al.*, 2004). But the primary benefit of using a celebrity endorser is heightened awareness for a brand. As Holman and Hecken (1983) have shown, a celebrity presenter will almost always increase recall for a brand. Of course, the presenter must be seen as a celebrity in the eye of the brand's target market. Also, brand recall, as opposed to brand recognition, should be the primary brand awareness objective (a point discussed in Chapter 11).

But in using a celebrity endorser the manager must be careful. As Percy and Elliott (2005) have pointed out, while a celebrity presenter may raise a brand's visibility, one must be equally concerned with the likely effect specific characteristics of the celebrity will have in relation to the underlying nature of the decision involved in choosing brands within a category. For example, with symbolic brands where the underlying purchase decision is positively motivated, for sensory gratification or social approval, the celebrity presented must be seen as likable; and the more highly involving the decision, the more the presenter must also be seen by the target market as similar to an 'ideal user'. In other words, with symbolic brands, not only must purchasers like and identify with the celebrity, they must also feel their social circle will also identify with the celebrity as positively representing the brand.

And of course, the use of a celebrity endorser for a brand must be carefully evaluated in relation to the generally high cost of securing the endorsement. Also, the risk of possible negative publicity associated with the celebrity must be weighed.

Choice heuristics

Studies have shown that consumers often make choices between brands based on simple rules-of-thumb, or choice heuristics, which short-circuit the process into an almost instantaneous decision. Heuristics such as 'buy the cheapest brand' and 'buy the brand I feel warm about' are the most common for fmcgs (Hoyer, 1984), while for leisure activities 'buy the brand my friends buy' is most common (Elliott and Hamilton, 1991). In some product categories, pictographic thinking is very common, where consumers rely on package illustrations to infer attributes (Viswanathan *et al.*, 2005). Therefore before focusing on any particular heuristic it needs to be identified through research as being frequently used by consumers in the product category of interest. But once identified, communications can focus on providing the relevant information, preferably visually.

Surrogate indicators

Consumers often use surrogate indicators to simplify their choice processes, where hidden dimensions of a product are inferred from some visible attribute. A common surrogate in purchasing grocery products is small size = low price; however the implications of this for strategy are complicated by the use by some consumers of a large size = low price inference (Viswanathan *et al.*, 2005). Again, specific research must be carried out before making decisions about pack sizes.

Market beliefs

As well as using heuristics based on aspects of the product, consumers also use more generalized beliefs about companies, advertising, and shops to guide their decisions. Some widely held market beliefs include beliefs such as 'when in doubt, a well-known brand is a safe choice', 'bad brands just don't survive', 'hard-sell advertising is associated with low-quality products', 'larger shops offer better prices than small shops' (Duncan, 1990).

Meaningful differentiation from meaningless differences

As discussed in the previous chapter, the BrandAsset Valuator studies identify differentiation and relevance as the core elements in building brand strength. However, for low-involvement brands in highly competitive markets, having a real source of differentiation in the product's functional attributes is very difficult to achieve and sustain. However, an intriguing study has demonstrated that it may be possible to differentiate a brand on the basis of irrelevant attributes (Carpenter *et al.*, 1994). Alberto Natural Silk Shampoo is differentiated by including silk in the shampoo and advertised as 'We put silk in a bottle'. This suggests that the consumer's hair will be silky, but there is no known benefit of adding silk to a shampoo. Experimental studies have shown that consumers will use a meaningless difference to aid decision-making, but most importantly it seems that a premium price increases the differentiating effect as consumers infer from the price that the (meaningless) differentiation is in fact valuable.

Behavioural processes

Brand repertoires

Using data from large-scale consumer panel studies, Ehrenberg and his associates have shown that in many fmcg markets, rather than buying only one brand—solus brand loyalty—consumers regularly buy from within a small number of competing brands: their brand repertoire. Within this set of brands they seem to buy at random and the brands usually share some physical characteristics. Interestingly, when asked about their buying behaviour consumers frequently over-estimated their loyalty when compared to their recorded actual purchases. See Table 8.1.

The implications of this are that the pursuit of solus brand loyalty may be fruitless in many fmcg markets, and the aim should be to build the number of consumers who have the brand in their repertoire. This why brand salience is such an important objective.

Penetration and purchase frequency

A major issue in deciding on strategy in fmcg markets is whether to focus on increasing penetration (new users) or increasing frequency of purchase (by current users). The

Table 8.1 Brand repertoires

Average frequencies of purchase of cereals in a year		
Brand	**Average purchases by buyers of stated brand**	
	Stated brand	**Other brands**
Nabisco Shredded Wheat (USA)	4	37
Nabisco Shredded Wheat (UK)	7	33
Kelloggs Corn Flakes (USA)	5	29
Kelloggs Corn Flakes (UK)	10	23

Source: Ehrenberg and Goodhardt (1979)

large-scale IRI study in the USA (1,251 brands, 14 fmcg categories, 82,000 households, over a two-year period) demonstrated that for brands which grew in the period, brand growth came largely from increased penetration, accounting for 75% or more of all growth (McQueen *et al.*, 1998). However, purchase frequency increases were important too, playing some role in growth for 76% of brands and being the predominant source of growth for 25% of brands. A further study has found convergent results, penetration being the primary growth driver, especially for brands that showed dramatic growth (Baldinger *et al.*, 2002).

If we look at the differences between large and small brands, we find that the larger the brand, the more likely it is to grow through purchase frequency, although penetration still contributes most. However, small brands with low penetration make up a sizeable proportion of many fmcg categories, and these brands grew almost exclusively through penetration. See Table 8.2.

The IRI study also classified the consumer panel data according to patterns of purchasing, resulting in five types of purchasing behaviour. See Fig. 8.1.

These buyer segments contribute to brand growth differentially, and brands have different profiles of the various buyer types. Brands dominated by 'loyals' gain most growth from increased frequency of purchasing; they also tend to be the biggest brands. At the other extreme, brands with a lot of 'light users' get most of their growth from penetration gains and are extremely vulnerable as the 'light users' are likely to buy a different brand every time they enter the market (Stockdale, 1999). See Table 8.3.

The implications for strategy are that all brands should attempt to increase penetration, but that large brands have less room to grow through this strategy and must also concentrate on increasing purchase frequency. It is also vital to understand the profile of consumer segments for any specific brand in order to target appropriate efforts towards major segments.

Table 8.2 The effect of brand size on growth mechanics

Brand Year 1 Penetration %	Percentage contribution to growth		
	Penetration	Frequency	Percentage of brands
0–5	92	8	23
6–10	77	23	34
11–30	68	33	32
30+	54	46	11

Source: Adapted from McQueen *et al.*, (1998)

Five types of buying behaviour:

- Long-term brand loyals
- Deal selectives
  - Who buy brand leaders on offer
- Rotators
  - Heavy users with large brand repertoire
- Price driven
  - Buy cheap brands and anything on offer
- Light users

Source: Adapted from Stockdale (1999)

Fig. 8.1 All customers are not equal

Table 8.3 Deconstruction of brand growth

Brands by buyer types	Contribution to growth		% of Brands
	Penetration	Frequency	
Loyals	15%	85%	15%
Deal selectives	50%	50%	17%
Rotators	68%	32%	20%
Price driven	75%	25%	29%
Light users	100%	0%	19%

Source: Adapted from Stockdale (1999)

Managing consumer perceptions

A consumer's perceptions of a brand are based on their history with the brand, including advertising, packaging, actual usage experiences, etc., and these perceptions can be refreshed and reinforced by associating the brand with new goals and usage situations or by encouraging category substitution (Wansink and Huffman, 2001).

Refreshing favourable perceptions

New information is most easily learned when it is related to what is already known, and it can be quicker and less expensive to re-activate existing associations than to create new ones (Deighton, 1984). An excellent example of going back to what differentiated the brand originally and bringing it up to date is Nestlé's Yorkie bar, which was originally launched in the UK in 1976 at a time when Cadbury had been reducing the thickness of their brand leader Dairy Milk bar in response to raw material cost rises, rather than increasing the retail price. Nestlé took advantage of this opportunity by launching a bar that was a much thicker shape and associating the brand with a large muscular truck driver biting down on the bar. The same truck driver image was used in TV advertising for many years. The brand was refreshed by a return to the male-oriented position with a more contemporary feel: 'It's not for girls'; 'Not for handbags'; 'Not available in pink'. This was carried through to the packaging and created much word-of-mouth through media attention.

Extending favourable perceptions

The creative use of product development can be instrumental in extending a brand's current perceptions into a new space. United Biscuits' Penguin chocolate biscuit, originally launched in 1932 and essentially unchanged for nearly 70 years, was recently extended into Penguin Flipper Dipper, a dipping product, intended to capitalize on the 'dipping' explosion within the snacking market. It comprises chocolate flipper-shaped biscuits with a chocolate and vanilla-flavoured dip, moving the basic consumer perceptions into a new product form.

New usage situations

There is clear evidence that associating a brand with new usage situations can increase sales, sometimes dramatically. A famous example is Arm and Hammer Baking Soda, which, when a decline in home-baking led to a drop in sales, was marketed as a deodorizer for refrigerators, and sales 'skyrocketed' (Wansink and Gilmore, 1999). Campbell's condensed soups have long been promoted on the pack as for use as a base sauce in cooking casseroles.

Penguin Flipper Dipper

Encouraging category substitution

A related strategy is to promote a brand as a substitute for products in other categories. For example, Danone yogurt was promoted as a substitute for high-fat eggs and oil in baking. Kellogg's Special K breakfast cereal was promoted for use not just at breakfast but as an afternoon or evening snack. This was later followed by new product development to create Special K bars, which resulted in greatly increased sales without damage to the core cereal product.

Walkers gave away over 7 million free books to schools. Image supplied by Walkers.

Real users

A new approach to managing perceptions of fmcg brands has been the use of 'real people' in advertising. The established brand of soap Lever Fabergé's Dove 'received significant publicity when it asked real women to strip down to their underwear to advertise its Body Firming range of products. Using the strapline "As tested on real curves" the poster version proclaimed "It wouldn't be much of a challenge to firm up the thighs of size 8 supermodels, would it?" ' (Mediaweek, 2003). Conspicuously, the women in the Dove campaign were not impossibly beautiful, unattainable perfect models, and as a consequence the communication was more believable. Lever Fabergé claimed that sales doubled after the campaign.

Cause-related marketing

A very powerful way to influence consumers' perceptions of fmcgs is to associate a brand with a 'good cause'. A recent study has found that 98% of consumers are aware of at

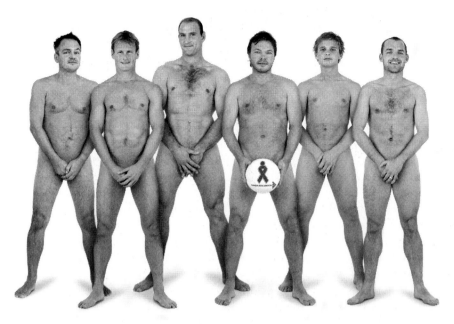

Photography by Rankin

least one cause-related marketing programme, and 83% have participated in at least one programme; 48% of consumers showed an actual change in behaviour, saying they switched brands, increased usage or tried a new product as a result, and 46% said that it improved their perceptions by making them feel better about using the product or service (Brand Benefits, 2003/4).

The Walkers Snacks (a PepsiCo Foods company) Free Books For Schools campaign involved consumers collecting tokens from packets of potato crisps and donating them to their local participating schools. The programme 'caused a huge collecting frenzy never witnessed before, reaching over 80% of the UK population' (Business in the Community, 2005). Over 7 million free books were given to schools over a five-year period, involving 85% of UK schools.

Gillette supported Cancer Research UK's Tackling Testicular Cancer campaign in 2005 by including leaflets in 18 million razor blade packs and promoting the BlueBoy awareness badge. The campaign also featured a risqué photograph of celebrities including famous footballers and rugby stars taken by celebrity photographer Rankin.

Managing choice situations

New distribution outlets

Snapple and Lipton's Iced Tea have extended their reach by accessing vending machines, as have video rental firms, and Taco Bell and Pizza Hut have been successful with their mini-stores inside supermarkets and convenience stores (Wansink and Huffman, 2001).

New packaging

Heinz introduced child-friendly containers and revolutionary colours ('Blastin' Green' and 'Awesome Orange') in its EZ Squirt ketchup, which revitalized a dormant category. Individual-servings packages have increased demand for a variety of products such as fruit drinks, coffee, and cheeses. The detergent market has seen positive consumer response to 'liquitab' gel sachets, and 'powerball' tablets have been well received in the dishwashing market, both adding some new appeal to markets very low on consumer interest.

Multiple shelf placements

Consumers often settle into a 'shopping script' that only includes a limited number of aisles in the supermarket (Hoyer, 1984). By placing pasta, Bolognese sauces and Parmesan cheese not only in their respective product categories but also together in a 'tonight's meal' section, supermarkets can make it easy for consumers to put a meal together. Similarly, consumers with allergy problems cam find a whole range of products free from gluten, wheat or dairy products in the 'Free From' section in Sainsbury's supermarkets.

Increasing purchase quantities

Studies have shown that it is possible to increase the actual amount a customer buys of a product either through effects on the desired quantity or through reducing the perceived price (Wansink *et al.*, 1998).

Quantity limits

Paradoxically, limiting the amount of a product that a customer can buy increases the number purchased, e.g. setting a limit that customers can only buy twelve cans of soup per person leads to a larger quantity being purchased than without the quantity limit.

Quantity cues

Giving a cue as to how many to buy, e.g. 'buy ten for the weekend' or 'buy five for the family', can also result in increased purchase quantities.

Price perceptions

Larger packages can reduce consumers' perceptions of unit price. This is often the operation of a market belief that 'larger package means lower price per unit'.

Increasing usage quantities

Promotion effects

Promotion can help increase purchase quantity with what is known as a *loading device*. Such promotions are aimed at changing the minimal purchasing pattern by encouraging the consumer to 'load up' on the brand by purchasing more than usual. This can be one with price-offs at the point-of-purchase, or with special 'price packs' where a reduced price is printed as part of the brand's label. Additionally, special bonus packaging may be used where more of the product is offered at the regular price.

Loading promotions are an effective strategy when it is known that a competitor is about to enter the market with a new product or new version of an existing product because it effectively removes people from the market, discouraging them from trying the new offering.

Increasing the amount a customer buys can also result in increased usage of a product.

Stockpiling

Studies show that household stockpiling can increase usage frequency, particularly in the categories of snacks and beverages (Wansinck and Deshpande, 1994). This effect is most pronounced if the products are visible in the house.

Packaging effects

Possibly as a result of reducing price perceptions, larger pack sizes can also increase usage rate.

Increasing the size of the opening is one way to increase usage quantity. For example changing to 'big-mouth' bottles resulted in increased consumption of Mountain Dew. This has become a widely used strategy in many food and drink categories.

Advertising effects

Advertising can help increase usage quantity in two ways: it can encourage new use situations or it can make the brand and category salient through tactical media scheduling.

Usage expansion advertising is most effective when it frames the new use as a complement to existing behaviour, e.g. 'Eat Campbell's soup for breakfast because it is as hot and nutritious as it is with lunch' (Wansink and Ray, 1996).

Scheduling can also have an impact on consumption by making the brand top-of-mind when the consumption decision is being made. For example, Campbell's soup runs its radio ads just before lunch and dinner times, and also has standing instructions for radio stations to run specially developed 'Storm Spot' ads during bad weather (Wansink and Huffman, 2001).

Building brand loyalty

Whereas with symbolic brands, loyalty is based on the meaning of the brand and the strength of its emotional connection with the consumer, with functional brands with low consumer involvement, loyalty is usually seen as being a factor that can be increased through reward schemes.

Loyalty programmes

There has been a proliferation of loyalty programmes in which consumers are offered incentives in exchange for repeat business, and there is some evidence that they can be successful with low-involvement products and services, particularly if the incentives overlap with brand meanings (Roehm *et al.*, 2002). It is likely that a programme that tries to restrict the operation of double-jeopardy behaviours like buying from within a brand repertoire will be inefficient (Dowling and Uncles, 1997). However, low and moderate reward programmes that target light users may generate cost-effective incremental sales (Wansink, 2003).

Raising consumer involvement

However, it may be possible to create some degree of loyalty in fmcg markets through raising consumer involvement. An example is the development by Lever Fabergé's Ponds skin-care brand of a membership programme around the 'Pond's Institute'. Originally an 'advertising fiction', the Pond's Institute aims to build bonds with customers by providing the reassurance required by consumers in this category. It has been developed into a vehicle for relationship marketing as customers have access to a range of services including email access to a qualified skin-care consultant (Miller, 2001). Kodak used SMS to access holiday-makers while they were clubbing in Ibiza, sending text messages containing DJ listings and discounts on disposable cameras.

CHAPTER SUMMARY

In this chapter we have emphasized the vital importance of top-of-mind awareness and brand salience to a functional brand. We have discussed a range of ways in which brand associations can be built up through pre-conscious and minimal cognitive processes using all elements of communication. We went on to consider behavioural processes to increase penetration and/or frequency of purchase, and then discussed ways of managing consumer perceptions. We ended with a consideration of how the choice situation can be managed, and approaches to building brand loyalty.

DISCUSSION QUESTIONS

1 What are the effects of brand salience on consumer behaviour?

2 When might mere exposure and classical conditioning be used effectively?

3 How can brand strategy lay down somatic markers?

4 How can colour be used in brand strategy?

5 Why must a celebrity endorser be used carefully?

6 When should brand strategy favour increasing purchase frequency?

7 How can existing favourable consumer perceptions be refreshed?

8 How can advertising be used to increase usage quantities?

CASE STUDY

The Launch of Roundup Weedkiller

Monsanto is a large international manufacturer of agrichemicals entering into the Australian consumer gardening market with a glyphosate brand that consumers did not need and the trade did not want. The ambitious target for Monsanto was that the brand should sell at a premium to the competition, and achieve full distribution and full profitability within the first 12 months after launch.

The daunting marketing problem

The problems facing the launch were considerable. First of all, the market is completely dominated by the brand Zero, with a sales market share of 60%. Secondly there was nothing at a product level to differentiate the Monsanto brand from its 65 competitors. Thirdly consumers claimed to be entirely satisfied with their current brand's performance and saw no need for another brand of weedkiller. The retail trade and the nursery industry similarly saw absolutely no need for another glyphosate brand, especially if it was going to come from Monsanto, as they believed that the market was flat and would not grow.

The marketing opportunity

To meet Monsanto's objective for the launch was to be a formidable task. It was clear the brand-to-be would have to find a new positioning in the market which *created* a consumer need, and thereby compete with Zero and overcome apathy in the trade.

The brand

Qualitative research examined a whole host of glyphosate formulations, names, packaging types, labelling styles, positioning statements and selling propositions for the brand-to-be and the opportunity for the brand was defined as shown in the table below.

The advertising opportunity and the launch

Advertising was going to be crucial. The brand had to be seen as more efficacious than it actually was to get the trial it needed and to sell at a premium to the brand leader. Furthermore, with a share of voice for Zero of 86%, the advertising needed all the impact it could muster to stand out and be seen.

Name	Roundup
Target market	Buyers of chemical weedkillers, primarily Zero buyers, 40 years +
Product range	375 ml ready to use, trigger pack/825 ml ready to use, trigger pack/3 litre ready to use, trigger pack/125 ml concentrate/1 litre concentrate
Pricing	40% premium to competition
Positioning	The most effective range of lawn and garden weedkillers available
Proposition	Nothing kills weeds faster
Support	Fast-acting formulation to accelerate plant browning and wilting
Personality	Professional, friendly and efficient

Roundup was launched in August 1994 using a combination of TV, point-of-sale and PR. The television campaign ran for six weeks, featuring a single TVC called 'Monster' in which the two screaming kids announce to their dad their discovery of unwanted weeds in their back garden. Dad then swiftly kills off the 'ugly' weeds with a Roundup 825 ml trigger spray, the commercial ending with the proposition 'Nothing kills weeds faster. Guaranteed'. The majority of consumers knew little or nothing about agricultural Roundup. The few that had seen or used the product regarded it as effective but as also perhaps environmentally dodgy, unsafe to humans, difficult to use and only for big jobs. The 'Monster' idea was therefore ideal because it clearly explained what this new brand is, what it is *for*, and how safe and easy it is to use, hence the back garden, the flowers and the kids.

Point-of-sale, packaging and labelling all reinforced the speed of kill message and the tone of voice of the advertising. To stand out from the competition, new pack shapes were designed and all material was branded. Lastly, PR was used to generate a ground swell of consumer and trade interest in the brand. Key media commentators were invited to the company's horticultural site to view at first hand the effectiveness of fast-acting Roundup in a 'green' environment. A gardening writer product mailing was also undertaken. Consumers do not buy weedkiller on a weekly basis, they buy it twice a year. TV and PR were therefore used to generate awareness for the brand and to predispose consumers to it prior to a later purchase occasion. POS, packaging, and labelling were then designed to promote the purchase decision itself at the point-of-purchase.

The launch results were outstanding! Roundup became the second largest selling brand and the second biggest weedkiller brand in Australia. It reached 68% brand awareness, a fact that positioned Roundup as the second most recalled brand in the market. Moreover, trial levels rose to 17% and the propensity of all buyers to purchase increased to 28%. It also reversed the trade apathy, and as a result key retailers who had initially refused to stock the brand are now signing national contracts with Monsanto.

Isolating the effect of advertising

The launch was a startling success, but what role did advertising play in contributing to this happy situation? Looking into the different elements of the marketing mix, we can probably conclude that they were not responsible for the gains in sales and distribution. More specifically, pricing played no role in driving the increase in sales since it remained constant at a premium to Zero for the duration of the campaign. The performance of the new product formulation cannot have driven sales. Consumers on average purchase 1.8 packs of weedkiller p.a., and so it is unlikely that repeat purchase due to a different 'fast-acting' formulation would have driven sales nationally over a six-week period. It is also unlikely that word of mouth could travel quickly enough to generate such a rapid rise in sales. It might be hoped, however, that word of mouth will work to sustain sales in the longer term by introducing new users to the brand via recommendation. Whilst seasonality influenced sales volumes, it could not account for the gain in share Roundup achieved against the competition, and the climatic conditions should have militated against the success of a new launch.

The effectiveness of the advertising

So how did the advertising work? Without the insights afforded by good qualitative research to evaluate the advertising, it is difficult to fully understand *how* and *why* the advertising worked. It is certainly true the advertising succeeded in getting noticed, but how effective was it at communicating on strategy and in prompting trial? Taking into consideration the following we perceive that advertising was performing as intended:

- The right selling message was getting through to consumers.
- The advertising seemed to be saying all the right things about the brand and generating higher scores than Zero on all key brand attributes.
- Trial and propensity to purchase were more than twice as high amongst advertising-aware consumers than amongst those who had not seen the campaign.
- The advertising was working in meeting the positioning and strategy defined for the new brand. It was achieving this against a flurry of reactive competitive activity, and doing so with a share of voice in the market of only 14%.

Conclusion

Roundup was launched in September with limited distribution, limited ranging and at a 40% premium to Zero, the market leader. By the end of December it was the second-best selling weedkiller in the country. This was a particularly impressive achievement given the tough market conditions and the fact that the brand has no *real* advantage whatsoever over the competition.

Of all the different elements in the marketing mix, it seems reasonable to single out advertising as the key driver behind the success of the launch. Roundup became profitable four months after the brand's launch and within this period the sales revenues covered *all* Monsanto RPD's costs.

Source: WARC, AFA, Advertising Effectiveness Awards 1994, The Launch of Roundup Weedkiller
Edited by Natalia Yannopoulou

Discussion Questions

1 What are the main challenges for a low-involvement brand, such as Roundup?
2 What other ways of increasing its brand awareness could Monsanto have used?
3 How would you describe Monsanto's brand strategy regarding Roundup and what would you suggest as future actions?
4 What other methods could be used to position Roundup in the market, besides advertising?

FURTHER READING

- The classic text based on analysis of over 20 years of panel data is Ehrenberg, A.S.C. (1988), *Repeat-Buying: Facts, Theory and Applications*, Oxford: Oxford University Press.

- A useful discussion of how to utilize a wide range of physical stimuli is Lindstrom, M. (2005), *Brand Sense: How to Build Powerful Brands Through Touch, Taste, Smell, Sight and Sound*, London: Kogan Page.

- An account of P&G's success at inventing and sustaining a vast range of functional brands in markets around the world is Dyer, D. *et al.* (2004), *Rising Tide: Lessons from 165 Years of Brand Building at Procter and Gamble*, Boston: Harvard Business School Press.

REFERENCES

Areni, C.S. and Kim, D. (1993), 'The influence of background music on shopping behavior: classical versus top-forty music in a wine store', in L. McAlister and M.C. Rothschild (eds.), *Advances in Consumer Research*, Vol. 20, Provo, UT: Association for Consumer Research, pp. 336–40.

Baker, W. (1999), 'When can affective conditioning and mere exposure directly influence brand choice?', *Journal of Advertising*, 28, 4, 31–46.

Baldinger, A., Blair, E., and Echambadi, R. (2002), 'Why brands grow', *Journal of Advertising Research*, January/February, 7–14.

Brand Benefits (2003/4), *Cause Related Marketing*, http://www.bitc.org.uk.

Bush, A., Martin, C., and Bush, V. (2004), 'Sports celebrity influence on the behavioral intentions of generation Y', *Journal of Advertising Research*, March/April, 108–18.

Business in the Community (2005), *Cause Related Marketing Award for Excellence*, http://www.bitc.org.uk.

Carpenter, G., Glazer, R., and Nakamoto, N. (1994), 'Meaningful brands from meaningless differentiation: the dependence on irrelevant attributes', *Journal of Marketing Research*, XXXI, August, 339–50.

Damasio, A. (1994), *Descartes' Error: Emotion, Reason and the Human Brain*, New York: Quill.

Deighton, J. (1984), 'The interaction of advertising and evidence', *Journal of Consumer Research*, 11, 763–70.

Dowling, G. and Uncles, M. (1997), 'Do customer loyalty programs really work?', *Sloan Management Review*, 38, 4, 71–82.

Duncan, C. (1990), 'Consumer market beliefs: a review of the literature and an agenda for future research', *Advances in Consumer Research*, 17, 729–35.

Ehrenberg, A. and Goodhardt, G. (1979), *Essays on understanding buyer behavior*, New York: J. W. Thompson.

—— Barnard, N. and Scriven, J. (1997), 'Differentiation or salience', *Journal of Advertising Research*, November, 7–14.

—— Barnard, N., Kennedy, R., and Bloom, H. (2002), 'Brand advertising as creative publicity', *Journal of Advertising Research*, July/August, 7–18.

Elliott, R. and Hamilton, E. (1991), 'Consumer choice tactics and leisure activities', *International Journal of Advertising*, 10, 4, 325–33.

Heath, R. (2001), *The Hidden Power of Advertising: How Low Involvement Processing Influences the Way We Choose Brands*, Henley-on-Thames: Admap Publications.

Holman, R.H. and Hecken, S. (1983), 'Advertising impact: creative elements affecting brand recall', *Current Issues in Research and Advertising*, 157–72.

Howard, J.A. (1977), *Consumer Behavior: Application of Theory*, New York: McGraw-Hill.

Hoyer, W. (1984), 'An examination of consumer decision making for a common repeat purchase product', *Journal of Consumer Research*, 11, 822–9.

Keller, K., Heckler, S., and Houston, M. (1998), 'The effects of brand name suggestiveness on advertising', *Journal of Marketing*, 62, 1, 42–52.

McQueen, J., Sylvester, A., and Moore, S. (1998), 'Brand growth', in J.P. Jones (ed.), *How Advertising Works*, London: Sage.

Mediaweek (2003), *Strategic Review: Getting Real to Boost a Brand*, http://www.mediaweek.co.uk/.

Miller, J. (2001), 'Building bonds with packaged-goods consumers', *Admap*, November, 22–5.

Miller, S. and Berry, L. (1998), 'Brand salience versus brand image: two theories of advertising effectiveness', *Journal of Advertising Research*, September/October, 77–82.

Milliman, R.E. (1982), 'Using background music to affect the behavior of supermarket shoppers', *Journal of Marketing*, 40, 3, 86–91.

Morgan, A. (1999), *Eating the Big Fish*, Chichester: John Wiley.

North, A.C., Hargreaver, D.T., and McKendrick, J. (1999), 'The influence of in-store music on wine selection', *Journal of Applied Psychology*, 85, 2, 271–6.

Osgood, C.E., Suci, G. and Tannenbaum, R.H. (1957), *The Measurement of Measuring*, Champaign: University of Illinois Press.

Percy, L. (1973), 'Determining the influence of color on a product cognitive structure: a multidimensional scaling application', in S. Ward and P. Wright (eds.), *Advances in Consumer Research*, Vol. 1, Provo, UT: Association for Consumer Research, pp. 218–27.

Percy, L. (2005), 'Unconscious processing of advertising and its effects upon attitude and behaviour', in S. Diehl, R. Terlutter, and P. Weinberg (eds.), *Advertising Communication*, Proceedings of the Fifth Internationial Conference on Research in Advertising, Saarland University, Saarbrücken, Germany.

Percy, L. and Elliott, R. (2005), *Strategic Advertising Management*, 2nd edn, Oxford: Oxford University Press.

Roehm, M., Pullins, E., and Roehm, H. (2002), 'Designing loyalty-building programs for packaged goods brands', *Journal of Marketing Research*, XXXIX, May, 202–13.

Romaniuk, J. (2003), 'Brand attributes: "distribution outlets" in the mind', *Journal of Marketing Communications*, 9, 73–92.

Rossiter, J.R. and Percy, L. (1997), *Advertising Communication and Promotion Management*, New York: McGraw-Hill.

Stockdale, M. (1999), 'Are all consumers equal?' in J.P. Jones (ed.), *How to Use Advertising to Build Strong Brands*, London: Sage.

Viswanathan, M., Rosa, J., and Harris, J. (2005), 'Decision making and coping by functionally illiterate consumers and some implications for marketing management', *Journal of Marketing*, 69, January, 15–3.

Wansink, B. and Deshpande, R. (1994),' "Out of sight out of mind": the impact of household stockpiling on usage rates', *Marketing Letters*, 5, 1, January, 99–100.

—— (2003), 'Developing a cost-effective brand loyalty program', *Journal of Advertising Research*, September, 301–9.

—— and Gilmore, J. (1999), 'New uses that revitalize old brands', *Journal of Advertising Research*, March/April, 90–8.

—— and Huffman, C. (2001), 'Revitalizing mature packaged goods', *Journal of Product and Brand Management*, 10, 4, 228–42.

—— and Ray, M. (1996), 'Advertising strategies to increase usage frequency', *Journal of Marketing*, 60, January, 31–46.

—— Kent, R., and Hoch, S. (1998), 'An anchoring and adjustment model of purchase quantity decisions', *Journal of Marketing Research*, 35, 1, February, 71–81.

Yalch, R.F. and Spangenburg, E. (1993), 'Using store music for retail zoning: a field experiment', in L. McAlister and M.C. Rothschild (eds.), *Advances in Consumer Research*, Vol. 20, Provo, UT: Association for Consumer Research, pp. 632–6.

9

Brand Stretching and Retrenching

1 Product and brand portfolio management strategy guide brand stretching and retrenching strategy.

2 The brand hierarchy comprises company brands, group brands, and single brands.

3 Category development index and brand development index help inform brand stretching and retrenching strategy.

4 Master brands have led to significant changes in product and brand portfolio management.

5 When to use source versus endorser branding strategies.

6 Brand extensions are different from line extensions.

Introduction

When talking about brand stretching and retrenching, one is dealing with a *branding strategy*, one that considers a number of elements related to the existing brands in a company's product portfolio (or sometimes just a single brand) and the best way to use those brands (or an individual brand) in order to maximize the overall potential of the company. This can involve quite complex branding strategies, utilizing multiple brand names and positionings over an entire product portfolio; or simply a brand strategy dealing with one brand. In the end, a brand stretching strategy is part of the overall strategy for developing and nurturing a strong overall equity for the brand, building upon a brand's equity to strengthen the overall product portfolio; and a retrenchment strategy looks to the elimination of brand extensions or the retirement of a brand, again to strengthen the overall product portfolio.

Before discussing the various ways one can think about brand stretching and retrenching strategies, it would be a good idea to consider just what is meant by such things as product and brand portfolios, and how they are related to one another. This is important because it provides the framework for understanding brand stretching and retrenchment strategies.

Product and brand portfolios

Everyone knows what a product is. A company's *product portfolio* is how marketers often describe the collection of different products they market in a category, and this will include individual products as well as product lines. A *product line* is a group of products within a single product category that are closely related to each other in some way, usually because they are seen as being used for the same thing. Brands too may be described in terms of portfolios and lines. A *brand portfolio* reflects the various brands marketed by a company, again within a particular product category; and a *brand line* is all of the products marketed under a single brand name.

One way to think about the interrelationships implied here (as Keller has) is in terms of a grid, with all of the products a company markets running along the top and the brands for each product listed below (Keller, 1995). Fig. 9.1 illustrates this for the products marketed by Levi-Strauss. Looking along the rows reflects the product portfolio, and looking down the columns, the brand portfolio.

It is important to think about products and brands in this way, because looking along a row is really looking at the current *brand extension* strategy of the company. What this partial example for Levi-Strauss shows is that when they made the decision to market cotton trousers, they decided *against* marketing them as Levi's. While they did initially introduce them under a Levi's umbrella (Levi's Dockers) in order to borrow and build upon the existing equity in the Levi's brand, now the brand stands alone, and in fact has spawned its own line extensions.

Looking at the brands for each product in the grid, one gets a feel for the branding strategy used by a company for the products it markets. In our example Levi-Strauss has

PRODUCT PORTFOLIO

	Denim pants	Non-denim pants	Shirts	Jackets	Other
	Levi's	Dockers	Dockers	Levi-Strauss Signature	
	Levi's 501	Levi-Strauss Signature	Levi-Strauss Signature		
	Levi's Engineered Jeans				
	Other				

(Left axis label: BRAND PORTFOLIO)

Fig. 9.1 Levi-Strauss partial product and brand portfolio grid

	Hatch	Notch	Sports coupe	Roadster	Pickup	Off-road
Luxury		Bentley, Lamborghini, Bugatti	Lamborghini			
Upper		Audi				
Upper middle		Audi				Audi
Middle		VW, SEAT				
Compact	Audi VW, SEAT	VW, SEAT Škoda	Audi			
Small	VW, SEAT Škoda	VW, SEAT Škoda			VW, SEAT Škoda	
Mini	VW, SEAT					

Fig. 9.2 Volkswagen partial product portfolio circa 2001

chosen to use the Levi's brand name as a group brand (which will be discussed below), providing an umbrella for all their jeans, and trading upon the original equity in the brand.

Fig. 9.2 illustrates Volkswagen's product portfolio as it existed in 2001. Most people are likely to know that Audi is part of Volkswagen, but not that such diverse brands as Bugatti, Lamborghini, and Bentley are also a part of Volkswagen. They have laid their product portfolio out with the various types of vehicles in the category across the top (the products) and the market segments in the category down the side, with their various brands inserted in the grid where appropriate. As it shows, Volkswagen as a corporation has deep penetration with several brands in a number of segments; and at the same time, there are a number of vehicle types where they only offer one brand, and two segments (mini and upper) where there is limited coverage. Perhaps the primary reason for having multiple brands within a category is to satisfy different market segments. Barwise and Robertson (1992) discuss several other reasons for doing so.

A look at this product portfolio suggests any number of areas where Volkswagen as a corporation could consider brand extensions via either line extensions for a particular brand for other vehicle types or an extension to additional segments. But it should be clear that not all their brands would be appropriate for extending into just any area. Would it make sense to extend Bentley into the mini segment, or Lamborghini into off-road? Hardly. The brand image and equity must *fit*, something that will be dealt with at length later.

Brand hierarchy

Brand names may be used in many ways, depending upon the branding strategy. As already seen in the brief Levi-Strauss example, Levi's is used alone as a brand name for jeans and to help introduce a new product (Levi's Dockers); and it is also used in combination with sub-brands of jeans (Levi's 501). This suggests, as many people have pointed out, that brands may be thought about in terms of a hierarchy. We will be looking at this hierarchy in terms of company or parent brands, group brands, and single brands. A *company brand* identifies the parent company, brands like Daimler-Benz or Unilever. A *group brand* is a brand name that is used in more than one category, brands like Yamaha that are used

Image supplied by Yamaha Factory Racing

to market such diverse products as pianos and motorcycles. At the bottom of the hierarchy are *single brands*, where the brand name is restricted to a single product category.

In practice, this hierarchy is not always so clear cut. When you think about Nestlé what comes to mind? Was it chocolate, or perhaps coffee? That is what most people are familiar with. In fact, one of Nestlé's very earliest advertising slogans was 'Nestlés makes the very best, chocolate'. Obviously, Nestlé is a chocolate brand, but is there such a thing as Nestlé coffee? No, but of course they are well known for such soluble coffee brands as Nescafé, Taster's Choice, and Gold Blend. Returning to chocolate, most people are probably also familiar with Nestlé Crunch bars. Consider this for a minute. What is the brand name? Nestlé, Crunch, Nestlé Crunch? And what does this say about the business they are in? If Nestlé is a brand of chocolate, what are Nestlé Crunch ice cream bars? Taking this further, how does one deal with the fact that Nestlé is, or has been, in a lot of other businesses, such as wine, non-dairy creamers, and frozen foods (under such brands as Berringer, Carnation and Findus)? And what about the more intangible aspects of a company's image (cf. Barich and Kutter, 1991; Hatch and Schultz, 2001)? This is really the focus of this chapter: branding strategies that help managers determine when and how a brand should be stretched or retrenched.

Thinking about branding strategies within a brand hierarchy helps make sense out of how brand names can be used, and this is essential before one can begin to consider how to stretch or retrench a brand. Does it help understand Nestlé's brand strategy? Not if one is looking to place Nestlé as a brand into one of the hierarchical classifications. But it does help to see the various ways in which Nestlé *use* their name. They use it as a single brand in the chocolate confection category; they use it as a group brand in chocolate confection and coffee (as well as other categories); and they use it as a company brand. *Why* it is used in various ways, why the Nestlé brand name has been stretched in different ways over the years, is all about (or should be) how the brand equity of the name Nestlé contributes to building the brand equity of each brand name with which it is associated in the company's product and brand portfolio.

One of the authors of this book worked with Nestlé on a project where they were looking into ways to expand their overall product portfolio. They wanted to know into what additional product categories consumers felt a number of Nestlé single and group brands could believably be stretched. They were looking along the rows of the product-brand grid to see if any current categories in the product portfolio could benefit from a new product introduction under another Nestlé brand (broadening it as a group brand), or if one of these brands made sense being stretched to an entirely new product category for Nestlé, thus expanding the overall product portfolio. For example, would a line of Taster's Choice coffee-flavoured confections make sense to consumers (moving Taster's Choice into the confections category where Nestlé already markets several brands); or what about a line of Taster's Choice baking products, moving the brand into a new category for Nestlé?

At issue is whether or not the images of one of these brands is compatible in people's minds with a different product category. In other words, does the current equity of the brand easily transfer to another product? While this will be dealt with in more detail throughout the chapter, at this point it is important to see how the idea of hierarchies and product and brand portfolios helps frame stretching (and retrenchment) branding strategies.

Levels of branding

A critical consideration in developing brand stretching strategies is the *level* at which a brand chooses to be positioned. At its most basic, considerations of level reflect brand hierarchies, but the question goes much deeper than this. What is the optimum level at which a brand should be positioned in order to optimize value to the consumer as well as profit for the company? This is a fundamental *strategic* issue that must be continuously revisited as a company looks for competitive advantage. Depending upon where a brand is now, any number of strategic questions might be raised. Does it stay where it is seen as the 'leader', or move the brand into new categories? Should it 'brand' a product or service that it provides, but has not marketed as a brand? In many areas of technology consumers are often not aware of the company behind a product or service, for example the broadband source of their high-speed Internet connection or the satellite company providing their television signals.

This is often the case too with so-called 'ingredient' products, which may or may not be branded. Most people with computers are familiar with Intel and its Pentium processor. But are they aware of who makes other components in the computer? Would it, or could it make a difference to the manufacturer if these components were 'branded'? Would it make sense for Intel to change its brand level and introduce a line of Intel computers? Or to stretch even further and market a line of Intel cellular phones or perhaps hi-fi components? All these questions are dealing with brand level, and as Kapferer (2001) has pointed out, the problem of choosing a level, especially when considering brand life cycle, is addressed in terms of brand stretching even though it is not always understood by managers as such.

Answers to all these questions should be considered in terms of long-term strategic concerns such as how long any change in positioning level for a brand will sustain a competitive advantage, and how profit may migrate with changes in customer base (as Slywotzky has discussed (1998)).

Product portfolio management

This leads directly to the question of managing a product portfolio. The key to managing a product portfolio is taking a *long-term* view. Markets are dynamic, changing over time, and a company's product portfolio must take this into account. This means that top management must carefully consider the role of different brands, and the relationship among these different brands, in the portfolio *over time*.

Anticipating changes in markets and assessing gaps in the company's current portfolio can suggest possible areas for different branding strategies. How are brands likely to change over time? As consumer needs change, how likely is it that they will switch to other brands in an existing product portfolio (something Keller (1995) called 'migration' strategies)? And as they change, does the company already market products for these new needs? Anticipation of this type of evolution in need is reflected in the products offered by Anheuser-Busch over the years. As markets grew and changed, adjustments were made to the product portfolio. Originally, there was Budweiser. With the growth of imported beer, Michelob was added to the portfolio and positioned against the imports. As the brewery's production capacity increased, Busch Beer was added to attract 'regular beer' drinkers.

With the success of Miller Lite in the 1970s, the beer market in the US was significantly altered. There had been many, many attempts in earlier years to introduce lower calorie (and lower carbohydrate) beers, but none of them had been successful. Owing to all the previous failures by other brewers, Anheuser-Busch was very cautious about entering the market. They began by introducing something they called Anheuser-Busch Natural Light, with the emphasis on the company brand. But when they learned that the 'bar call' for the brand (the way people ask for a brand when ordering) was 'Busch Light' or even 'Bud Light', a decision was made to drop the Anheuser-Busch from the name, and focus on the word Natural. They dropped the emphasis on the company brand because there was still the concern, even though Miller Lite looked like a real success, that there could be *negative* associations from a lower calorie beer that could impact their regular Busch brand and premium, flagship brand, Budweiser. It was not until some time later that the Budweiser and then Michelob brands were extended with Bud Light and Michelob Light. At that point Natural Light was repositioned as a price brand with no marketing support.

This is a good example of an adjustment to a product portfolio to meet competitive change in a market place, while withholding brand extensions within existing product lines until the company is certain there will be no problems for the equity of their established brands. In the 1990s, with the popularity of 'micro-breweries' in the US, Anheuser-Busch again adjusted their product portfolio, adding new single brands such as Killian's Red *outside* of the umbrella the Anheuser-Busch family of brands.

Projected and actual changes in the market may also lead to retrenchment branding strategies. Product obsolescence, a glut of brands in a category, a new corporate focus, or changes in a market's dynamics may suggest it is time to eliminate certain brands or brand extensions from the portfolio. In some cases, a brand's equity may no longer provide potential growth because the market is now looking for different things. In extreme cases a brand's existing equity may in fact have a negative impact upon the product portfolio because of changing attitudes in the market. In such cases it will be necessary to retrench, and retire the brand.

The short-lived introduction of the New Coke brand in the 1980s provides an example of where the introduction of a new product to the portfolio was meant to lead to eventual retirement of the existing Coke product, with the new version eventually taking over the Coke brand name. It never happened because the market reacted in a strongly negative way, and New Coke was hastily withdrawn. What happened? The original reason for considering stretching the brand in this way came from research that suggested Coke was losing share to its main competitor Pepsi among younger cola drinkers. Pepsi was a somewhat sweeter product, so the decision was made to develop a product that was sweeter than the existing Coke, and preferred to Pepsi. As we have discussed, this could seem to be an appropriate response to a change in the market.

But it did not work. In all their product development and taste testing for New Coke, the company never considered the strength of the equity in the existing Coke brand. While New Coke was indeed preferred to regular Coke in all the taste tests, and to Pepsi, these were all *blind* taste tests where people did not know what brands were involved. When New Coke was introduced, it was now being compared with a Coke brand that came with 100 years of positive brand equity attached. People preferred the original Coke brand *because* – because it *was* Coke!

There can be no better example of the power of brand equity. In *any* consideration of brand stretching or retrenchment it is essential that the effect a brand's current equity will have in that branding strategy is understood. Original Coke was re-branded Classic Coke, and for a brief period of time was marketed with New Coke. In the end, however, it was New Coke that was retired. Classic Coke remained in the portfolio, and eventually returned to its original brand name, Coke.

Brand involvement

The importance of involvement with brands and its relationship with how they are seen in terms of product portfolio management and potential brand extensions has been considered in a rather interesting way by Kunde (2000) in something he talks about as 'corporate religion'. He looks at brands in terms of a hierarchy, much as we have been discussing it, but with more of an emphasis on involvement. At its most basic level, some consumers are thought to see a brand as nothing more than a product: washing powder is washing powder, whether Persil or some other brand. Other consumers, however, may invest a certain level of emotional value with a brand, involving them with the brand in such a way that it provides a competitive advantage, even when the brand is basically a commodity (very much along the lines of how brand equity is defined).

Next up the scale for Kunde is where a brand has actually achieved such a superior position in the market that it quite literally *becomes* the product category: this would include brands such as Kleenex, Hoover, and Xerox. In effect, consumers have replaced the function of the product with the brand. Finally, the ultimate goal for a brand in this scheme is to achieve what he calls 'brand religion', where a brand has extended its brand culture to a point where it becomes *essential* to the consumer. Kunde estimates that only about 10% of brands reach this level, and offers The Body Shop and Harley-Davidson as examples. The Body Shop sells a 'religion' based upon natural ingredients and environmental concerns; Harley-Davidson 'freedom'.

When to consider brand stretching or retrenching

In the earlier discussion of product portfolio management the subject of when to consider brand stretching strategies was introduced briefly, and examples of when to consider stretching (as in the case of Anheuser-Busch) or retrenching (the initial decision to replace Coke with New Coke) were described. But many branding strategies also result from opportunities that present themselves outside the traditional notions of product portfolio management: such things as co-branding, ingredient branding, or even how brands are distributed.

Reproduced with the kind permission of Harley-Davidson Europe Ltd

In the next section we will be looking at a number of ways one might look at and consider opportunities for brand stretching or retrenching. But before getting into specific strategies, we would like to talk about an old idea in marketing that is not discussed much any more, the idea of category and brand development indexes. Considering Category Development Indexes (CDIs) and Brand Development Indexes (BDIs) offers the manager a measure of the overall dynamic of the market, and where their brand 'fits'.

A CDI reflects the size of penetration into a product category. A low CDI indicates that the category does not enjoy widespread usage in the market. This will almost always be the case with new product categories; and often with older categories where new technology is leading to product obsolescence. But in some cases, CDIs are low simply because the market itself is small. A high CDI indicates that the product category enjoys strong penetration among most, if not all, of its potential market. BDIs reflect the same thing, only in relation to competitive brands in a category. A low BDI indicates that a brand has a low share relative to others in the category; a high BDI indicates a large share of the target market.

This is important when considering brand stretching strategies, because when brand managers look at their brand portfolio for a given category, there are a number of strategic questions to address related to the development of the category. These questions follow from the four possible combinations of CDIs and BDIs. A brand may find itself with a low BDI in a category with either a low or high CDI; or it may enjoy a high BDI in a category with either a low or high CDI. (These are, of course, not dichotomies in actual practice. A brand or category might fall anywhere along a continuum from high to low, but for purposes of discussion, we need only concern ourselves with high vs. low.)

Suppose a brand has a low BDI in an established category. If the brand has been around for a long time and has not been able to capture a larger share of the market, this very definitely opens up the possibility of stretching the brand in some way (even introducing a new brand rather than brand extension) in order to drive up overall share in the market for the company. This would certainly make sense in a category with a high CDI. But what if it has a low CDI? Would it be worth the effort to try and capture a larger share of a small market unlikely to grow? Would a new product innovation be likely to drive up the CDI? What if a brand enjoyed a strong BDI in a category with a low CDI? There would probably be very little incentive to stretch the brand, because it already enjoys a large share.

Newer product categories with low CDIs may have the potential for growth. Brand stretching strategies must then take into account *how* the category is likely to grow. With high CDIs, opportunities are obviously greater for brand stretching. If the category is not established, things change. Even with established product categories, managers must be looking at how their market is likely to change. This means they must *anticipate* change in their market and become proactive with their brand stretching strategy.

As should be evident, what is going on in the category will influence how the managers should approach brand stretching (and retrenchment) strategies. Whether or not one thinks in terms of CDIs and BDIs, brand stretching strategies will be influenced by how well developed the category is where a brand is marketed, and where that brand stands relative to its competitors in that category.

Evaluating stretching (and retrenching) opportunities

There are three fundamental questions that must be asked when evaluating opportunities for a change in branding strategy. First of all, does it make sense *strategically* for the brand and company in terms of its product and brand portfolio? Second, if it makes sense strategically, will the change '*fit*' in terms of the brand's equity? And finally, if the change makes sense strategically, and the brand logically fits into the new market, will it be *profitable*?

Strategically, there are many reasons a company might want to consider stretching a brand; or to retrench. They may wish to exploit a competitive weakness in the category by introducing sub-brands; fill a gap in the category or in new product categories for the brand; or position the brand for expected changes in either market structure (e.g. technological advances in the category) or in the target market (e.g. an aging population that could create more, or less, demand for a product).

Kraft, a major parent brand in its own right, which also owns such traditionally important parent brands as Nabisco and General Foods, offers a good example of a company that did not respond to changes in their key markets during the early 2000s (Ellison, 2003). For years, they were a master of brand extension, offering a never-ending line of 'new and improved' versions of their well-known brands, everything from Oreo and Chips Ahoy cookies to Jell-O and Maxwell House. But they failed to develop new products that private labels could not easily copy. By endlessly extending existing established brands they missed out on one of the most important changes in grocery store food dynamics in the late 1990s, the rising importance of 'healthy' foods such as cereal bars and foods with organic ingredients (to name just a few). As a result, they fell behind in the race to adjust their product portfolio, with a significant impact upon profit and share prices.

Regardless of the market issues involved, there are other strategic questions dealing with potential changes in the meaning of a brand that must be asked. If a brand is stretched into a new category, what is the potential for a change in the image or meaning of the brand? If it retrenches, and the brand is no longer associated with a particular product (especially if that product is the one with which the brand was originally associated), how might that affect the image of the brand for those products that remain associated with that brand name? Also, how recently has a brand been extended? And into what areas? If a brand is seen as moving into several new areas within a short time it could lead to brand identity confusion; whereas, if the brand is extended into the same categories, but over time, consumers might more easily assimilate the extensions.

In terms of 'fit', suppose a brand enjoys a strong image or equity for a particular benefit that on the surface seems logically transferable to another product category. With a strong reputation for killing germs, a hand and face soap manufacturer might consider stretching the brand into the household cleanser market. With a strong brand equity built upon killing germs, this should easily transfer to, say, a kitchen or bathroom cleanser. On the other hand, a household cleanser brand with the same strong image for killing germs in the kitchen or bathroom might not be a good fit for stretching into the hand and face soap market. If it works for a soap-to-household cleanser extension, why might it not work for a household cleanser-to-soap extension? While the key benefit is the same, there might very well be a perceptual problem in transferring the germ-killing equity from a product used on hard surfaces in the kitchen or bath to a soap that will be used on your face. Consumers must accept that an equity transfer makes sense, or the brand extension is likely to fail.

If there is a good strategic reason to consider brand stretching or retrenching, and a proposed extension 'fits' in terms of brand image and equity, it only remains to determine if the extension or retrenching will lead to better long-term profitability for the company.

Can any brand be stretched?

Abercrombie & Fitch provides an interesting example of the importance of brand equity in brand stretching. The company, now a chain of retail stores aimed at the '18–22 college guy who has a good body and is aspirational' (in the words of Chief Executive Mike Jeffries in 2002) (Branch, 2003), was once the legendary outfitter of Theodore Roosevelt (the famous 'Rough Rider' and later US President almost a century ago) and such luminaries as Ernest Hemingway. After passing through a number of changes in ownership, it was acquired by Limited Brands in 1988. They tried unsuccessfully to reposition the chain as a preppy, button-down-collar men's store. In 1992 they gave up and Mr Jeffries, a veteran of the fashion industry, took over the company and it became independent with a public shares offering in 1996.

Up to this point in its history, the company had turned from its original positioning as an outfitter for adventurers, with a successful brand extension into exotic location travel bookings, to a preppy apparel store for men. Under Mr Jeffries, the company pursued yet another positioning, entering the volatile world of youth fashion, utilizing on-the-edge, often homoerotic, sexual imagery. Promotions featured partially clad young men, often in provocative poses. Initially successful, the imagery was pushed further and further out, offering thong underwear for girls with words such as 'eye candy' on the front, and a feature on group sex, heterosexual as well as homosexual, in their quarterly 'magalog' (this last proved too much and led to it being discontinued at the end of 2003). Men defected from the brand in droves.

In an effort to stretch the brand and reach younger consumers, a group of 'abercrombie' stores was launched for children, and Hollister stores for younger teens. The brand extension for kids utilized a rather clever device, creating the extension by simply utilizing a lower case 'a' in the name. For the so-called 'tweens' market, a completely new brand, Hollister, was created. Unfortunately, these brand stretching efforts did not help the overall bottom line. The parent brand had itself become too narrowly focused, and along with the controversy over its marketing communication, the company was experiencing its fourth consecutive significant drop in same-store sales in early 2004.

What does this case suggest? To begin with, it illustrates the potential problems that a complete repositioning of a brand can bring, abandoning its established equity. Establishing a new position without any positive carry-over from a brand's equity in effect is the same as introducing a new brand, but with the burden of possible confusion in the market *because* of the brand's established equity. In terms of brand stretching, it shows that stretching a brand to reach a broader market does not always work, even with a well-known brand. The problem was, even though the name was well-known, the parent brand was seriously weakened by its ever-more confrontational and unconventional sexual imagery. To the extent that it was building an equity, that equity hardly made sense in providing credibility to its sub-brands: group sex and homoerotic images for pre-teens? Add to this the fact that such equity was itself subject to the vagaries of youthful fancy and fashion, and one can understand the difficulties.

As one analyst put it, by pushing the edge of fashion the brand also pushed away many of its customers out of the brand. But Mr Jeffries was unmoved: 'If I exclude people—absolutely. Delighted to do so' (Branch, 2003). With a parent brand in trouble because of its narrowly focused positioning, it becomes almost impossible to successfully stretch the brand. And in the case of Abercrombie & Fitch, add the fact that they were spending only about 2% of revenue on marketing and advertising compared with an average of 10% among other youth-oriented marketers, and it becomes very difficult to build and sustain a successful brand, let alone stretch it.

Retrenching strategies

Just as brand stretching decisions centre on considerations of long-term profitability for the company, so do retrenching strategies. As market dynamics change, with the growth of strong competitors or the introduction of new products, a brand may simply no longer be able to compete. Situations where a manager might want to consider retrenching were discussed earlier, and examples offered where it made sense to eliminate a brand. But in addition to the normal attrition of brands owing to market conditions, many companies have begun to incorporate retrenching strategies as a part of their overall marketing strategy.

In recent years many large consumer marketers have taken a serious look at their brand portfolios and retrenching strategies, eliminating many marginal brands. This trend has been particularly evident among large multinational marketers as they not only eliminate marginal brands from their portfolios, but eliminate many local and regional brands as well, concentrating on consolidating their strongest brands. While retrenching at the local level by global marketers may undermine a firm's ability to satisfy particular market segments and cater to individual market differences, there can be significant cost savings. Ongoing shareholder pressure for cost reduction and such things as the changing retail environment (e.g. consolidated distribution) have all contributed to the loss of marginal and local brands.

Master brands

One result of this retrenching has been the rise of something known as *master brands*; or perhaps the rise of master brands has led to these retrenching strategies. Regardless of which came first, there is no question that the creation of master brands has led to significant changes in product and brand portfolio management. The trend to master brands has included everything from consumer durable manufacturers like Philips to fmcg marketers like Cadbury. In the late 1990s, Unilever embarked upon a course to retrench, trimming its global brand portfolio of some 1,400 brands by 75% to 400. Even ingredient brands like DuPont's Teflon have undertaken a master brand strategy, refocusing on marketing and promoting the technology as a single, core, non-stick brand worldwide; and then extending into new categories like apparel, upholstery, and carpeting.

In many ways, a master brand is just another way of thinking about sub-branding and brand hierarchy. For example, Unilever's Bestfoods division took one of its more formidable brands, Hellman's mayonnaise, and positioned it as a master brand in 2003. They then extended it, using the brand as an umbrella for their Wish Bone salad dressings, as well as several new categories. This push for master brands at the cost of eliminating marginal brands, and sub-branding others, leads to significant downsizing, with corresponding cost savings. In one of many retrenchings as they eliminated more and more brands while

Cadbury Trebor Bassett

creating new master brands, Unilever cut some 8% of its Bestfoods staff, eliminating 130 marketing, sales, and finance positions in 2003 (Thompson, 2003).

Along with downsizing of staff, another consequence of this trend towards master brands has been a radical rethinking and realignment of marketing communication strategies, budgets, and advertising agency affiliations. In 2003, Unilever North America's President announced that only 200 of the surviving 400 brands in their brand portfolio were likely to receive advertising support. In fact, it was reported that the real goal for the company was to identify as few as 50 'power brands' that would receive heavy advertising levels (Thompson, 2003).

Beyond the strategic issues involved in the creation of a master brand, when considering a retrenching strategy there are very real organizational issues that must be considered. With the wrong corporate culture, the likelihood of successfully developing a master brand is low. Where do brand issues fall on top management's priority list? Is attention paid to branding by senior management outside marketing departments? Are there communication channels within the organization that encourage interdivisional or interdepartmental cooperation? How will decisions for a master brand be made? Are there procedures in place that enable the optimization of marketing funds between the master brand as parent and sub-brands? These are just a few of the questions that must be satisfactorily addressed if a company is considering the creation of a master brand (Upshaw and Taylor, 2000).

Creating master brands is more and more common today as a retrenching strategy. However, it must be carefully considered, not only in terms of a company's product and brand portfolio, but as just discussed, also in terms of the company's organizational structure and its ability to effectively manage a master brand.

Brand extensions

Earlier the idea of hierarchy in branding strategy was introduced, and it was noted that it is not always so clear-cut as one would like. Before talking more specifically about brand extensions, it would be well to take a closer look at this idea. As suggested, at the top of the hierarchy are company brands, which may or may not be a part of the positioning for all the brands marketed by that company (as evident in the Nestlé case). Next come group brands, which may be used in a wide variety of ways. In some cases they may be subsumed under a company brand (e.g. in the case of something like Kellogg's Frosties), or on their own they could be used to cover a wide variety of products. Last are single brands, used within a single category, and often used to cover a number of different products within a category, for example with L'Oréal, which markets such items as hair products, perfumes, and cosmetics under the L'Oréal brand name.

But as with most things discussed in this chapter, it is never quite so straightforward. Consider the case of L'Oréal. While it acts as a single brand in the personal care category, it is also a group brand as part of Elsève and other sub-brands, and also a 'hidden' company brand behind Lancôme, another of its brands. So when considering a brand extension, just what is the 'brand' being extended? The key, of course, is to remember that branding policy is a *strategic* decision aimed at optimizing the promotion and marketing of a product.

Although brand extensions have been mentioned several times in this chapter, what exactly is a brand extension? The idea of brand extensions in marketing is certainly not new (cf. Gamble, 1967), even if research into brand extensions is relatively recent. Basically, it is nothing more than adding an existing brand name to a new item in a line, or perhaps a new or revised version of a product. Consumer packaged goods companies use brand extensions, retail stores extend their 'brands' to other types of outlets, and services or other businesses extend their names to cover a variety of different products or activities under the same 'brand' name. Brand extensions may be accomplished using a single brand name, a group brand, or a company brand. Perhaps the most important reason for considering adding a brand extension is to capitalize on existing strong brand awareness and positive brand equity, but there are other reasons as well:

- Brand extensions can create excitement in the market, for the consumer as well as the trade.

- Brand extensions can offer the appearance if not the actual consequences of positive change.

- Brand extensions can help meet new market demand, and they can also provide new competitive advantages.

Brand extensions can be close, logical extensions of the original product, or they can mark a complete change. When Gucci extends its brand from high-fashion clothing and accessories to sunglasses, it is a logical extension; when it moves into cosmetics, it is moving further from its origin. Other high-fashion houses such as Armani and Hugo Boss extended their high-priced brands to more mid-priced boutiques, Emporio Armani and Boss. Even a traditional brand like Harley-Davidson, founded in 1903 and for many years in the mid-20th century the only manufacturer of motorcycles in the US, found it useful to maximize its strong brand image and introduce a number of brand extensions, including a line of MotorClothes and licensed products!

Obviously, brand extensions, brand stretching, can occur anywhere along the brand hierarchy. At issue is where and how a brand extension makes the most sense within the product and brand portfolio. For example, will it improve overall brand image or reduce risk for consumers (Milewicz and Herbig, 1994)? Will it produce economies of scale in terms of more efficient use of marketing expenses, versus the value of a new brand name (Sullivan, 1992)? This is tied tightly to how the brand extension will be *positioned*. In our definition of brand hierarchy, we have identified three rather general and straightforward brand levels. Others have taken a more detailed view of branding strategies. Kapferer (1997), for example, offers six different levels of possible branding strategies. While he makes some very useful distinctions, for most purposes this is probably more than we need to be concerned with. However, the distinction he makes between what he calls 'source' brands and 'endorser' brands is worth noting.

Briefly, Kapferer describes a *source brand* as one where products are directly named, while a company brand acts as a guarantee of the product's quality. An example would be Tommy Hilfiger's Freedom line of perfume. The brand extension is Freedom, but the source assuring the customer of the brand's quality is Tommy Hilfiger. On the other hand, an *endorser brand* is one that acts as a guarantee of quality for a wide range of products, possibly ranging over a variety of lines as was noted with Yamaha.

What makes this distinction so important for brand stretching strategies is that the benefit structure driving the brand equity of the source or endorser brand, and the benefit structure underlying the potential brand extension, should be considered in terms of which of these two potential branding strategies makes the most sense for the individual product. The choice, of course, will depend (primarily) upon the product or brand portfolio strategy, as well as the perceived strength of the potential equity in the brand extension's positioning. It will be this equity trade-off that should drive the choice.

This distinction reflects a critical difference in brand architecture, which is important for how a brand is marketed (Kapferer, 1997). A *source* branding strategy provides a *direct* parent-product link: source brand name plus brand extension. An *endorser* branding strategy projects greater independence between the parent-endorser and the extension: brand extension from the endorser brand. The higher the level of someone's involvement with a product, the more likely they are to have a strong focused idea of what benefit they want from that product. This means they are more responsive to a single, stand-alone brand or an *endorser* brand, where the specific positioning is more likely to be unique and reflective of the specific benefit(s) for which they are looking. Those with lower levels of involvement with the category tend to be looking for more general benefits, and are more likely to look for the reassurance that comes with a strong *source* brand (assuming the source parent brand is indeed seen as the guarantor of quality or value related to the brand extensions).

These brand extension opportunities may be found in either a line extension of the existing product, an extension within the category where the brand is currently marketed, or a new category altogether. Brand extensions offer the opportunity to reach or better serve specific segments within a market in the case of product *line extensions* or *category extensions*; or to reach new markets with extensions into new categories. The key to success in either case is the compatibility of the equity in the brand name with the proposed brand extension.

Line extension

Brand extensions may be introduced as either a line extension or category extension (Farquhar, 1989). If considering a line extension for a brand, both brand stretching and retrenching strategies for the line as a whole must be considered. As a result, adding items to a line will increase market penetration, but it will also increase costs. Even if the proposed line extensions can be produced using the same manufacturing facility, it adds to the burden of overall production; and there will always be additional marketing costs. The projected increase in overall sales for the brand must more than cover its costs; it should also increase overall profitability. While there may be tactical considerations that might excuse lower profitability in the short term (e.g. to meet a competitive threat), long-term strategy should aim for increased profitability for the brand from the line extension.

Another issue to be concerned with when considering line extensions is the possibility of a change in a brand's image as the line expands. One must be very careful here. Recall the discussion earlier of Anheuser-Busch's concern for their flagship brand Budweiser if they were to introduce a Bud Light, deciding first to introduce a new brand (Natural Light) into the category. More is not always better. In fact, with brand extensions within a product line it is often a good idea to consider a retrenching strategy as well, retiring some existing items from the line, as new extensions are added. A good example of this is with lines of prepared food products. Because of something the industry refers to as 'flavour fatigue' most pre-pared food companies will regularly extend their line offerings, while at the same time eliminating some items from the line. Aside from issues of overall profitability if the line is too long, there is also the very practical issue of distribution to be considered. Just because a brand offers a long line of items does not mean that the trade will stock all the items. Brand stretching within a product line often must be coupled with retrenching.

Category extensions

Category brand extensions may occur either within the product category where a brand is already marketed, or in an entirely new category for the brand. In terms of brand hierarchy, if the extension is within a product category where the brand currently has a presence, the existing brand will become a parent or company brand (if it is not already one), and the new introduction a sub-brand, either as part of a source or endorser brand strategy. If the exten-sion is outside the category where the brand is currently marketed, it may also become a sub-brand in the same way, or simply a group brand.

As discussed earlier, a company or product brand is one where the brand identifies the par-ent company, such as L'Oréal or Nestlé, and is associated with one or more sub-brands. Group brands are those where the same brand name is used in more than one product category, such as Harley-Davidson or Yamaha. And as was also discussed, while this hierarchy (including single brands) provides a good way to look at brand stretching strategies, in reality there are many variations and permutations possible (and likely). For example, Kapferer (1997) has six models of branding strategies, and he also posits nine positioning alternatives within them.

The number of brands or sub-brands offered by a company within a product category is often referred to as the *depth* of a company's brand strategy. The obvious reason for offering different brands within the same product category is to address the needs of different seg-ments within the market (as we saw with Volkswagen). In terms of brand stretching, the issue is whether to extend an existing brand from another category or to introduce a sub-brand of an existing brand in the category. Of course, there is always the option of creating an entirely new brand. The decision will be based upon the broader considerations of the company's branding strategy.

Advantages of brand extensions

Almost all companies at one time or another will be actively involved in brand stretching. It is in the nature of markets to evolve, and this requires ongoing evaluation of the product and brand portfolios. Inevitably, this will lead to brand stretching (or retrenching). Brand stretching with extensions makes sense, primarily because of the advantages associated with being able to transfer a brand's existing equity to an extension. While there can be risk here, as we have already seen, when there is a positive fit there is the potential for real advantages (see Fig. 9.3).

- Reduces the cost of new product introduction through easier distribution, building brand awareness faster, creating positive brand attitude faster
- Reduces risk of trial
- Increases customer base
- Stronger overall brand attitude for parent brand
- Increased extension opportunities

Fig. 9.3 Advantages of brand extensions

Building positive brand attitude from scratch for a new brand introduction takes time, and a great deal of marketing resources. Introducing a brand extension rather than a new brand significantly reduces the cost of a new product introduction from a marketing standpoint. It is the existing brand awareness and brand attitude that facilitates the introduction. Because the brand name is a known entity, gaining distribution is easier. Because the brand name is known, building awareness for the new product is easier. Existing brand attitude means there is an equity base already established to form the foundation for positive attitudes towards the new product, significantly reducing marketing communication costs for advertising and promotion.

In addition to these marketing efficiencies, there are a number of other benefits to brand extensions. Because the brand name is familiar, it facilitates the acceptance of the new product by reducing perceived risk in trying it on the part of the consumer. Because the new product is likely to address a new customer segment, the customer base for the brand is likely to increase, along with the potential for trial of the parent brand by these new customers. And when successfully implemented, there is the opportunity to build an even stronger overall brand attitude for the parent brand. Finally, by extending the brand to a new product, it opens up the opportunity for additional extension from that new product.

Disadvantages of brand extension

For the most part, if a brand extension is carefully considered, along the lines discussed, there are no significant disadvantages. However, if the extension has not been carefully considered, there is a real potential for problems. In fact, what are advantages when brand extensions are well considered can often become *dis*advantages with a bad brand stretching strategy (see Fig. 9.4).

It has been noted how existing brand knowledge can help facilitate building brand awareness and brand attitude for an extension, but when not well considered, that same positive understanding of the brand could lead to confusion over just exactly what the brand is all about. This can really be a problem when consumers do not readily see the congruence between the equity of the parent brand and the new product. If a high-fashion line like Chanel were to extend its brand into the active participation sportswear category, it could very well cause confusion with the haute couture image of the brand. This would be especially true if they were to extend as a group brand, using only the Chanel brand name, and even if they were to extend with a sub-brand using a source strategy, for

- Potential consumer confusion
- Cannibalization of parent brand sales
- Limited extension opportunities

Fig. 9.4 Disadvantages of brand extensions

example, 'Chanel Sport'. While the potential for confusion might be less with an endorser sub-branding strategy, something along the lines of 'Excell, active sportswear from Chanel', people are not likely to see any logical association with Chanel's long-established high-fashion brand equity. High fashion is simply not likely to be an important benefit for the active sportswear worn by someone running a marathon or working out in a gym, with the possible exception of a very small segment of the market.

But even if a small segment of the market was interested in wearing high-fashion active sportswear, one must consider what the overall impact would be upon the existing market for Chanel. Would someone spending thousands of euros for a Chanel dress want to see the brand associated with people perspiring in a heavy workout? Not very likely! This example should underscore how important it is to consider the 'fit' of any brand extension.

Helmut Panke, chief executive of BMW (in 2004) put this in an interesting way. When asked in an interview 'For you, as a CEO, are there any special responsibilities you have for maintaining or building your brand image?' he replied: 'As provocative as it sounds, the biggest task is to be able to say "No". Because in the end, authentic brand management boils down to understanding that a brand is a promise that has to be fulfilled everywhere, at any time. So when something doesn't *fit* [our emphasis], you must make sure that that is not done' (Boudette, 2003). He went on in that interview to illustrate the point by talking about an internal debate on their product portfolio. 'There is a segment in the market which BMW is not catering to and that is the minivan or the MPV segment. We don't have a van because a van as it is in the market today does not fulfil any of the BMW group brand values. We all as a team said no. We will not bring a van.'

There are other advantages that might become disadvantages if a brand extension strategy is not well considered. For example, while a known brand can often help secure distribution for a new product, if a brand already has a strong presence in a market, it could meet with resistance from the trade, particularly if there are numerous or particularly strong brands already in the category. While this is especially true for line extensions (particularly with fmcgs where, with different sizes and variations, a brand could easily market twenty or more items in a line), it can also be a problem for brand extensions within a category. If you are a brand like Nivea, with an extensive line of skin-care products in the beauty aid category, and decide to stretch the brand into the already crowded cosmetic market with a line of lipsticks and fingernail polish, you could very well meet with resistance from the trade.

While carefully planned brand extensions should increase the customer base, there is the possibility that a new product introduction will actually reduce the overall customer base, either through a negative effect upon overall brand attitude for the parent brand (as above) or through cannibalization of the existing brand franchise. Cannibalization occurs if a new product is seen as a preferred alternative to the parent brand by those who currently buy it. Even if the extension attracts new customers to the brand, if it cannibalizes the existing base, the dynamics of the brand will change significantly. This may not be a bad thing if the new configuration increases profitability overall for the brand, but it will require a new overall brand strategy and marketing plan. In effect, the brand extension becomes the parent brand, and the original brand the sub-brand, and this new situation would need to be carefully evaluated in terms of the company's product and brand portfolio strategies.

Finally, if a new product is introduced as a brand extension, this means it will not have the potential for its own unique identity, and it will have limited opportunities for extensions in its own right. In many situations, this is not a problem. But it is something that should be carefully considered. It is important to think well beyond the short term when considering a brand extension. The company may be sacrificing future opportunities by limiting a new product to the umbrella of a parent brand. There are many advantages to well-considered brand extensions, but managers must always be aware of the fact that these same advantages could become disadvantages.

Considering options for a brand extension

To help put all this into perspective, consider a situation that confronted Nestlé a few years ago (and with which one of the authors was involved). The Findus division, which markets frozen prepared foods under that brand name and under the Lean Cuisine brand, was considering the introduction of a new line of frozen prepared foods specifically positioned for lunch. With the introduction of refrigerators and microwaves for employee use in many offices, this seemed like a natural expansion for them. But how should it be positioned in terms of branding strategy?

Nestlé was considering using the Lean Cuisine brand in some way. But would it make more sense to introduce it as a line extension of Findus, and not consider Lean Cuisine at all? Or would it be better to introduce a stand-alone single brand called Lunch Express? What would you recommend? They were initially keen on a sub-branding strategy using an endorser strategy with Lean Cuisine as the parent: Lunch Express from Lean Cuisine. They wanted to trade upon the strong market position of Lean Cuisine with its already high levels of brand awareness and brand attitude. But consider Lean Cuisine's brand equity. It centres on good-tasting products that are calorie-controlled for people watching their weight. This would limit the market for Lunch Express, as well as *significantly* limiting the potential for any future Lunch Express brand extensions.

Using an endorser or source brand strategy with Findus would have made more sense because it would not be limited to calorie-controlled products, but its brand equity in the market was not as strong as Lean Cuisine. We argued for Lunch Express to be a new single brand from Nestlé because it opened the opportunity for addressing both those looking for calorie-controlled products and those not concerned with watching their weight, with product lines oriented to both markets. Also, it would open the opportunity for brand extensions into a number of other areas. Importantly, this would enable the brand to expand into non-frozen foods, everything from snacks to beverages. In the end, Nestlé decided against introducing the new product, opting instead for advertising their existing Findus and Lean Cuisine product lines as 'great for lunch', and promoting the idea with a portable freezer pack so you could carry them to the office.

As this case illustrates, branding strategy requires a great deal of strategic thought and planning. The matter must be looked at from many aspects, not just short-term profitability. Where would such a move fit within the company's overall product and brand portfolio strategy? Does it make strategic sense for the brand? Will the proposed extension 'fit' in terms of brand equity congruence? What are the advantages of such an extension; and what disadvantages might there be? Carefully considered, brand extensions will strengthen the overall brand position; when not well considered there is the potential for serious long-term problems.

Brand stretching in a postmodern world

In recent years, a number of marketing academics have linked many of the ideas of postmodernism with marketing. Stephen Brown (1995) has written that postmodernism provides a way of looking at the dramatic changes that are taking place in the marketing arena, and that it is very much in tune with contemporary marketing sentiment. We are not so sure of that, but certainly Baudrillard's suggestion (in Brown, 1995) that 'image is all', and more important than reality (in fact *is* reality), is consistent with the importance of understanding a brand's equity in making brand stretching decisions. Recall that brand equity reflects that which attains to a brand over and above its intrinsic qualities. In other words, its 'image'.

One of the arguments made in discussions of postmodernism and marketing is that owing to the frantic, uncertain nature of life in a postmodern world, brands can provide an anchor, especially long-established brands. In a world increasingly taken up with hyperreality (the postmodernist would argue), the stability offered by brands with a positive equity and history can provide a bit of stability. In terms of brand stretching strategy, this would suggest that extending existing, well-established brands could have an advantage over the introduction of a new brand name.

Beyond this, the reality, such as it is, of a postmodern world (again the postmodernist would argue), creates an ideal environment for 'retrospection', the recycling of fashion. This notion is perhaps best typified by postmodernism in the arts, and most especially in architecture. Nowhere do we see the idea of postmodernism on firmer ground. Postmodern architecture uses traditional materials and styles, but combines them in unique, innovative ways. Usually informed by classical or neoclassical styles, various elements of these traditions are combined to provide a new but familiar look. The results may not be pleasing to the traditionalist's eye, 'Hepplewhite and Chippendale in drag' (Hepplewhite and Chippendale were two leading 18th-century English cabinetmakers who defined the taste and style of the period), as quoted in Jencks (1989), but it reflects the idea that there can be no one style, no 'correct' style, in a postmodern world.

In looking for brand stretching opportunities, this idea of recycling earlier fashions must go beyond a simple revival of an earlier product or brand. In Stephen Brown's (1995) words,

Reproduced with the kind permission of Parker Pens

it should reflect 'a retrospective inclination to appropriate and recycle past styles in an ironic or parodic manner'. The new brand extension will be informed by the old, but with a twist; the world of retro marketing. In the late 1990s, and continuing into the early 2000s, there was an ongoing stretching of established brands with extensions reflecting earlier versions of the brand: Parker pens, Hobbs coffee percolators, Vimto, Converse All Stars, Ovaltine; the list goes on and on.

This 'look back' has been especially true for the automotive market. Chevrolet revived its old Impala name plate, but as a 'sportier' model rather than a staid family saloon; Daimler-Chrysler introduced the PT Cruiser, a small-scale reproduction of a 1940s-like estate wagon, with a raked look reminiscent of a 1950s 'hot rod'; and the Mini Cooper was revived. In each case, the company is reaching back to find a brand extension, yet the resulting product does not duplicate the original. This is especially true for the Mini Cooper. While it may resemble that old much-loved vehicle, the new version carries a hefty price tag. The same is true of the retro Ford Thunderbird. One senses the 1955 original, it has the mesh-like grille and hood scoop reminiscent of the original, and it uses the original T-bird logo. But side-by-side, they are very different vehicles. And like the Mini Cooper, this is one expensive automobile. With the Mini Cooper and T-bird, the search for a sense of stability in nostalgic brands is anything but cheap.

Consider one more example. Levi's are almost synonymous with jeans, and we have used them as an example several times in this chapter. Yet their share of market plunged significantly during the 1990s. The company, long the dominant brand in the market, had lost its focus. It had stretched itself into every conceivable niche for jeans, and was no longer seen as unique. The many brand extensions had begun to erode the original brand equity. Among other attempts to reverse declining sales and revive the brand, it looked back to its heritage. The company reacquired an original pair of their jeans from the 1880s that had been found in a coal mine, and reproduced it as a limited edition extension at US $400 a pair! In addition, they significantly retrenched, eliminating many extensions. Those retained, along with new brand extensions (such as the limited edition Nevada jeans described above), were positioned more consistently with the brand's original equity. The results arrested the slide in sales, and have made the company more competitive.

CHAPTER SUMMARY

In this chapter we have looked at brand stretching and retrenching within a strategic context, placing them within the broader framework of product and brand portfolio management. We looked at how an evaluation of both category and brand development can help suggest how a manager approaches brand stretching and retrenching. Next, we addressed the fundamental questions that must be asked when considering a change in branding strategy: does it make strategic sense; does it 'fit' in terms of a brand's equity; and will it be profitable? Then we looked at what is involved in brand extensions, and discussed different ways of dealing with a brand extension strategy. Various advantages and disadvantages associated with brand stretching and retrenching were presented, and the fact that what begins as an advantage may end up a disadvantage. Finally, we looked at branding strategy in light of postmodern thinking.

DISCUSSION QUESTIONS

1 How does product and brand portfolio management influence the development of brand stretching and retrenching strategy?

2 Discuss the idea of brand hierarchy and its role in branding strategy.

3 What criteria are important when making a brand stretching or brand retrenching decision? Are some of these criteria more important than others?

4 Think of two or three brands you feel are likely candidates for brand stretching, and discuss why and what direction you think it would make sense for them to 'stretch'.

5 Pick two or three brands that you feel could or should not be stretched, and discuss why.

6 How does the concept of a master brand fit with retrenching?

7 Discuss the difference between a brand extension and a line extension.

8 When does it make more sense to use a source rather than endorser branding strategy, and when an endorser rather than source?

9 When can a brand extension advantage become a disadvantage?

CASE STUDY

The White Stuff: How Advertising Helped Stretch Hovis Without Breaking it

Hovis, a brand owned by British Bakeries, moved into the white bread sector in 1991. This movement would have threatened Hovis' original values and the reputation for homely brown bread; yet, it successfully transferred Hovis from a brown bread specialist to a bread leader. This case demonstrates how British Bakeries capitalized on its Hovis brand by guiding it safely into uncharted territory: the white bread market.

In 1886 Hovis started its life as 'Smiths Patent Germ Bread'. This was soon changed to Hovis from the Latin 'hominis vis' (strength of man) which was used to symbolize wheatgerm bread, bread that was related to Hovis' original idea of nutrition and health. Advertising played a strong role in the growth of the brand and many famous campaigns have been associated with Hovis over the years. In 1916 'Don't say brown, say Hovis'; in 1936 'Have you had your Hovis today'; in 1954 'Hovis is the slice of life'. All in all, perhaps the most famous advertising of all for Hovis started in 1973 (and lasting for 20 years thereafter) when the 'Boy on the Bike' campaign first appeared executing the thought and the line: 'Hovis. As good for you today as it's always been.'

No other food is as integral to the British diet as a loaf of bread. It was a massive market worth just under £2 billion, 60 million loaves a week. The problem was that bread was not something consumers think about very much because it was taken for granted. With the notable exception of the small speciality bread sector (£100m) it was a habitual purchase and little time was spent at the bread fixture. 60% of the total market was own label and branding appeared to be pretty unimportant especially in the huge standard white sliced sector which was very close to being a classic commodity market. There was, however, an exception to this general rule within white bread—which represents 70% of the total market. This was the white premium sector worth about £200 million, about 18% of total white bread value. It was created in the late 1980s with the launch of Allied Bakeries' Kingsmill brand. British Bakeries followed with Mother's Pride Premium, but they failed to gain sufficient distribution to challenge Kingsmill. In addition, against a background of decline in the natural environment of brown bread, the Hovis brand was capitalized on by British Bakeries as an opportunity for corporate growth. The company decided to use the strength of the Hovis brand to attack this important submarket. In 1991, British Bakeries launched Hovis White—using the renowned brand to support a non-brown product for the first time.

Yet Hovis' entry to the white bread segment stimulated some concerns. These concerns were clear and significant: Could a premium brand still remembered for 'Don't say brown, say Hovis' take a step into territory seen as the very antithesis of all of Hovis' homely, nutritious and wholesome values without weakening its own character and strength? And would the white bread buyer see a Hovis White as a credible product? However, a number of factors conspired towards a Hovis White launch. First, research indicated that people lacked a meaningful grammar for understanding the bread-relating terms, such as fibre, wheatgerm, and granary. Faced with such insecurity and a plethora of own-label products, consumers looked on Hovis as a trusted signpost, shorthand for good, reliable baking. Second, research also confirmed the new topography of the bread market, where discrete segregation was becoming a thing of the past as products like softgrain and mildbake blurred the traditional brown/white boundary. Third, for British Bakeries it was imperative to secure the Mother's Pride Premium listings and support *one* brand effectively against Kingsmill. The strongest brand to fight that battle (it was felt) was Hovis, which had potentially a more attractive franchise than Kingsmill. And finally, an AGB Repertoire Analysis confirmed that 85% of Hovis buyers were already buying white bread and over a quarter were purchasing Mother's Pride. Following this thread, British Bakeries saw a huge growth opportunity available to turn Hovis into the definitive bread brand. Hovis' first task, therefore, was to launch Hovis White as a credible product in its own right at the same time as reassuring existing Hovis (brown) consumers that their brand had not changed for the worse.

Hovis White was launched in July 1991. The launch was supported by a new execution in the 'Boy on the Bike' advertising style called 'Stages In Life', featuring an elderly Hovis enthusiast reminiscing about how he was brought up on Hovis from boy to man. Set in the present day it captured his memories of Hovis in his past life (using flashbacks); he says that Hovis had always been part of his life, so he would probably get used to the idea of a new Hovis white bread. The music, voice over and filmic style were the same as the core 'Boy on the Bike' campaign.

The initial burst of advertising lasted six weeks from 1 September until mid-October 1991. The advertising was not only very visible in itself, but contributed to a high degree of spontaneous awareness of the brand. More importantly, though, a range of evidence, qualitative and quantitative, suggested that the advertising, in communicating the historical antecedents of Hovis White, gave the new product a credible legitimacy—in the words of the qualitative debrief, it was a 'contemporary reaffirmation of a traditional ideal'.

> 'It was about the little boy who has grown up with Hovis brown bread, he was going into his desk to nick a bite of this sandwich, then again when he's sitting on a stone wall, then again when he's an old man, I think he's with his wife and he's now eating Hovis white bread. That Hovis can change with the times. That they are willing to try new things.'

24, DE / Millward Brown

> 'They were advertising white Hovis. This old boy said he had had Hovis all his life and was amazed to find they were producing white Hovis; he thought he might get used to it. That they were up to date and white Hovis is as good as brown.'

61, AB / Millward Brown

> 'Hovis now makes a white loaf that is made with all the quality and goodness that Hovis has always had.'

MI Qualitative Research

Within a market that was essentially flat, Hovis White made an immediate sales impact. It not only recovered the Mother's Pride Premium sales base, but exceeded it rapidly. Despite being massively outspent by its chief rival in the premium white sector, the Hovis White commercial succeeded in announcing a new, unexpected Hovis variant at the same time as re-presenting essential Hovis characteristics in a more modern and universally relevant tone. Within three months Hovis White achieved a 3% share of the market and was approaching Kingsmill on 5% (the gap might have been eroded more quickly were it not for Kingsmill's barrage of advertising throughout Hovis White's launch period). Within eight months, Hovis stood as the biggest single brand in the bread market. Moreover, the brand reached its proposed positioning, having bona fide (premium) white credentials based on popularity and family acceptability alongside the inherited (brown) values. A subsidiary benefit was that the Hovis Brown image also showed a positive response to the Hovis White advertising.

The ideal brand is one where the link between brand values and product values is seamless. That Hovis has succeeded as the strongest, most durable brand in the market is a direct result of the way in which advertising has built a formidable bridge between brand and product values. It has been argued that, as well as retaining endangered distribution from its British Bakeries stablemate, the Hovis White advertising has successfully announced a new and unexpected Hovis variant at the same time as representing essential Hovis values in a more modern and universally relevant tone. Nevertheless, it achieved this balancing act without jeopardizing its heritage or credibility. More than this, it reinforced and rejuvenated its past in a way that only hindsight could consider straightforward—and this while being spectacularly outspent by its main competitor. The brand's business base now caught up with the power of its imagery and identity.

Sources: WARC, IPA Effectiveness Awards 1992, The White Stuff: How Advertising Helped Stretch Hovis Without Breaking It, by Anthony Tasgal (Historical information is referenced from WARC, Relaunching the white loaf from the brown bread company, 1996, by Mo Fisher)

Edited by Hazel H. Huang

Discussion Questions

1 What were the possible reasons for British Bakeries' launch of Mother's Pride Premium before Hovis White?

2 What were the advantages and disadvantages of British Bakeries' determination to launch Hovis White?

3 How did the advertising help Hovis gain credentials in the white bread sector and reinforce its inherited values in the brown bread sector?

4 What is the difference between Hovis positioning itself as a brown bread specialist and then as a bread expert? How did the change in position help Hovis to break through its concerns regarding launching Hovis White?

FURTHER READING

- For a good overview of product and brand portfolio management see Aaker, D.A. (2004), *Brand Portfolio Strategy*, New York: Free Press.

- Aaker and Keller provide evidence for a two-step consumer evaluation of brand extensions when they first determine the 'fit' between the parent brand and the extension before then deciding whether or not to apply their attitudes towards the parent brand to the extension in their January 1990 *Journal of Marketing* article 'Consumer evaluations of brand extensions', 84, 27–41.

- Tony Apéria and Rolf Back provide a brand overview of models appropriate for use when considering brand extensions (among other brand management issues) in their book *Brand Relations Management*, Copenhagen: Copenhagen Business School Press.

- Master brands and their relationship to brand extension strategy are discussed in Farquhar, P.H., Han, J.Y., Herr, P., and Ijiri, Y. (1992), 'Strategies for leveraging master brands: how to bypass the risks of direct extensions', *Journal of Marketing Research*, 4, 3, 32–43.

REFERENCES

Barich, H. and Kutter, P. (1991), 'A framework for image management', *Sloan Management Review,* Winter, 94–104.

Barwise, P. and Robertson, T. (1992), 'Brand portfolios', *European Management Journal*, September, 3, 277–85.

Boudette, N.E. (2003), 'BMW's CEO just says "no" to protect brand', *The Wall Street Journal*, 26 November, B1.

Branch, S. (2003), 'Maybe sex doesn't sell, A&F is discovering', *The Wall Street Journal*, 12 December, B1.

Brown, S. (1995), *Postmodern Marketing*, London: Routledge.

Ellison, S. (2003), 'Kraft's state strategy', *The Wall Street Journal*, 18 December, B1.

Farquhar, P. (1989), 'Managing brand equity', *Marketing Research*, September, 1, 24–33.

Gamble, T. (1967). 'Brand extension', in L. Adler (ed.), *Plotting Marketing Stragegy*, New York: Interpublic Press Book.

Hatch, M.J. and Schultz, M. (2001), 'Are the strategic stars aligned for your corporate brand?', *Harvard Business Review*, February, 129–34.

Jencks, C. (1989), *What is Postmodernism?* 3rd edn, London: Academy Editions.

Kapferer, J.N. (1997), *Strategic Brand Management*, 2nd edn, London: Kogan Page.

—— (2001), *Reinventing the Brand*, London: Kogan Page.

Keller, K.L. (1995), *Building, Measuring, and Managing Brand Equity*, Upper Saddle River, New Jersey: Prentice Hall.

Kunde, J. (2000), *Corporate Religion*, London: Financial Times, Prentice Hall.

Milewicz, J. and Herbig, P. (1994), 'Evaluating the brand extension decision using a model of reputation building', *Journal of Product and Brand Management* 3, 1, 39–47.

Sanderson, C. (2002), 'New old Levi's', *Esquire*, September, 46–5.

Slywotzky, A. (1998), *Value Migration*, Paris: Village Mondial.

Sullivan, J.L. (1992), 'Brand extensions: when to use them', *Management Science*, 38, June, 793–806.

Thompson, S. (2003), 'Best foods strategy results in shakeup', *Advertising Age*, 7 July, 3.

Upshaw, L.B. and Taylor, E.L. (2000), *The Masterbrand Mandate*, New York: John Wiley & Sons.

Volkswagen website (2003).

10

Branding Services and Managing the Corporate Brand

➡ **KEY CONCEPTS**

1 Products and services can be placed on a tangibility spectrum which emphasizes positioning by a focus on either evidence or image.

2 The importance of managing brand touchpoints through the touchpoint chain.

3 The vital role of employees in influencing customer perceptions.

4 The vision-culture-image gap analysis model.

5 Understanding an organization's stakeholders and their orientation.

6 The role of corporate stories in building a culture and motivating employees.

7 Developing corporate brand strategy appropriate to different stakeholder groups.

8 Developing emotional connections to stakeholders through corporate stories, symbols and sponsorship.

9 Internal brand communications and living the brand.

Introduction

Although the range of brand strategies detailed in Chapters 7 and 8 apply equally to service and corporate brands, there are some special considerations due to the intangibility and person-dependence of a service and the need to manage the corporate reputation perceived by stakeholders, especially employees. We will discuss these special considerations and the implications for creating a bond between the employees and the brand as well as the role of corporate culture and strategic vision. Before going on, some clarification is required of the terms 'corporate brand' and 'corporate reputation'. Whereas many writers have moved from talking about B2B brands to using corporate reputation as a portmanteau term, in theory we would like to make a distinction between a corporate brand, where the major focus is on customers and employees, and corporate reputation, where the major focus is on a wide range of stakeholders, particularly the media, government and financial markets. However, in practice this distinction is hard to maintain so here we will use both terms interchangeably.

The nature of services

If we place goods and services along a continuum from pure good to pure service, we can see that the customer's ability to make rational, evidence-based choices declines the more service elements are involved. See Fig. 10.1.

A pure good has *search qualities*, which means potential buyers can evaluate the quality of the good before purchase using product and market knowledge. Many goods include service elements and have *experience qualities*, which mean they can only be effectively evaluated after purchase and during use, and this leads to consumers using brands to reduce risk. For example, they may do this by favouring national brands over private label brands when the product category is perceived to be high in experience qualities (Batra and Sinha, 2000). But a pure service only has *credence qualities*, which means that even after purchase and use customers cannot make clear judgements based on evidence but have to

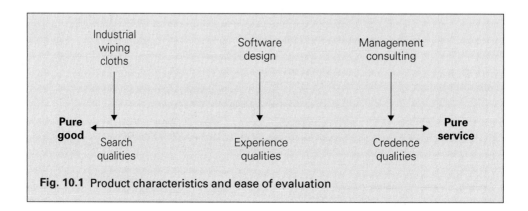

Fig. 10.1 Product characteristics and ease of evaluation

believe in the quality of the service. This means that services are high in perceptions of risk, and coupled with their intangibility, inseparability and heterogeneity (Zeithaml, 1981), they are replete with problems for both customers making choices and managers delivering consistent quality. This is particularly true for labour-intensive services, as the greater the involvement of human beings in the production of a service the greater the variability in quality and the more consumers must rely on trust. For example, front-line service employees are often the lowest paid in the organization, may be part-time and have low motivation.

The intangibility of services refers to the fact that they cannot be touched or inspected or tried out in advance. This means that customers are generally forced to depend on surrogates to assess what they are likely to get; they rely on promises of satisfaction and the marketing effort must provide metaphorical reassurance in advance. Promises, being intangible, have to be 'tangibilized' in their presentation; metaphors and symbols become surrogates for the tangibility that cannot be provided or experienced in advance (Levitt, 1981). For example, insurance companies pictorially offer to put you 'under an umbrella' or place you 'in good hands'. Products can be analysed by the degree of intangibility and positioned on a product tangibility spectrum from products that are tangible dominant, like salt, to those that intangible dominant, like education. See Fig. 10.2.

When a product is largely a physical reality and tangible dominant then the emphasis in market positioning should be on presenting evidence, but when a product involves many service elements and is intangible dominant then the focus shifts to a market positioning focusing on intangible abstractions or image (Shostack, 1977). The more intangible elements there are, the more companies must search for all forms of evidence, no matter how trivial, that might be used to tangibilize the offer and influence customer perceptions. This is illustrated in Fig. 10.3.

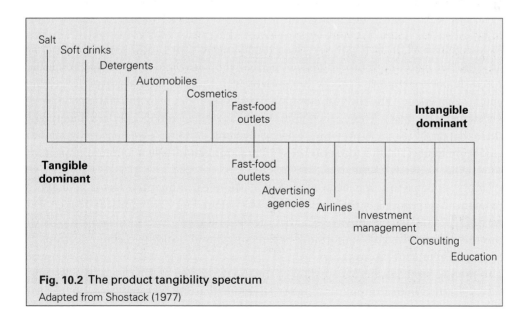

Fig. 10.2 The product tangibility spectrum
Adapted from Shostack (1977)

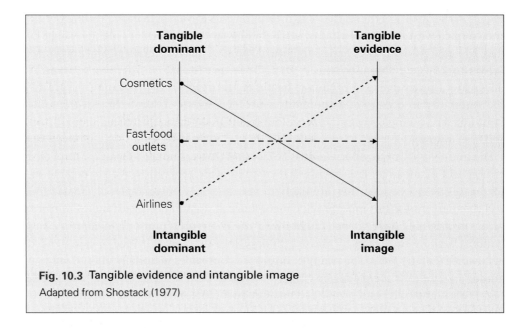

Fig. 10.3 Tangible evidence and intangible image
Adapted from Shostack (1977)

Visible elements often have a strong influence on perceptions: colour, logos, and architecture can all be utilized to help a customer evaluate an intangible service. People can also be used as evidence, lawyers are 'packaged' in dark, pin-stripe suits, doctors 'packaged' in white coats, UPS drivers in brown uniforms. A strong brand can provide potent surrogate choice criteria, replacing the intangibility with perceptions of a cohesive compelling brand story which is delivered through multiple *touchpoints* (Berry and Lampo, 2004).

Managing brand touchpoints

A touchpoint is all the different ways that a brand interacts with and makes an impression on customers and other stakeholders, in particular on employees (Davis and Longoria, 2003). Brand touchpoints can be categorized into the pre-purchase experience, the purchase experience, and the post-purchase experience, and sum to the total experience of a customer with brand. These touchpoints can be identified and located in a touchpoint chain that can be managed over time to deliver dynamic customer experience programmes guided by market data to focus on those interactions that have maximum impact on customer perceptions (Hogan *et al.*, 2005).

Employee behaviour has been identified as the most influential factor in shaping consumers' perceptions of their most- and least-preferred service brands, and as services are just as intangible for employees as they are for customers (Davis and Longoria, 2003) this underscores the vital importance of directing brand-building communications at employees as much as at customers.

In the UK, retail brands occupy four of the top ten places in the Harris 'Best Brands' survey (Harris, 2006). Communicating with its more than 300,000 employees can be seen as one of the important factors behind the success of Tesco, number five in the Best Brands

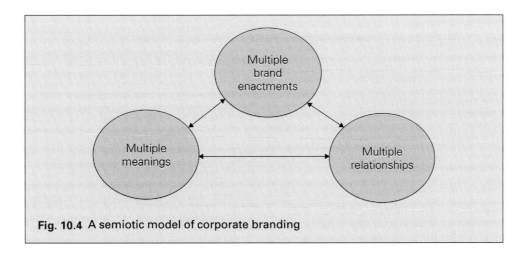

Fig. 10.4 A semiotic model of corporate branding

list, and which is now operating in 13 countries across the world including China, Poland, South Korea and Japan. A great deal of effort is devoted to communications with staff, partly through their website, which gives details of the wide range of benefits available to staff and examples of how the store's brand values have delivered benefits for the community as well as the employees (www.tesco.com/EveryLittleHelps/csrourpeople.htm).

However, as we argued in Chapter 3, brand communications are about the production of meaning as opposed to the transmission of messages, and this has been developed into a semiotic model of multiple corporate brand enactments that occur each and every time an organization interacts with its employees and its customers through touchpoints (Leitch and Richardson, 2003). This is illustrated in Fig. 10.4.

The key point here is that the brand is co-created by its customers and the organization's employees as a service is produced and consumed and that this process is continuously evolving and can be a rather unpredictable process. So managing brand touchpoints is actually about managing meaning and this is a very complex process. We will discuss this later when addressing the idea of living the brand.

Corporate reputation: vision, culture and image

In order to understand the relationship between the organization and its employees we need to utilize concepts from organizational behaviour, in particular, the concepts of strategic vision and corporate culture. These concepts have been added to the familiar concept of corporate brand image and proposed as the foundations of corporate branding by Hatch and Schultz (2003), who articulate the need to manage all three simultaneously.

Strategic vision expresses top management's aspirations for the company, while corporate culture involves the internal values, beliefs and basic assumptions that embody the heritage of the company and the way that employees feel about the organization. Corporate image is the set of perceptions held by a range of stakeholders including customers, employees, stockholders and the media. Together all three can be seen as components of corporate reputation: see Fig. 10.5.

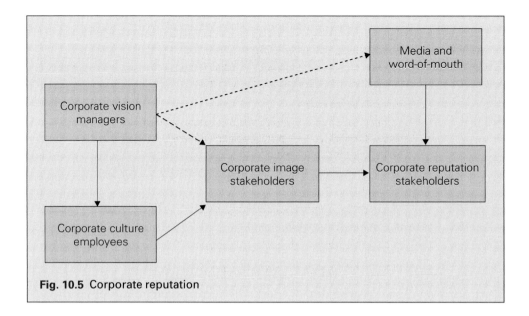

Fig. 10.5 Corporate reputation

The major influences on corporate image are employees, who in turn are influenced by management, but management may also have a direct influence on image through corporate communications.

Vision-Culture-Image gap analysis

Hatch and Schultz (2001) propose an alignment analysis model which identifies key problem areas where gaps arise between the component parts. They frame their Vision-Culture-Image gap analysis toolkit as a series of questions. See Fig. 10.6.

A key issue in this analysis is understanding who are the organization's stakeholders and what are their relative needs.

Stakeholder groups

A useful four-groups typology has been proposed by Dowling (2001) of groups that may all have different functional and emotional relationships with an organization and therefore hold different perceptions of it.

Customer groups

Customers analysed by their needs into different needs-based segments.

Functional groups

Employees, trade unions, suppliers, distributors, service providers.

- Vision-Culture Gap
  - Do employees know the vision?
  - Does the company practise what it preaches?
  - Does the vision inspire all the sub-culture?
- Image-Culture Gap
  - What images do stakeholders hold of the organization?
  - How do employees and stakeholders interact?
  - What are the touchpoints?
  - Do employees care what stakeholders think?
- Image-Vision Gap
  - Who are the most important stakeholders?
  - What do they want?
  - Are you communicating effectively with them?

Fig. 10.6 Vision-Culture-Image gap analysis

Normative groups

Government, regulatory agencies, stockholders, board of directors, trade associations.

Diffuse groups

The media, special interest groups, community members.

Stakeholder orientations

Not only are there many stakeholders, but each stakeholder group may be looking for very different things from the organization. Customers' major interest may be quality and reliability, whereas employees may be most interested in being able to trust the organization. Investors may be focused on credibility whilst community groups may be concerned about responsible behaviour. Analysing where to concentrate efforts can be helped by mapping stakeholders on a power/interest matrix (Johnson and Scholes, 2001). See Fig. 10.7.

Whilst the Vision-Culture-Image gap analysis approach is a very useful way to understand issues that require attention, we will discuss some other approaches to corporate reputation management later.

Corporate culture and the corporate brand

A seminal distinction between espoused values (what organizations may claim in mission statements) and values-in-use (how organizations actually behave) was made by Schein (1992) and underlines the idea that if the values underlying a corporate

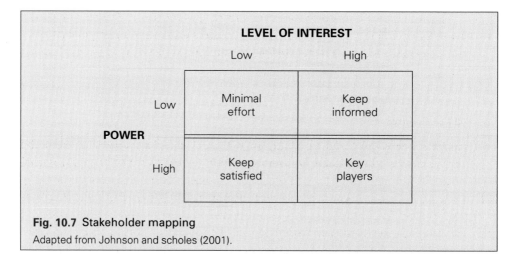

Fig. 10.7 Stakeholder mapping
Adapted from Johnson and scholes (2001).

brand are to be 'more than romanticism' (Hatch and Schultz, 2003) they must be rooted in the lived experience of the employees. It is not sufficient simply to articulate the brand values to employees, but requires them to be involved in the development of the corporate brand values (de Chernatony, 2002). This means that to manage the corporate brand we also need to understand the tacit mental frameworks and taken-for-granted assumptions that are used by employees to make sense of their world and the role which symbols and stories play in this sense-making process (Czarniawska, 1997).

Organizational theorists argue that corporate stories which are effective in motivating employees need to achieve two fundamental outcomes: credibility and novelty (Barry and Elmes, 1997). Van Riel (2000, p. 164) maintains that credibility can be best achieved by corporate stories that are perceived by both internal and external stakeholders as 'illustrations of the centrality and continuity of the organization' while novelty has to express 'distinctiveness compared with players in the same or a comparable league'.

A further element in corporate culture which becomes important for the brand is the area of symbolic management: 'post-industrial organizations create emotional bonds and messages attracting and maintaining managers, employees and network partners' (Larsen, 2000, p. 203); and the corporate identity is symbolized by artefacts such as logo, name, style and other emergent cultural symbols (Hatch and Schultz, 2000). Both stories and symbols must be part of developing a corporate brand.

Developing corporate brand strategy

In developing a corporate brand strategy, organizations have the same two basic alternatives of functional versus symbolic strategies. Recent research in corporate branding has focused on the organization's corporate ability in comparison to its corporate social responsibility (Dacin and Brown, 1997; Berens *et al.*, 2005). Different strategies may be appropriate for different stakeholder groups, e.g. customers may be most concerned about corporate ability to deliver quality products and services and thus a functional strategy is most appropriate; while employees and community groups may be most interested in socially responsible behaviour and thus a symbolic strategy may be most appropriate.

Functional strategy

The objective here is to build associations in the minds of stakeholders about the company's expertise in products and services: such factors as superiority of internal research and development and the resulting technological innovation, manufacturing expertise, and customer orientation. For example, UPS makes claims about its supply-chain expertise and responsiveness, while Airbus emphasizes its non-stop innovation. Santander Bank, like many financial and consulting firms, uses the expertise of their employees. In particular, perceptions about an organization's innovativeness and trustworthiness have a marked effect when the purchase is considered to be of high risk, e.g. in expensive or high-technology markets (Gurhan-Canli and Batra, 2004).

Basic factors important in the functional strategies discussed in Chapter 8 are also relevant to corporate brand strategies.

Brand salience

Dominating the mindspace of the market is vital for many corporate brands, and advertising and promotions play an important role here, as do word-of-mouth, media mentions and increasingly the Internet and blogs. Sponsorship of sports and cultural activities can play a part in building and maintaining brand awareness with stakeholders, but perhaps its greatest role is with employees (Hickman *et al.*, 2005) and we will discuss this later.

Differentiation

Perceptions of differentiation are just as important for corporate brands as for product brands, and the same factors discussed in Chapter 7 are vital here: that the brand is different from other brands, that this point of difference is unique to the brand, and distinctive in that it is worth paying for. Increasingly, it appears that symbolic strategies that focus on emotional aspects may offer the most scope for differentiation.

Symbolic strategy

Corporate social responsibility (CSR) has leapt up the agenda of many stakeholders, not least financial and governmental groups (Marquez and Fombrun, 2005) and the websites of more than 80% of the Fortune 500 companies address CSR issues (Bhattacharya and Sen, 2004). CSR encompasses environmentalism, commitment to diversity in hiring and promoting, commitment to community support and commitment to social causes, and has been suggested as a form of brand insurance for global brands (Werther, 2005). However, a recent study suggests that building stakeholder relationships through CSR programmes, other than with customers, is not yet a priority for the majority of major firms (Knox *et al.*, 2005).

Although the fifteen approaches to symbolic brand strategy discussed in Chapter 7 can all be applied to corporate brands, particularly brand mythologies, we want to focus on developing emotional connections to stakeholders through corporate stories and symbols and through sponsorship.

Stories

Boje (1991) argues that organizations are essentially storytelling systems, in which stories are 'the preferred sense-making currency of human relationships among internal and external stakeholders'. Based on narrative theory, Barry and Elmes (1997) argue that successful stories can obtain credibility by the use of materiality, that is they become effective if conveyed in physical modes e.g. video, PowerPoint; however they also suggest that the most significant organizational discourse is communicated verbally, as also argued by Boje (1991). A further aspect of credibility through materiality is by reference to the everyday life of the CEOs as human beings, which allows stakeholders to identify more closely with the company; for example Anita Roddick, previously CEO of The Body Shop, and Lee Iacocca at Chrysler made the companies take on a human face (Barry and Elmes, 1997). However, they suggest that over time as organizations become more interdependent, corporate stories may shift away from a focus on agency and self towards a more communitarian focus on relationships with others. When building a corporate story, the question of authenticity becomes an important factor.

Reproduced with the kind permission of The Body Shop International plc

Authenticity and credibility

Beyond basing the story on the realities of the organizations and simply telling the truth, what is required is to communicate transparency and integrity to stakeholders (Ind, 2003). Moore (2003, p. 116) argues that authenticity can be achieved by under-promise and describes the TV documentary series Airline, which features the everyday problems of ground staff handling easyJet customers and their problems: 'With no investment in CRM and frequent-flyer pseudo-loyalty, they seem to have created a more realistic relationship with customers.' There is recent evidence that credibility for a wide range of organizations in different markets can be enhanced through emotional perceptions of *openness* (Maathuis *et al.*; and Sikkei, 2003). 'Not only do your customers want to talk with real people inside your organization, but your employees are desperate to talk with real customers. They want to tell them the truth' (Levine *et al.*, 2000, p. 92).

Symbols

Symbols 'have the power to encapsulate the senses . . . the symbol can in a magical way summarize the idea of an entire corporation', and a corporate brand and visual identity can become a rallying point for staff: 'Employees, wherever they lived and worked, whatever their social, cultural or religious background, could identify with the whole enterprise' (Olins, 1989, pp. 73, 82). But symbols are not just visual devices which represent the corporate identity, they also include symbolic behaviour by management and employees. The old idea of 'walking the talk' (Peters and Waterman, 1982) is still a vital factor in building the corporate brand inside the organization, as is also attested to by Collins and Porras (1998) in their study of visionary companies driven by a core ideology that also had to be performed symbolically. Leadership behaviour matters, and we will come back to this when discussing living the brand.

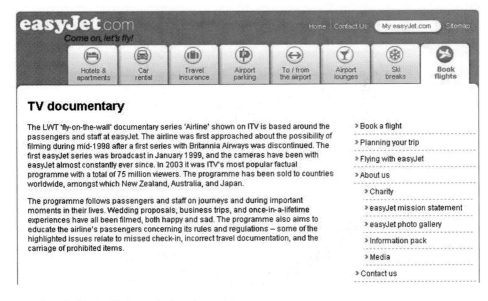

Reproduced with the kind permission of easyJet

Sponsorship

Despite the huge amount of money spent by organizations in sponsoring sports and cultural events, there is little research that demonstrates that it has a long-term effect on the corporate brand. However, recent studies of sports sponsorship point to its potential role in building positive perceptions in both customers and other stakeholders, but particularly employees. Customers can form positive attitudes towards a brand, more likely to occur as identification with the sponsored team increases (Madrigal, 2000). Employee morale can be improved by sports sponsorship and it works as a form of internal communication, altering and enhancing a company's culture at different levels of the organization, helping management to communicate company values of 'strength' and 'winning' to employees, and creating a bond between front-line employees and customers (Hickman *et al.*, 2005).

Living the brand

Building a corporate brand demands that major attention be paid to employees, bringing them along with the brand strategy so that they understand it, believe in it and also practise it in their behaviour towards customers and other stakeholders. 'Living the brand' (Ind, 2001) means transforming every member of the organization into a brand champion. This is not an easy task. A survey of US employees found that they believed that 'only 66% of company leaders are trying to do what is best for their customers, and even fewer, only 44%, believed corporate leaders are trying to do what is best for their employees' and 19% are 'actively disengaged' from their employer (Gallup, 2002). Internal branding communications are part of the answer, and Mitchell (2002) outlines some key principles. He suggests that people have limited tolerance for branding and visioning initiatives, but at certain 'turning points' when the company is facing challenge or change, employees are seeking direction and an internal branding campaign 'can direct people's energy in a positive direction by clearly and vividly articulating what makes the company special'. Internal and external messages have to be linked in 'two-way branding' that harmonizes the employees' experience of the brand with what customers are being told. An example is IBM's e-business campaign, which was not aimed just at potential customers and other external stakeholders but was just as much aimed at bringing employees to the idea of the Internet as the future of technology. He points out that employees have brand 'touchpoints' too and that their everyday experiences with the company must be managed to ensure that the brand strategy, and the research behind it, informs their actions. Here symbolic management practices play an important role, as does the company policy. For example, the award-winning US convenience store chain QuickTrip's customer-service appraisal system and the reward structure emphasizes the team performance in satisfying and delighting customers. 'If a mystery shopper is especially impressed with a particular employee, everyone on staff at the store during the shift receives a bonus, because the company believes that individual rewards would undermine the message that all employees contribute to the customer's experience' (Bendapundi and Bendapundi, 2005).

A 'living the brand' programme was implemented successfully at Airtours Holidays, a UK package holiday company. This was aimed at changing the internal culture of the company in order to deliver the corporate brand strategy of quality customer service. An internal 'values programme' was planned to support an external repositioning campaign and involved all 2,500 employees in a sustained effort involving communication and training, with appraisal and reward structures being brought into line with the brand values. A key factor was developing employees' pride in working for the company, which came from line managers behaving in ways that were consistent with the brand such that a majority of employees agreed that 'overall, our corporate brand reflects what it's like to work here' (Stanier, 2001).

The employer brand

An organization that has a strong brand can use the brand to attract and retain employees: 'Developing an "employer brand" is increasingly seen as a winning strategy for managing all aspects of employee relationships' (Economist, 2001). It can reduce the costs of employee acquisition, improve the relationship between employees and employer and extend the average length of employee retention, and allow companies to attract high-calibre staff at lower salaries than competitors with weaker employer brands (Ritson, 2002). McKinsey Consulting, itself a formidable employer brand, advocates that employers must think of recruits as customers and use sophisticated market analysis techniques to identify key rivals and what corporate attributes matters most to specific types of recruits (Hieronimus *et al.*, 2005). Similarly, Philips, the giant electronics company, is actively engaged in a battle to attract talent using both internal and external research to uncover attraction and retention factors and then building these into an employer brand strategy of 'touch lives everyday', which was piloted in China and is now being rolled out around the world (Leeuwen and Pieters, 2005). The key point is that the strategy highlights the actual employee experience at touchpoints through the employment lifecycle.

Managing the corporate brand image/reputation

A critical approach to measuring and managing corporate brand image/reputation is proposed by Dowling (2001, p. 212), who recommends going beyond the 'scorecard' approach of the Fortune Most Admired Companies survey or its equivalents to collect as much information as the budget will allow on detailed measures of the images and reputations held by various stakeholder groups of the organization and its competitors, and 'an indication of the characteristics of an ideal organization' in the relevant industry. From here, the management process is to close any identified gaps through managerial action and then use communication to change the perceptions of the stakeholder groups.

The process of detailed measurement, monitoring and management has been developed into a commercial product by MORI, whose Reputation Centre offers a research-based approach to understanding the views of key stakeholder groups, and the measurement and monitoring of perceptions over time. They have particular expertise at accessing the perceptions of government at both national and European level, which is a key issue for many multinational corporate brands.

CHAPTER SUMMARY

In this chapter we have focused on the issue of tangibility, which is such a feature of service brands and how brand touchpoints can be managed. We have emphasized the importance of employees in influencing customer perceptions of the brand, and how organizational culture can be developed. We have shown that corporate brand strategy must be appropriate for different stakeholder groups, and discussed the role of corporate stories, symbols and sponsorship.

DISCUSSION QUESTIONS

1 Why are services high in perceptions of risk?

2 How can risk perceptions be reduced?

3 How can people be used as evidence?

4 Why must brand-building communications be directed at employees?

5 Why is it important to understand an organization's shareholders' orientations?

6 How can brand salience be built for a corporate brand?

7 How can authenticity be communicated to stakeholders?

8 How can sponsorship be used to create a bond between employees and customers?

9 How can an organization become an employer brand?

CASE STUDY

Creating a Culture of Brand Engagement from Scratch

Over the years, a lot has been talked about the 'democratization of wealth' in the UK. The statistics tell us that one in every twelve adults in Britain has £50,000 or more in liquid financial assets. An ideal market for the diverse providers of financial services to target? Yet, until recently little effort had been made to address the requirements of this substantial sector of the population. Why? Because those requirements are phenomenally diverse. The 'mass affluent' are anything but a mass market and the response of much of the financial services industry to this market has been to adopt a lowest-common-denominator approach: 'What do all these people have in common? Money. So let's offer them more.' But such an approach overlooks a key feature of the mass affluent—they do not value their wealth *as* wealth. Financial services should be about providing opportunities to manipulate that money in a whole range of ways—however individuals choose—in a fashion that sits comfortably with their lifestyle choices. So—unusually for the financial services industry—we set about building distinctive brand values into the very heart of our business. The picture of our target customers informed every decision at every stage of the development of Inscape.

They're all around us

The first thing we had to realize about the mass affluent was that these are the people we see every day. They come from a wide range of social backgrounds: 34% are C1, 14% C2 and 50% A/B. They include a lot of women and people from ethnic minority backgrounds. The source of their wealth also varies, although in 40% of cases it has been built up through a salary. At present approximately two-thirds are men, 50% are aged between 45 and 65 and 44% are retired or working part-time. In addition, and as a result of the diversity of their experiences, these people's aspirations, desires and behaviour are also quite distinct, as are their attitudes to financial services. Their only consistent and distinctive characteristic is their attitudes to their wealth. Wealth for the mass affluent is a means to an end—it is about opportunity.

Representation for the 'mass affluent'

In terms of financial services, what the 'mass affluent' segment requires is a service provider who understands this fundamental driver and is capable of responding to it.

These individuals have three options for their financial services: red carpet retailing in the high street, elitist banks or independent financial advisers. A retail bank cannot effectively address the needs of this market. Generic products are inappropriate for people with very specific, highly individual requirements. And high-street banks do not offer the high-quality investment expertise demanded by these people. By contrast, the elitist banks, which are familiar with and proficient at managing substantial wealth, are perceived as the preserve of 'old money', offering a particular kind of service to a particular class of people with whom the mass affluent simply do not identify. In theory, a middle ground does already exist, in the shape of the independent financial adviser, but many IFAs have no brand equity to call on to act as guarantor of their proficiency.

Something new, something different

Looking at the market, it was clear to us that there was a need for a new approach. We knew the kind of services our customers would respond to: high-quality investment strategies that control risk while producing attractive rates of return, expert management, good, astute advice, technical accuracy and appropriateness, and a high standard of communication through a unique customer experience. To deliver financial services expertise, we recruited from the very best fund managers in retail banking—Abbey National. But for us, their skills alone were not enough to develop the kind of company we were looking for. The whole customer experience had to be different. So to achieve such a radical transformation of business processes meant that we had to build a new culture of brand engagement from scratch.

Brand-building from the inside out

The first stage in the development of the Inscape brand was the creation of the core concept of 'True Wealth, Open Minds', which is at once a promise of a different kind of financial advice and a commitment to a different kind of customer. 'True Wealth' describes our customers' pursuit of goals through their financial arrangements other than simply swelling their bank balance. 'Open Minds' refers to the many and varied approaches they have to living their lives. While for us at Inscape, 'True Wealth, Open Minds' expresses our commitment to making the most of our customers' assets. As for 'Open Minds', that simply means that, whether a customer is a

22-year-old pop star wanting to put money away for their children's education, or a septuagenarian surfer saving for a trip to Australia, we won't bat an eyelid.

However, to realize this brand strategy, we needed to look at how the 'True Wealth, Open Minds' concept would manifest itself in the real world. Firstly, Inscape will democratize investment management opportunities, by opening up an unrivalled range of investment management opportunities based on customers' needs for the the 'mass affluent' sector. Secondly, we aim to demystify investment by providing customers with accessible, intelligible information so that they can make up their own minds about our performance. Thirdly, we are committed to delivering on standards of service through the comprehensive implementation of a brand strategy that enables customers to engage with the brand and make the promise a reality. That, of course, is a challenge, as in the past differentiation in the financial services sector has been almost exclusively on price.

Rolling out the brand

With a brand strategy in place, we looked to Circus to help us execute it. Circus adopted an all-round approach with the objective of ensuring consistent and comprehensive implementation. As an example, let us look at the physical environment of our Client Centres. We had to break away from the traditional aesthetics of either impersonal, plasticky booths or oak panelling and dark green leather upholstery. Our Centres had to defy pigeon-holing by prospective customers and indicate a serious, business-like attitude. Our first six advice centres were situated just off main streets in major towns. Din Associates were brought in to design the interiors, which are professional, modern and informal. Staff feel the environments are well suited to their style of working and they engender a strong feeling of pride—it is clear that the offices have been designed especially for their working needs and have not simply been bought off the shelf. Initial client responses were encouraging—they find the offices bright and welcoming, different from and more professional than the standard high-street bank, yet not at all intimidating.

Our marketing included national advertising and direct mail. We needed to ensure that the promises we made to customers—'Wealth management for the privileged many'—were precisely what we, and importantly our staff, understood we would be offering. The diverse range of people represented in the posters and print ads was an accurate reflection of the initial research on which we had based the business.

Fundamental to the practical implementation of our brand strategy are our people. Ultimately it is our staff, through their encounters with prospective customers, who are the primary agents of the Inscape brand. Many of the team we brought together to create the company have been involved since the inception of the Inscape brand. They have helped build and sustain an excitement and a commitment to Inscape that would have been hard to achieve any other way. To ensure that all new staff have the skills to act as representatives of the Inscape brand, they are selected for their communication and listening abilities, as well as their financial expertise.

Getting engaged

Circus created a range of customized tools to facilitate the process of engagement within the new business, both prior to launch and as we grow in the future. The main focus of these tools was to introduce a true one-to-one customer service ethic aligned with customers' needs, not with the products we wanted to sell. We used a Brand Tool Kit to introduce staff to the brand. The kit is used by a small group and a facilitator to explain the brand's principles and values, and then to invite participation to promote active understanding and appropriate application in various circumstances. There is also an interactive CD-ROM that introduces staff to the potential range of customers, including vox-pops from a broad section of our target group. A Q&A section assesses each user's understanding of the brand and, in turn, their ability to engage the customer. Lastly, there is a further 'brand aide' in the form of a pack of postcard-sized cards, featuring references to the brand's values, some relevant quotes and inspirational sayings, and the imagery that represents the brand, in order to help the brand stay top-of-mind.

Source: WARC, Market Leader, Issue 13, 2001, Creating a Culture of Brand Engagement from Scratch
Edited by Natalia Yannopoulou

Discussion Questions

1 How did Inscape build its brand identity?

2 How did Inscape respond to the challenge of intangibility?

3 What are the key factors that contributed to the creation of Inscape's Brand Engagement culture?

4 What challenges will Inscape face in the future and how can they be addressed?

FURTHER READING

- The nature of services and the special challenges posed for their marketing is discussed by Gronroos, C. (2000), *Service Management and Marketing*, 2nd edn, Chichester: John Wiley.

- A comprehensive text about corporate reputation is Dowling, G. (2001), *Creating Corporate Reputations*, Oxford: Oxford University Press.

- A US approach to corporate reputation is given by Fombrun, C. (1996), *Reputation: Realizing Value from the Corporate Image*: Cambridge: Harvard Business School Press.

REFERENCES

Barry, D. and Elmes, M. (1997), 'Strategy retold: toward a narrative view of strategic discourse', *Academy of Management Review*, 22, 2, 429–52.

Batra, R. and Sinha, I. (2000), 'Consumer-level factors moderating the success of private label brands', *Journal of Retailing*, 76, 2, 175–91.

Bendapundi, N. and Bendapundi, V. (2005), 'Creating the living brand', *Harvard Business Review*, May, 124–32.

Berens, G., van Riel, C., and van Brugger, G. (2005), 'Corporate associations and consumer product responses: the moderating role of corporate brand dominance', *Journal of Marketing*, 69, 3, 35–47.

Berry, L. and Lampo, S. (2004), 'Branding labor-intensive services', *Business Strategy Review*, Spring, 15, 1 , 18–25.

Bhattacharya, C. and Sen, S. (2004), 'Doing better at doing good', *California Management Review*, 47, 1, 9–24.

Boje, D. (1991), 'The storytelling organization', *Administrative Science Quarterly*, 36, 106–26.

Collins, J. and Porras, J. (1998), *Built to Last: Successful Habits of Visionary Companies*, London: Random House.

Czarniawska, B. (1997), *Narrating the Organization: Dramas of Institutional Identity*, Chicago: University of Chicago Press.

Dacin, P. and Brown, T. (1997), 'The company and the product: corporate associations and consumer product responses', *Journal of Marketing*, 61, 1, 68–85.

Davis, S. and Longoria, T. (2003), 'Harmonizing your touchpoints', *Brand Packaging*, Jan/Feb, 17–23.

De Chernatony, L. (2002), 'Would a brand smell any sweeter by a corporate name?' *Corporate Reputation Review*, 5, 2/3, 114–32.

Dowling, G. (2001), *Creating Corporate Reputations*, Oxford: Oxford University Press.

Economist Intelligence Unit (2001), 'Building employer brands', *Business Europe*, May.

Gallup Management Journal (2002) http://gmj.gallup.com.

Gurhan-Canli, Z. and Batra, R. (2004), 'When corporate image affects product evaluations: the moderating role of perceived risk', *Journal of Marketing Research*, XLI, 197–205.

Harris Best Brands (2006), http://www.harrisinteractive.com.

Hatch, M. and Schultz, M. (2000), 'Scaling the Towers of Babel: relational differences between identity, image and culture in organizations', in M. Schultz, M. Hatch, and M. Larsen (eds.), *The Expressive Organization*, Oxford: Oxford University Press.

—— —— (2001), 'Are the strategic stars aligned for your corporate brand?', *Harvard Business Review*, February, 129–34.

—— —— (2003), 'Bringing the corporation into corporate branding', *European Journal of Marketing*, 37, 7/8, 1041–64.

Hickman, T., Lawrence, K., and Ward, J. (2005), 'A social identities perspective on the effects of corporate sports sponsorship on employees', *Sports Marketing Quarterly*, 14, 3, 148–57.

Hieronimus, F., Schaefer, K., and Schröder, J. (2005), 'Using branding to attract talent', *McKinsey Quarterly*, 3, 12–14.

Hogan, S., Almquist, E., and Glynn, S. (2005), 'Brand building: finding the touchpoints that count', *Journal of Business Strategy*, 21, 11–18.

Ind, N. (2001), *Living the Brand*, 2nd edn, London: Kogan Page.

—— (2003), 'A brand of enlightenment', in N. Ind (ed.), *Beyond Branding*, London: Kogan Page.

Johnson, G. and Scholes, K. (2001), *Exploring Corporate Strategy*, London: Prentice-Hall.

Knox, S., Maklan, S., and French, P. (2005), 'Corporate social responsibility: exploring stakeholder relationships and programme reporting across leading FTSE companies', *Journal of Business Ethics*, 61, 3, 7–28.

Larsen, M. (2000), 'Managing the corporate story', in M. Schultz, M. Hatch and M. Larsen (eds.), *The Expressive Organization*, Oxford: Oxford University Press.

Leeuwen, B. and Pieters, J. (2005), 'Building Philips' employer brand from the inside out', *Strategic HR Review*, 4, 4, 16–19.

Leitch, S. and Richardson, N. (2003), 'Corporate branding in the new economy', *European Journal of Marketing*, 37, 7/8, 1065–79.

Levine, R., Locke, C., Searts, D., and Weinberger, D. (2000), *The Cluetrain Manifesto*, London: Pearson Education.

Levitt, T. (1981), 'Marketing intangible products and product intangibles', *Harvard Business Review*, May–June, 94–102.

Maathuis, O., Rodenberg, J., and Sikkei, D. (2003), 'Credibility, emotion or reason?' *Corporate Reputation Review*, 6, 4, 333–45.

Madrigal, R. (2000), 'The influence of social alliances with sports teams on intentions to purchase corporate sponsors' products', *Journal of Advertising*, XXIX, 4, 13–24.

Marquez, A. and Fombrun, C. (2005), 'Measuring corporate responsibility', *Corporate Reputation Review*, 7, 4, 204–308.

Mitchell, C. (2002), 'Selling the brand inside', *Harvard Business Review*, January, 99–105.

Moore, J. (2003), 'Authenticity', in N. Ind (ed.) *Beyond Branding*, London: Kogan Page.

Olins, W. (1989), *Corporate Identity*, London: Thames & Hudson.

Peters, T. and Waterman, R. (1982), *In Search of Excellence*, New York: Harper and Row.

Ritson, M. (2002), 'Marketing and HR collaborate to harness employer brand power', *Marketing*, 24 October, 18–21.

Schein, E. (1992), *Organizational Culture and Leadership*, 2nd edn, San Francisco: Jossey-Bass.

Shostack, L. (1977), 'Breaking Free from Product Marketing', *Journal of Marketing*, 41, 73–80.

Stanier, M. (2001), 'Living the brand at Airtours Holidays', *Strategic Communication Management*, August, 28–31.

Van Riel, C. (2000), 'Corporate communication orchestrated by a sustainable corporate story', in M. Schultz, M. Hatch, and M. Larsen (eds.), *The Expressive Organization*, Oxford: Oxford University Press.

Werther Jr, W.B. and Chandler, D. (2004), 'Strategic corporate responsibility as global brand insurance', *Business Horizons*, 48, 4, 317–24.

Zeithaml, V. (1981), 'How consumer evaluation processes differ between goods and services', in H. Donnelly and W. George (eds.), *Marketing of Services*, Chicago, IL: American Marketing Association.

11

Brands and Advertising

 KEY CONCEPTS

1 Effective positioning requires selecting the optimum benefit and correct benefit focus.

2 Benefit selection should be based upon importance to the target audience, perceived ability to deliver, and doing so uniquely or better than competitors.

3 Brand awareness will be either recognition or recall based, depending upon how the brand decision is made.

4 Involvement in purchase decisions is a function of risk, defined in either fiscal or psychological terms.

5 Brand purchase decisions will be driven by either negative motives, where a problem is to be solved or avoided, or positive motives, where a reward is sought from the product.

6 Both involvement and motivation are critical to communication strategy for building brand attitude.

Introduction

The original meaning of the word 'brand' seems to derive from an Old Norse word *brandr*, which meant 'to burn' (Interbrand Group, 1992). Yet in the etymology of the word, this idea of branding as a 'permanent mark deliberately made with a hot iron' now takes second place to 'goods of particular name or trade mark' (NSOED, 1990). But does this really describe what is understood as a brand? The American Marketing Association describes a brand as a 'name, term, sign, symbol, or design, or a combination of them intended to identify the goods and services of one seller or group of sellers and differentiate them from those of competitors'. The AMA definition concerns the *reason* for a brand: to enable a person to identify one alternative from a competitor. All this is true, but a brand must be a *label* in the true sense of that word: something 'attached to an object to give information about it' (NSOED, 1990). The information about a brand in very large measure comes from its marketing communication, and it could be argued that without advertising there would be no brands.

Before going on, it is important to understand just exactly what we mean by 'advertising'. When we refer to advertising we are talking *broadly* about any marketing communication that is meant to reinforce brand awareness and build positive brand attitude, regardless of the way that message may be delivered. It is a strategic consideration. This means anything from store atmosphere, packaging, endorsements, and product placements to messages in more traditional mass media such as television, radio, posters, magazines and newspapers can be advertising. This is what is often referred to today as 'contact points' (Donaghey and Williamson, 2003).

In this chapter we will be considering the critical role that advertising-like messages play in strategic brand management, and how to develop effective brand positionings for marketing communication, and strategies for building brand awareness and positive brand attitude.

The nature of brands and advertising

When people think of brands, they usually think of products they buy: Coke, Cadbury, Ford, Hoover, Persil, Mars. But just about anything can be 'branded' as we have already seen. Products, services, corporations, retail stores, cities, organizations, even individuals can be seen as 'brands'. Remember, a brand name is meant to embody information about something, information that represents an added value, differentiating it in a marked way from alternatives. A brand name is meant to trigger in memory positive associations with that brand. Politicians, hospitals, entertainers, football clubs, corporations, they all want their name, their *brand*, to mean something very specifically to their market. It is how they wish to be seen, and how they wish to be distinguished from competitive alternatives.

Coca-Cola and the Dynamic Ribbon are registered trademarks of the Coca-Cola Company

Positioning

Why do some people shop at 'better' stores when they can buy identical (brand name) products for much less at a discount store? Clearly, price is not the most important consideration in their shopping decisions. They are looking for something else, but how do they know where to find it? They rely upon their knowledge or experience of different retail stores to direct them to stores where they expect to find what they want. This *image* or understanding of the store in their mind is cued by or communicated by the store name, the *brand*. In marketing a retail store, one may want people to feel it always offers the lowest price, or the widest variety of merchandise, or the most enjoyable shopping experience. This is known as *positioning*, and it is the critical first step in developing advertising for establishing a brand.

Brand attitude

The idea of a brand as a label is really the key. A brand provides *information*, and that kind of information comes from marketing communication. Think about a brand you know. What comes to mind when you think about it? No doubt a great deal more than the fact that it is a particular type of product. Perhaps you were thinking about how much you like it, that it is well-known, or that it is 'one of the best'. All these thoughts reflect something that is called *brand attitude*. A brand name represents everything you know about a particular product and what it means to you. It provides a convenient summary of your feelings, knowledge and experience with the brand. It means you do not need to spend a great deal of time 'researching' a product each time you are considering a purchase. Your evaluation of the product is immediately reconstructed from memory, cued by the brand name. In many ways, building and ensuring a continuing positive brand attitude is what strategic brand management is all about, and this is largely accomplished with advertising.

The effect of a positive brand attitude leads to *brand equity*. Brand equity, as already discussed in Chapter 5, represents an *added value* to a product in the consumer's mind, enhancing the overall value of that product well beyond its merely functional purpose. In trying to understand what the relationship between a brand and advertising is all about, it will pay to briefly consider brand equity again now. Think about chocolate for a minute. Basically, chocolate is chocolate. Or is it? Are some *brands* better than others? Why? What about washing powder? They all get the job done, and use the same basic ingredients. Or do you think some do a better job than others? What about toothpaste, or vodka, or under-wear? Where do the differences among brands in these product categories come from? How much of the difference is 'real' versus perceived? Why do you prefer one brand over another, especially if, when looked at with a coldly objective eye, there is very little, if any, actual difference in the products?

This underscores that to a large extent a brand is not a tangible thing at all, but rather the sum of what someone knows, thinks, and feels about a particular product. In a very real sense, brands only exist in the minds of consumers, but that does not make them any less real. It is the job of a brand manager to effectively manage how consumers see their brand versus competitive alternatives, and they do this with advertising.

Positioning brands in communication

The idea of 'brand positioning' can mean many things. It could refer to where a brand is seen in a category relative to its competitors; it could refer to the benefits or 'images' associated with a brand. Kotler has defined it in terms of enabling a brand to occupy a 'distinct and valued place' in the mind of the target consumer (Kotler, 2003). All these meanings are important and must be considered when thinking about how to specifically position a brand when talking about it in advertising and other marketing communication. This is usually summarized in a *positioning statement* that addresses the benefits a brand offers a specific target audience in order to satisfy a particular need.

Before looking at how to develop an effective positioning statement, we need to understand two basic types of positioning: central vs. differentiated positioning. A *centrally positioned* brand must deliver all the main benefits generally associated with the product category. This means that a centrally positioned brand may be described as the 'best brand in the category' and it would be believable because people see it as offering all the main benefits they are looking for in that type of product. Centrally positioned brands are generally category leaders, and they do not need to continually list their benefits. For example, a category leader might simply position itself as 'the best'. Of course, people must believe this. A central positioning can also work if a brand is seen as doing as good a job as the category leader, especially if it is lower priced.

All other brands should adopt a *differential* positioning, where one looks for an important benefit that consumers believe the brand offers, and does a better job than other brands. This is where the correct positioning strategy is so important, and that will be addressed in the rest of this section.

Brand positioning may be thought of as a 'supercommunication' effect that tells the potential customer what the brand is, who it is for, and what it offers. This reflects the relationship between brand positioning and the two core communication effects of brand awareness and brand attitude. Brand awareness and brand attitude will be discussed later in the chapter. Strong brand awareness (for almost any brand) must be generated and sustained with marketing communication. It is marketing communication, and advertising in particular, that builds and maintains *brand salience*. It is not enough for a brand to be recognized. If it is to be successful, a brand must occupy a 'salient' position within the target audience's consideration set. In fact, the strength of a brand's salience is one indicator of the brand's equity. (A useful measure of this is the ratio of top-of-mind recall to total recall among competitive brands in a category, as discussed in Chapter 6.)

In Chapter 6, we raised some key questions about measuring brand attitude: Who exactly *is* the target audience? Is everyone looking for the same thing, or the same things all the time? What is important, and to whom? How are brands seen to deliver on the things important to the target audience? As we said then, answers to these questions are critical if marketing communication is to positively affect brand attitude, and they are part of developing an effective positioning strategy.

Obviously, a brand must also be linked to the correct target audience, which means that the target audience for the brand should *immediately* understand that the advertising is talking to them. But as Percy and Elliott (2005) have pointed out, the key is understanding brand awareness and brand attitude. The link between a brand and category need, what people are looking for, is what brand awareness is all about. A brand must be positioned in its marketing communication in such a way that when the need for such a product occurs, that brand comes to mind. Then, the brand must be linked to a benefit that provides a motivating reason to consider it (the global benefit of 'best' in the case of a centrally positioned brand). It is this link between the brand and benefit that lies at the root of building positive brand attitude, which in its turn builds positive brand equity.

Benefits play a central role in effective positioning for marketing communication. But as already suggested, benefits are related to brand attitude, and brand attitude is what drives purchase motive. 'I love Cadbury' is an *attitude* about Cadbury that connects the brand in the consumer's mind with a likely reason to buy: sensory gratification. Where does this brand attitude come from? It is the result of one or more beliefs about the *specific benefits* Cadbury is seen to offer. Effective communication strategy requires an understanding of what that belief structure is, and how it builds brand attitude. One might think of this as an overall summary judgment about a brand, and it follows the most widely used model of attitude, the expectancy-value model (introduced in Chapter 6).

Within the overall positioning that results from this understanding of how benefits and their importance build brand attitude, the manager must determine what the benefit emphasis and focus should be, which we take up in a later section. But, it is important first to remember that purchase motive is really the *underlying* basis of why a benefit is seen as important. Purchase motives are the fundamental 'energizers' of buyer behaviour. As a result, an effective positioning must reflect the correct motive, the one associated with why consumers in the category are *really* buying *particular* brands.

It is also important to distinguish between motives that drive product category decisions rather than brand decisions. People may buy lower calorie foods because they are watching their weight (a negative motive), but buy particular brands for more taste-related reasons (a positive motive). This is an absolutely critical distinction. Benefits like low in calories or fat relate to negative motives like problem-solution or problem-avoidance, and are unlikely to drive *specific brand* purchases. Someone may be looking for a lower calorie product, but probably *not* at the expense of taste. The reason this is such an important point is that positive motives suggest marketing communication where the execution itself actually becomes the product benefit, as we shall see in the section on brand attitude strategies later in this chapter. When dealing with positive motives a truly unique execution is required where the brand owns the 'feeling' created by the advertising for the brand. Advertising can't prove a brand is more stylish or popular, but it can make people *believe* it is.

Benefit selection

The benefits a brand emphasizes in marketing communication should be selected according to three major considerations: importance, delivery, and uniqueness (Percy and Elliott, 2005). *Importance* refers to the relevance of the benefit to the underlying motivation. A benefit assumes importance *only if* it is instrumental in helping meet the consumer's purchase motivation. *Delivery* refers to a brand's perceived ability to provide the benefit. *Uniqueness* refers to a brand's perceived ability to deliver on the benefit relatively better than other brands. As Boulding *et al.* (1994) have pointed out, this uniqueness must be seen in the message about the benefit. What one is looking for are one or two benefits, relevant to the underlying motive, that can produce a perceived difference between alternative brands. These benefits should then be emphasized in a brand's marketing communication.

A note in passing. We are talking about *perceived* delivery and uniqueness. Just because a brand may not now be thought to provide benefits that could optimize purchase against important motives does not mean this perception cannot be created (unless, of course, it stretches the consumer's understanding of the brand, which is one reason it is necessary to fully understand current brand equity).

How can this idea of importance, delivery, and uniqueness be used to actually come up with the best benefits to use in a brand's positioning? One arrives at an optimum benefit selection by utilizing the assumptions of the expectancy-value model of attitude (Fishbein and Ajzen, 1975). The model assumes that a person's attitude toward something (A_b) is the sum of everything they know about it (b_i) weighted by how important each of those things are to them (a_i). The connection with the three benefit selection considerations is implied by the a_i and b_i components of the model. The importance of a benefit in brand selection is represented by a_i, and the belief that a particular brand can deliver the benefit is represented by b_i. Applying the model to the importance and delivery of brand benefits in effect computes an approximation of brand attitude (A_b).

In Chapter 6 we presented an example of how the expectancy-value model can be used in understanding and measuring brand equity. Perhaps another example here will help us see this more clearly in terms of positioning. Suppose you were looking to buy a new car, perhaps after receiving a promotion with a big increase in salary. Some of the things you might be considering in making a choice are: safety, value, mileage, power, stylishness, exciting envy. Obviously, this does not represent everything you might consider, but it will serve for our example. In order to determine what your attitude might be toward different automobiles you are considering, following the expectancy-value model, one would need to know how important each of these considerations is to you, and whether or not you feel a particular automobile delivers that benefit.

Look at Table 11.1. Here is a hypothetical example of how the market might see Volvo vs. BMW in terms of the six potential benefits we are considering. The importance weights represent how important the market considers each characteristic when making a new car choice: if it is considered essential, it is weighted a 3; a 1 if considered desirable, but not essential; and if it is important, but not as important as the other characteristics, it receives a weight of 0. (This is not an arbitrary weighting scheme, but reflects relative importance weights as we discussed in Chapter 6.) The beliefs that Volvo or BMW deliver on the potential benefits are represented as: definitely deliver rates a 3, does an okay job receives a value of 1, and if it is not seen to deliver the benefit, a 0.

Table 11.1 Comparative expectancy-value model of attitude for Volvo vs. BMW

	Importance weight (a_i)	Beliefs (b_i)	
		Volvo	BMW
Safe	3	3	1
Value	1	1	0
Mileage	0	1	0
Stylish	3	0	3
Powerful	1	1	1
Exciting envy	1	0	3
$A_0 \sum_{i=1}^{6} (a_i)(b_i)$		11	16

Reproduced with the kind permission of BMW (UK) Ltd

Reproduced with the kind permission of Volvo Car Corporation

Looking at the attitude scores, Volvo is an 11 and BMW a 16. So what do these scores mean? According to the expectancy-value model, multiplying the importance weight times the belief score for each potential benefit, and adding them up, provides a sense of the *relative* strength of attitudes towards Volvo vs. BMW. What these scores tell us is that people hold a more favourable attitude towards BMW than Volvo. Looking at why, the key difference is on perceptions of 'style'.

The two most important benefits (remember this is only a hypothetical example) are 'safety' and 'style'. Volvo definitely delivers on safety, while BMW is seen as doing an okay job. But in terms of 'style', BMW definitely delivers while Volvo doesn't at all. If you were the brand manager for Volvo, what would you do? The best course would be to try and change this perception. If people could be persuaded that Volvo did even an okay job in terms of 'style', overall attitude would increase to a much more competitive level with BMW (14 vs. BMW's 16 compared with the current 11 vs. 16).

This example should illustrate how the idea of finding important benefits, related to the underlying motives driving choice, that the brand can deliver, is tied directly to people's attitudes towards the brand. That is why this is so important to positioning. One is looking for the one or two benefits most likely to positively affect brand attitude. The idea of uniqueness is related to trying to come up with benefits that the brand can be seen as delivering *better* than other brands. In this example, Volvo uniquely delivers 'safe' while BMW uniquely delivers on 'style' and 'exciting envy'. Because Volvo's overall attitude is lower than BMW's (again, in this example, not necessarily in the 'real world'), it must position itself against BMW's strength in order to find parity because of the importance of 'style' to people, while *maintaining* its unique position in terms of 'safe'.

Finding the best benefits to emphasize in positioning a brand is critical to its success, and using something like the expectancy-value model offers a powerful tool for identifying such benefits in terms of the three important criteria: importance, delivery, uniqueness. This can be done by doing research among the target audience to identify those things that are important in making choices, and how competitive alternatives rate in terms of delivering on them. With the results of the research in hand, it will be possible to evaluate potential benefits for emphasis in a brand's communication positioning in terms of:

- building or reinforcing a unique position in terms of important benefits;
- taking advantage of a competitor's weakness on an important benefit;
- emphasizing important benefits the brand delivers better than its major competitors;
- increasing the importance of a benefit the brand delivers better than its competitors (if it is not already considered 'essential');
- minimizing the importance of benefits the brand does not deliver as well as its competitors.

Benefit focus

The overall positioning of a brand basically chooses a location for the brand in the consumer's mind. The benefit selection analysis helps decide which benefit(s) to emphasize.

After that, the manager must decide what aspect of the benefit to concentrate on in the execution of marketing communications.

Up to now the term 'benefit' has been used in a rather general way. We have considered a benefit as any potential positive or negative reinforcer for a brand, in line with our definition of brand attitude as representing the overall delivery on the underlying motivation. Since a 'reinforcer' is anything that tends to increase a response, benefits as we have been talking about them underlie and help increase brand attitude. Now we will consider benefits in more detail, distinguishing between attributes, benefits as subjective characteristics, and as emotions (a distinction made by Percy and Elliott, 2005).

Thinking about the underlying motive as 'why the consumer wants a brand', benefits may be expressed in terms of:

- *attributes*, objective components of the product;
- *characteristics*, the subjective claims made about the product; or
- *emotions*, the feelings associated with the product.

A brand, for example, may offer attributes that the consumer may or may not think of as a benefit. Subjective claims in their turn may have various emotional consequences or antecedents, depending upon the underlying motive.

All marketing communication presents or implies a 'benefit' as either an attribute, subjective characteristic, or emotion as defined above. The key to *effective* communication is using the appropriate benefit *focus* (Rossiter and Percy, 2000). At this point it must seem that things are overly complicated, but this really is a powerful way of 'fine-tuning' a positioning, and not nearly as confusing as it may appear.

Throughout this discussion of positioning mention has been made of the importance of the underlying motives associated with why people make particular choices. A brand's marketing communication, to be effective, must be consistent with this underlying motive. This will be dealt with more in the next section when we look at brand attitude strategies. But to understand the importance of getting the benefit focus right, it is necessary to relate it to whether a decision is positively or negatively motivated. When motives are positive, a brand's advertising and other marketing communication must address the target audience's 'feelings' in some way: e.g. 'I want to feel sexy', or 'I want to really impress her'. On the other hand, when motives are negative, information of some kind must be offered in order to address a problem: e.g. 'How can I get these stains out?', or 'What's the best investment for retirement?'

A brand's positioning, as presented in its marketing communication, must reflect this fundamental distinction between positive and negative motivations. The way this is done is through the benefit *focus*. When the motive is positive, the benefit focus should bear the *emotional consequences* of the benefit, and when the motive is negative, the benefit focus should be *directly* on the benefit. How is this done?

When dealing with a positive motivation, the focus should be either on an *emotional* benefit alone or on the *emotion* that results from a *subjective characteristic of the benefit*. Suppose you are a brand manager at Mars and you are trying to reposition Bounty bars. You could focus entirely on an emotional benefit like 'Pure Pleasure', or use a subjective characteristic like 'Taste of the Tropics' to support an emotion, such as: 'With Bounty's taste of the tropics you will experience pure pleasure.' We are *not* suggesting this would actually be the creative used (we wisely leave that sort of thing to creative experts), but *strategically* this line illustrates how for the positive motive driving candy bar brand choice (sensory gratification) one can focus on either an emotional benefit alone or an emotional benefit resulting from a subjective characteristic of a benefit.

On the other hand, when dealing with a negative motivation, the focus should generally be on either an *attribute* of the brand supporting a *subjective characteristics of the benefit*, or a *negative emotion* that is resolved or eliminated because of a subjective characteristic of the benefit. The brand manager for Anthisan Plus sting relief spray would be dealing with a - negative problem-solution motive. One benefit focus option would be to utilize an attribute of the product like 'anaesthetic' to support a subjective characteristic like 'fast relief': 'Our anaesthetic action means fast relief.' Another option would be to resolve a negative emotion such as *annoyance* at how long it takes for relief after applying most sting relief products with the *fast relief* of Anthisan Plus: 'No more annoying wait for relief from insect bites with the fast relief of Anthisan Plus.' Again, these are *strategic*, not creative examples, but they should illustrate how to focus on the benefit when dealing with negative motivations.

Which benefit focus to use within the options available for a positive or negative motivation will depend upon the specific benefit structure involved, and what is known about the strength of the various aspects of the potential benefit in positively effecting brand choice. This, of course, is addressed during the benefit selection process.

Positioning statement

We have looked at the important relationship between the brand and why people need it, the key to effective brand awareness. We have discussed the need to establish a link between the brand and its benefit, providing a motivating reason to consider the brand. We have seen how to optimize benefit selection by looking at its importance to the target audience, how well the brand is seen to deliver benefit and where it can do it uniquely, and we have learned how to focus on that benefit in the advertising. These steps are summarized in Table 11.2. Now the manager is ready to write a positioning statement.

In its simplest form, a positioning statement follows a format similar to: _____ is the brand for (target audience) that satisfies (category need) by offering (benefit). This may be refined somewhat as follows:

For the target audience, the brand

1. satisfies why people need it
2. by providing a motivating reason to consider it,
3. emphasizing in its advertising an optimum benefit
4. with a focus consistent with the motivation driving behaviour in the category.

Returning to the hypothetical example for repositioning Volvo discussed earlier, a positioning statement might read as follows: 'For people looking for an upmarket

Table 11.2 Steps for positioning a brand in marketing communications

Step 1:	Relate the brand to category need for effective brand awareness
Step 2:	Relate the brand to an overall benefit to build positive brand attitude
Step 3:	Select a specific benefit in terms of its importance, delivery, and uniqueness
Step 4:	Correctly focus upon the benefit relative to the appropriate motivation driving behaviour in the category

automobile, Volvo provides a sense of pride in ownership and its advertising should emphasize 'style' as a subjective characteristic benefit supporting an emotion benefit focus.' A more detailed discussion of the positioning statement may be found in Rossiter and Bellman (2005).

Now it is time to look at how to develop the best communication strategy to deliver a brand's positioning.

Brand communication strategy

We have seen how a brand is a 'label' for something that helps someone identify a particular product, and is associated in memory with what is known and felt about it. That knowledge and those feelings help define a brand's 'equity', which is built and nurtured by how it is presented in marketing communication, how it is *positioned*. We have also seen that how a brand is positioned in its advertising and other marketing communication relates directly to the two universal communication objectives, brand awareness and brand attitude.

Positioning establishes the link in the consumer's mind between the brand and category need, why you want the product. When a need for the product occurs, the managers want their brand to come to mind. This is what brand awareness is all about. But how can a company ensure it is their brand that comes to mind and not a competitor's? Positioning also establishes the link in memory between a brand and what it offers, its benefit(s). But how can this be done? Answering these two questions is what brand communication strategy is all about.

Brand awareness

What is meant by 'brand awareness'? When someone goes shopping for something, they are likely to buy a brand with which they are familiar. But how did they settle on that particular brand? Did they see it on the shelf, or did they specifically ask for it? Or did they go to the store with that brand in mind? Were they also familiar with other brands that they did not buy? How familiar? How many? A number of very important principles about brand awareness are suggested by these questions.

Consider these last questions for a moment, the ones dealing with brand familiarity. If someone is to name all the brands of pain relievers they can think of, how many are likely to come immediately to mind? Most people will think of one or two, possibly three, but not more. Yet as they consider the questions, additional brands are likely to come to mind. This difference between what is immediately thought of and those that come to mind later reflects something called *salience*. Brands that immediately come to mind are said to be salient. People generally know about a lot more brands than are salient at any one time. A company really doesn't care that much if someone knows about their brand if it is not salient. For a brand to be purchased, almost always it must be one that comes to mind immediately. This is why getting the link between the brand and the category need correct in positioning is so important, and forms the basis for brand awareness strategy in advertising. It is this link that establishes salience for the brand in memory.

The other questions posed above reflect the three ways brand awareness works, depending upon how someone actually makes a purchase in a brand's category. In many situations (almost all fmcg), people choose a brand after it is 'recognized' at the point-of-purchase. In other situations, they must 'recall' the brand they want in order to ask for it. And in yet other situations, they may think about wanting a particular brand before shopping, then be reminded of it when it is recognized in the store; or recall it when they get to the store so they can ask for it. These situations define the two fundamental types of brand awareness: recognition and recall (Table 11.3).

Recognition brand awareness

If you stop to think about it, for most of the things people buy they spend very little time thinking about them: toothpaste, snacks, detergent, pain relievers, soft drinks, washing powder. These are all products purchased as a result of something John Howard (the father of the study of consumer behaviour) called *routinized response behaviour* (1977). Someone sees the product in a store and decides they want it or are reminded that they need it.

When the purchase decision for a brand is made like this, the appropriate brand awareness communication objective is *recognition* brand awareness. Basically, this means visual iconic learning (Rossiter and Percy, 1988). In such cases a brand's advertising must present the brand as it will be seen at the point-of-purchase. In most cases this means it will

Table 11.3 Brand awareness strategy

Recognition brand awareness   When the purchase decision is made at the point-of-purchase, where the need for the product is stimulated by seeing the brand
Recall brand awareness   When the brand name must be remembered (or recalled) once the need for the product occurs

be necessary to clearly feature the package in all advertising for the brand. It also means that when recognition is the brand awareness communication objective, radio should not be used in the media mix since one obviously cannot 'see' the package as it will appear in the store. An exception to this rule would be if recognition of the brand occurred from *hearing* the brand name. This would be the case with such things as insurance or financial services companies, or in fact any product that is marketed via telemarketing. When called on the telephone it would be necessary for you to recognize the brand name if you were to seriously give it any consideration.

Recall brand awareness

While most of the things bought in stores occasion recognition brand awareness, there are many situations where one must remember the brand name in order to ask for the product. For example, when a waitress in a restaurant asks what kind of beer a customer would like, they must recall the brand they want from memory. In fact, before they arrived at the restaurant they had to recall the restaurant name from memory. They decided they wanted to eat out, and considered what they were in the mood for (category need). That need was associated with or linked in memory to a salient set of restaurants, and they picked one from that 'considered set'. It is very unlikely they decided to go out to eat, then drove around until they recognized a restaurant where they would like to eat.

In situations like this where someone must pull the brand name from memory in order to make the purchase (or utilize the service), *recall* brand awareness is the appropriate brand awareness communication objective. This depends upon verbal paired-associated learning (Lee and Ang, 2003). When recall is the brand awareness communication objective, advertising for the brand should repeat the brand name as often as practical, but *always* linked to the category need. Repetition is important because associative learning is more difficult in a cluttered environment (Kent and Allen, 1993). In fact, the association should be need first, then brand. The advertising sets up the need, then provides the brand to satisfy the need. This is what helps establish the appropriate links in memory between the need and the brand so that when the need occurs in 'real life', the brand will come to mind.

This linkage is critical if the brand is to be successful. Unfortunately, many brand names in and of themselves do little to help consumers associate the name with the category need. As a result, brand names are subject to what neuropsychologists call 'blocking', that all-too-familiar experience of recognizing someone but not being able to remember their name (cf. Schacter, 2001). The information is in memory, and in fact retrieval cues may even be in place that one would expect to trigger recall, but the name remains tantalizingly out of reach when needed. The reason people often have trouble remembering someone's name is that names are difficult to retrieve from memory because they tend to be isolated from conceptual knowledge. After all, what *is* an Elliott or Percy? Without a strong association in memory with something specific that is linked to the effort to remember a name, it will be hard to recall.

Just like proper names, brand names may be 'blocked', especially if they are not well integrated with a specific category need. There must be immediate associations in memory between the need and brand if it is to be recalled when that need occurs, and it is advertising's job to build and sustain that association. Another potential problem, if the links in memory are not strong, is that competitive brands with stronger associations will more likely be recalled, blocking recall of our brand. This is why it is so important to create a *unique* identity for a brand in its advertising and other marketing communication in order to avoid potential confusion in memory with other brands. This is especially true when a brand is not the market leader.

Brand recognition and recall

What if the manager is not sure if the purchase decision is driven by recognition or recall? Or what if in some situations recognition drives purchase and sometimes recall drives purchase? If someone goes to the shops for a bottle of gin, they are likely to 'recognize' the brand they want and purchase it. But if they are in a restaurant and ask for a gin and tonic, what if the waitress asks what brand of gin they would like? It would be necessary to recall the desired brand from memory. When someone is not sure, or if both types of decision-making situations are likely, the brand's advertising must take *both* recognition and recall brand awareness communication objectives into account. This means that a clear indication of the package as it will be seen at the point of purchase must be present, as well as a strong need–brand link established.

Brand Attitude

Brand attitude was discussed in the section on positioning, and in Chapter 6 when we talked about measuring brand equity. Remember, it is basically brand attitude that forms and sustains brand equity, and it is marketing communication, especially advertising-like messages, that helps form brand attitude. In the discussion of positioning it was pointed out that brand attitude provides the link between the brand and the benefits associated with it, and that effective positioning identifies what benefit(s) to include in advertising along with what the focus should be. But simply identifying what benefits to talk about in advertising is only the first step in formulating communication strategy for brand attitude.

There are two fundamental considerations that must be taken into account when developing a brand attitude strategy: involvement and motivation (Table 11.4). These two criteria go to the heart of how and why people make product choices, and as a result must guide how we approach marketing communication for a brand. These issues are discussed

Table 11.4 Brand attitude strategy

Involvement
The degree of 'risk' (fiscal or psychological) associated with the purchase decision, whether low or high, determines whether the message must be accepted or believed (high involvement) or only a tentatively positive attitude created (low involvement).

Motivation
Understanding the motivation during the purchase decision, whether it is positive or negative, determines how to focus upon the brand's benefit.

in some depth in our *Strategic Advertising Management* text (Percy and Elliott, 2005), but they deserve some explanation here. The issue of involvement is important because it influences what is needed to successfully process a message. Motivation is critical because it dictates how the benefit must be treated in the execution of a brand's advertising.

Involvement

Involvement reflects the degree of *risk* perceived by people when deciding whether to buy or use a product or service (cf. Nelson, 1970). This perceived risk can be seen in terms of either psychological risk or fiscal risk, but in either case is specifically associated with the target audience. For most of us, buying casual clothes is a relatively low-involvement decision. They do not cost a lot of money, and we generally dress to please ourselves. Not so, however, with young teenagers. For them, a great deal is at stake, making the choice of casual dress a high-involvement decision. They would not be caught dead wearing something of which their peers did not approve. This suggests that the level of involvement in a product decision will be very much a function of how the target audience looks at the purchase.

The reason it is so critical to be concerned about involvement in terms of advertising and brand attitude strategy is that it affects the degree of acceptance or believability required in the message. When dealing with low-involvement situations, when the target audience sees little or no risk in the purchase, it is not really necessary to completely accept the message as true. If a person thinks it *might* be true, something Maloney (1962) called 'curious disbelief', they will form a *tentatively* positive brand attitude. They can try the product, based upon this tentative belief, because if it turns out not to be true, they haven't lost much. But if it was true, and they did like the product, then a more permanent positive brand attitude will begin to develop. But when the target audience feels there is some risk in the purchase decision, they need to be certain of their choice before they make the purchase. With high-involvement decisions, the target audience must believe the message and accept it as true. This helps them form a positive brand attitude *prior* to actually making a purchase. As one might imagine, how one deals with the creative content of advertising will differ significantly depending upon whether one is dealing with a perceived low- or high-involvement purchase decision.

Motivation

Psychologists suggest that all human behaviour is the result of a particular motivation. While they may argue about what those motivations specifically are, there is general agreement that there are only a handful of different motivations involved. And again, while not all psychologists are in total agreement (some psychologists feel all motives are negatively oriented, that everything we do is to more-or-less 'solve' a problem in one way or another), most consider that some motives are positively originated and others negatively originated. This is the view that we take. While early thinking about motivation centred only on drive reduction, *both* drive reduction and drive increase are involved in behaviour (Wickelgren, 1977; Warr *et al.*, 1983).

The reason it is so important to understand what motivates people to purchase or use a product or service for brand attitude communication strategy is that if the advertisers do not know *why* the consumer wants it they will not be able to effectively relate benefits to the brand. This point was made in the last section in talking about benefit focus in positioning. When dealing with negatively motivated behaviour, advertising must focus directly on the benefit. But when behaviour is positively motivated, the advertising must deal with the emotional consequences of the benefit.

When considering negatively motivated behaviour, it is important to understand that this does not mean negative in the sense of being 'bad'. Negative motives generally deal with behaviour that is meant to solve or avoid a problem. A homemaker has a counter full of dirty dishes (problem) and needs washing-up liquid to get them clean (solution); or a father is worried about what will happen to his young family if he has an accident and can't work (problem), so he buys insurance (avoidance).

Positive motives generally involve seeking personal satisfaction or social approval. A person sees some pastries in a bakery window and buys some to enjoy (sensory gratification), or they buy a fancy new outdoor grill to impress their neighbours (social approval). Whether the motivation driving the behaviour of the target audience is positive or negative, it is important that advertising be consistent with the underlying motivation. And as we have seen, an important way of ensuring that is by using the correct benefit focus in the creative execution.

The Rossiter–Percy grid

Recognizing the importance of involvement and motivation in the development of effective brand attitude communication strategy, these two considerations have been used to define the brand attitude quadrants of the Rossiter–Percy grid (1997). Basically this grid provides a structure for identifying the appropriate creative tactics to be used in effecting positive brand attitude with advertising and other marketing communication, as well as the appropriate brand awareness creative tactics. It may be thought of, then, as four basic brand attitude strategy quadrants, for each of which an appropriate brand awareness strategy must be considered. This is important because *both* brand awareness and brand attitude strategy must be considered *together* for all advertising.

We have already talked about the basic differences between the creative tactics needed for recognition vs. recall brand awareness: clearly show the package as it will be seen at the point-of-purchase for recognition brand awareness, and provide a clear need–brand link for recall brand awareness.

Brand attitude strategies will reflect one of the four quadrants occasioned by combinations of involvement and motivation with the purchase decision. These brand attitude strategic quadrants are shown in Fig. 11.1. Notice that they label strategies for dealing with negatively originating motivations 'informational', and those dealing with positively originating motivations 'transformational'. These labels reflect the *general* goal of brand communication for negatively motivated behaviour to provide information to help solve or avoid the problem at hand, and for positively motivated behaviour to 'transform' your mood from a neutral or dull state to a more positive feeling resulting from enjoying a product or gaining social approval from purchasing it.

Before discussing the specific creative tactics suggested by the brand attitude communication strategy quadrants in the grid, we should point out that others in the past have proposed various 'grids' to help explain or identify types of marketing communication.

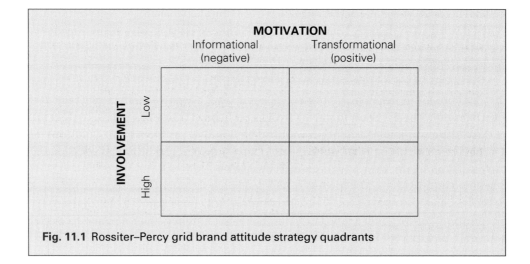

Fig. 11.1 Rossiter–Percy grid brand attitude strategy quadrants

Perhaps the best-known example is the so-called FCB grid introduced back in the 1960s. Despite many problems with this early formulation, many textbooks and marketing practitioners continue to refer to it. This is unfortunate, for there are serious problems with the ideas upon which it is built (Rossiter *et al.*, 1991).

The real strength of the Rossiter–Percy grid is that it helps focus the manager's thinking about a brand in terms of how its target audience makes choices in the category. What type of brand awareness is most likely? What is the perceived risk or involvement in the purchase or use of the brand? What motivates people to purchase products or services in the brand's category? Answers to these questions alert the manager to specific creative tactics that are likely to maximize the processing and positive response to the brand's advertising. We will now look at the four brand attitude strategy quadrants and see how they dictate significantly different creative tactics.

When dealing with low-involvement informational strategies, where there is little perceived risk in purchase and the motivation is negative, a wide variety of creative options are open. This is actually the easiest brand advertising to deal with, primarily because one does not need to convince the target audience, as pointed out when we talked about involvement. Remember Maloney's notion of curious disbelief? In fact, the target audience does not even need to like the advertising. The key is that the advertising provides some information, perhaps even exaggerated, to encourage the target audience to think the brand just might solve or help avoid a problem, so why not give it a try?

It does not matter that the attempt to persuade is so obvious, because there is so little risk in trying (Wood and Quinn, 2003). At the high-involvement level, when dealing with negative motives, there is a significant difference in creative tactics. Here the target audience *must be convinced* by what you say in the advertising. While in and of itself the message may not be enough to convince someone to purchase now, it must be believable, contributing to the building of a positive brand attitude. In order to ensure that a message will be believable, the benefit claims made must be consistent with how people currently think about a brand, its competitors, and the category in general. Otherwise, it leaves open the

Table 11.5 Brand attitude creative tactics

Low Involvement/Informational	Provide one or two clear benefits, even exaggeration of the benefit
High Involvement/Informational	Provide believable information about the brand that is consistent with the target audience's existing attitudes, careful not to over-claim
Low Involvement/Transformational	Key is the perceived emotional authenticity of the execution, and target audience must like it
High Involvement/Transformational	Emotional authenticity is critical, and target audience must personally identify with the feeling created

likelihood the target audience will consciously counter-argue the message (Gilbert, 1991). These tactics are summarized in Table 11.5.

When the underlying motivation driving category behaviour is positive, when dealing with transformational brand attitude strategies, the key to effective creative is *emotional authenticity*. This holds regardless of involvement. The target audience must identify with the advertising, and must like it. It is not unusual for the 'feeling' one gets from the advertising to become the actual brand benefit. In effect there must be increased arousal while processing the advert (Baumgartner *et al.*, 1997).

In one of the best examples of how this can work, the *taste* of beer is often more likely to be found in its advertising than in the bottle (at least in the US market). A study by one of the authors looked at taste evaluations for six then currently marketed beer brands in the US. In one test people knew what they were drinking, but in a second group the drinkers did not know what they were drinking. The results of their taste evaluations were 'mapped' (using a multivariate statistical analysis which positions the brands in relation to how similarly they are evaluated, in our case in terms of taste), and the results are illustrated in Figs. 11.2 and 11.3.

In Fig. 11.2 the results of the relationships between the six brands studied in terms of how similarly or differently beer drinkers evaluated the taste of each when they knew what they were drinking are shown. What was found is that on one side of the 'space', Coors and Miller Lite mapped rather close to each other, indicating that the beer drinkers felt they were rather similar in taste. In fact, Miller Lite is a lower calorie beer, and Coors tends to have a reputation as a 'mild' beer. Both are marketed as premium beers. In the middle of the space we find Budweiser and Pabst, each seen as tasting quite differently from Coors and Miller Lite, but also differently from each other. Budweiser is marketed as a premium beer, Pabst as a regular beer. Towards the right of the space we find first Colt 45, then Guinness Stout. Colt 45 is a malt liquor, and Guinness is, well, Guinness.

What does this 'map' tell us about how beer drinkers in the US evaluate the taste of these six brands? It seems that running left to right is a 'strength' dimension, with a vertical dimension more or less dividing what are seen as more premium beers from the one regular

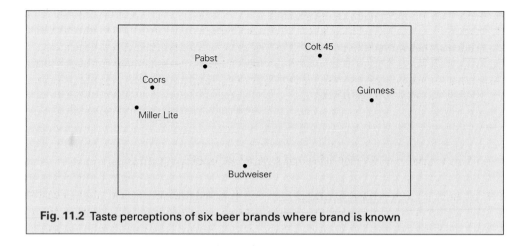

Fig. 11.2 Taste perceptions of six beer brands where brand is known

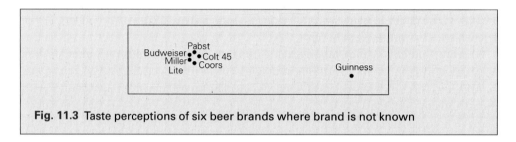

Fig. 11.3 Taste perceptions of six beer brands where brand is not known

beer, Pabst. Coors and Miller Lite are milder tasting beers, Budweiser and Pabst somewhat stronger, with Colt 45 stronger tasting yet, and Guinness the strongest or heaviest of all.

But how are these 'objective' tastes evaluated when the drinkers do not know what brand of beer they are tasting? A glance at Fig. 11.3 shows that, basically, with the exception of Guinness (which of course is not only a heavier tasting beer but also dark brown in colour), these drinkers could not distinguish between the taste of any of the other five brands. And remember, these ranged from the lower calorie Miller Lite to Colt 45 Malt Liquor, which contains over three times the alcoholic content of the other brands.

So where does the 'taste' of these beer brands come from? The advertising. When people know what they are drinking, they judge the taste in terms of the general positioning of the brands in their advertising. When they do not know what they are drinking, the objective characteristics of the brands (with the exception of Guinness) are not different enough to be distinguished.

One can see from this example how *advertising* can actually become a brand's benefit. This is the way transformational advertising 'works'. The emotional authenticity of the advertising, the result of how it is creatively executed, becomes linked in memory with the brand. With low-involvement decisions, when the brand is recognized at the point of purchase, the feelings from the advertising are re-experienced, and that becomes reason enough to consider the brand. With high-involvement transformational strategies, the only real difference is that the target audience must *personally identify* with the experience conveyed by the advertising. This is what convinces them (remember, accepting the message as true is needed with high-involvement decisions) that they too will experience these same positive feelings, helping to build positive brand attitude, leading to purchase or use of the product or service. In fact, it has been argued that such emotional responses are a necessary precursor to subsequent top-down cognitive justifications for such decisions (Dijksterhuis *et al.*, 2005).

Insights from tracking studies of brand-advertising effects

Almost all brands monitor their performance in terms of sales and market share, but it is also important to relate this performance to the brand's marketing communication. While the manager must always keep in mind that there is rarely a one-to-one correspondence between advertising and sales (because of the influence of other components of the marketing mix such as price and distribution, to say nothing of competitive activity), it is still important to understand the *extent* to which a brand's advertising is accomplishing its communication objective and contributing to the brand's success.

One of the best ways to gain an understanding of the relationship between a brand's advertising and market performance is with continuous tracking. This can be expensive, especially in large markets, but the information it can provide is critical. But as with all market research, it must be done correctly. This is not the place to go into the best methodologies for continuous tracking, but when it is done well, a great deal of valuable information will be available for better strategic management of a brand.

To give you some idea of what can be learned about brands and advertising from continuous tracking, we will briefly look at some insights gained from actual studies. (These and many others are discussed in *Advertising and the Mind of the Consumer*, by M. Sutherland and A. K. Sylvester, 2000.)

How transformational brand attitude works

In the discussion of the Rossiter–Percy grid it was pointed out that strategies for building brand attitude when dealing with positively motivated behaviour, transformational strategies, the benefit is often implied by the execution, and takes time to build. This makes it very difficult to use standard advertising 'testing' to determine if your message is working. In the 1990s a new snack brand was introduced using a musical jingle that talked about a couple of general benefits that were not very differentiating (such as 'best'). The execution itself, especially the visual components and the pacing, however, was meant to imply that this was a 'modern' brand, the brand's primary positioning.

Not surprisingly, when asked what the message said, people responded with the benefits offered in the jingle. Very few talked about it being 'modern'. But transformational strategies take time to build, and this is just what happened. In a continuous tracking study, when people were asked 'Which brand or brands do you most associate with the description "a modern, up-to-date brand"?' the new snack brand was mentioned even though

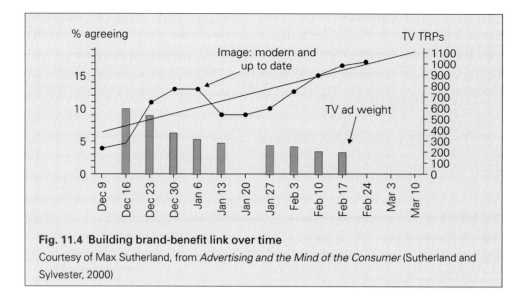

Fig. 11.4 Building brand-benefit link over time

Courtesy of Max Sutherland, from *Advertising and the Mind of the Consumer* (Sutherland and Sylvester, 2000)

people did not mention this as part of the message. And as seen in Fig. 11.4, this benefit association with the brand built over time.

This is a good example of how effective transformational advertising builds positive brand attitude, and how continuous tracking can measure its effect. If the brand manager relied only upon a traditional advertising 'effectiveness' study that only looked at what people felt the message 'said', it is likely the advertising would have been seen as a failure. It required *indirect* measurement, over time, with something like a continuous tracking study, to learn if the emotional authenticity of the execution was effective in associating the brand in people's minds with the desired benefit.

Building brand attitude for high-involvement products

By contrast, we know that for informational brand attitude strategies we must provide information, and that for high-involvement decisions the potential buyer must be *convinced* by the advertising (and other marketing communication) before making an actual commitment to purchase. And this brand purchase intention takes time to arrive at because someone is unlikely to be convinced the first time they see an advert. If managers for high-involvement products are not sensitive to this need for advertising to take time in order to fully convince the target audience to take action, they may give up on the brand because sales are slow to develop.

After launching a new high-involvement durable product, a company wanted to cut out advertising after only seven weeks because of disappointing sales results. But the company was conducting a continuous tracking study of the launch, and was convinced by the researchers that even though sales were below expectation, it was too early to give up. As seen in Fig. 11.5, this was a smart decision. Each time the brand was advertised, a positive increase in brand attitude and intention to buy occurred, and eventually sales did respond.

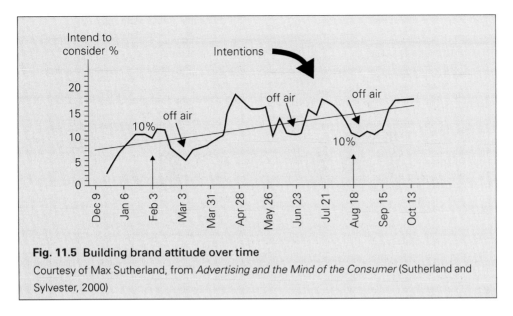

Fig. 11.5 Building brand attitude over time
Courtesy of Max Sutherland, from *Advertising and the Mind of the Consumer* (Sutherland and Sylvester, 2000)

Over time, there was a solid upward trend despite the inevitable fall-offs when there was no advertising, and the initial period of time required to convince those who formed positive intentions to actually purchase. Without a continuous tracking of what was going on the managers for the brand would not have had the kind of information they needed to make sound strategic decisions.

Brand awareness vs. trial

Brand awareness is critical for all brands, but especially so for new products. If people are not aware of a new brand, there is almost no chance they will try it. When introducing a new brand into the market, it is critical that not only sales are tracked, but also awareness of the brand. New products, especially low-involvement products, must generate trial quickly for a number of reasons. It is important to reach payout quickly in order to sustain market-ing budgets. But it is also important to capitalize on the 'newness' of the brand. With fmcgs, there are new product introductions all the time, and if you do not gain an early foothold, the brand is not likely to succeed.

Suppose a new brand is introduced, but after two months sales remain disappointingly low. Is it time to give up? It depends. If most of the target audience are aware of the brand, but have not tried, the answer is 'yes'. But what if only a few people are aware of the brand? That is the case we see illustrated in Fig. 11.6. After two months, awareness for this new brand was only 26%. This suggests that something is wrong with either the advertising itself or its media schedule. Brand awareness is the *easiest* thing to communicate about a brand, and the tracking results indicate it is not happening. If sales remain low after new advertising (or an adjustment in the media schedule) increases awareness, then it is time to pull the brand. But this decision cannot be made without a good understanding of how your advertising is working.

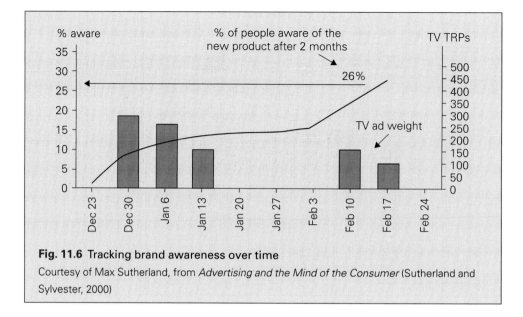

Fig. 11.6 Tracking brand awareness over time

Courtesy of Max Sutherland, from *Advertising and the Mind of the Consumer* (Sutherland and Sylvester, 2000)

Unexpected advertising effects

There is a fascinating aspect to how our minds work that psychologists call the *mere exposure* effect (Zajonc, 1968). If someone is simply exposed to something, they are more likely to prefer it to something to which they have not been exposed. Psychologists know this from conducting studies where they show people a set of random shapes or some other stimuli. Then at a later time, they show them a series of paired examples, one from the set they had seen earlier and one similar, but not seen, and ask which is preferred. Consistently people 'prefer' the one they had been exposed to earlier.

This same effect can occur with advertising. Fig. 11.7 illustrates how the popularity of a brand increased over time with advertising. The advertising execution reflected its 'taste and occasion suitability' positioning, but over time the number of people who felt that 'everyone seems to be drinking it' increased steadily. This increase in *popularity* for the brand was a function of mere exposure. Simply because it was seen advertised, the target audience felt the brand was more popular, even though this was not part of the creative strategy.

As just these four examples show, tracking studies (especially continuous tracking) can help managers better understand the effect their advertising and other marketing communication is having on the market, and this in turn enables the manager to make better strategic decisions for the brand. It is not enough to position the brand well and develop effective communication strategies. Managers must also monitor and evaluate how well the advertising itself, as well as other marketing communication, is contributing to a brand's success.

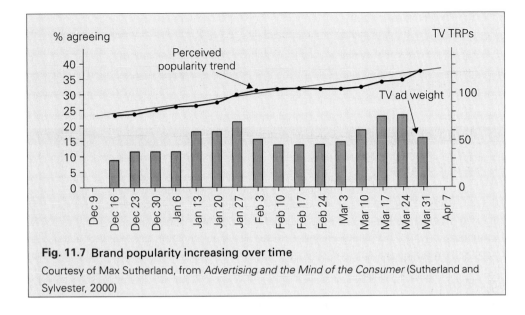

Fig. 11.7 Brand popularity increasing over time

Courtesy of Max Sutherland, from *Advertising and the Mind of the Consumer* (Sutherland and Sylvester, 2000)

CHAPTER SUMMARY

In this chapter we have examined how in many ways it is marketing communication, and advertising in particular, that define a brand for consumers. We looked at how to best position a brand versus its competition, utilizing benefits that are important to the consumer and that the brand can be seen as believably delivering, and ideally better than other brands. Based upon that positioning, a communication strategy is built around the correct focus upon the benefit, consistent with the motivation driving behaviour in the category.

We saw how brand awareness and brand attitude are critical communication objectives for all brand advertising, and how the correct use follows from the positioning. Brand awareness was seen as either recognition or recall based, depending upon whether in most purchase situations the consumer sees the brand and is reminded of a need, or whether the brand must be recalled when a need occurs. Finally, brand attitude strategy was seen as depending upon the level of involvement people have in the purchase decision, defined in terms of risk, and the underlying motivation that drives purchase behaviour in a category.

DISCUSSION QUESTIONS

1 How does a brand name communicate information about that brand?

2 Identify two or three centrally positioned brands, and discuss what makes them so.

3 Discuss how to differentiate a brand in its positioning, with particular emphasis on benefit selection.

4 How is benefit selection related to brand attitude?

5 Why is it so important to get the benefit focus correct in advertising?

6 Discuss the importance of understanding the motivation driving category behaviour to positioning and communication strategy.

7 Identify two or three brands you feel involve recognition brand awareness, and two or three brands recall, and discuss why.

8 What are the roles of involvement and motivation in brand attitude strategy?

9 Identify two or three brands for each of the four quadrants of the Rossiter–Percy grid, and discuss why they belong there.

CASE STUDY

Andrex: Sold on a Pup

If a league table of great British brands were to be compiled, Andrex would be there in the premier division, richly deserving its status as a 'superbrand'. However, it must be said that intuitively it is strange that a brand of toilet paper should be in a position to achieve this accolade. The esteem in which this brand is held by consumers does not seem to fit with the esteem of the product and its function! Our assertion in this case history is that this effect is due in a major part to a Labrador puppy, who has appeared consistently in Andrex's TV advertising since 1972.

Andrex's success

Andrex is by far the biggest and fastest selling brand in its market, and has been since the early 1960s when soft toilet tissue became the norm. No other brand has since then ever held a share in this market of over 12%. In the period since the puppy advertising began in 1972, Andrex has increased its Nielsen volume share from under 5% to over 30%.

Currently Andrex, even being the most expensive product available, is the UK's second biggest brand by value, as it sells 1.5 million rolls every day. It also has very loyal buyers, as one-third of Andrex buyers never buy any other brand. In addition, Andrex is significantly preferred by consumers in blind product tests, a fact that shows the product's 'added value', that is, the value attributed to a brand over and above its functional attributes. Bearing in mind the nature of the product, the size of this 'added value' is exceptional.

Puppy advertising

Toilet paper is inherently a low-interest, low-anxiety product. For this reason it was felt at the outset that if advertising were to work effectively for Andrex it needed to create its own interest. A primary requirement for advertising on this brand would be that it should generate high awareness, and get noticed. It was also felt that it was an equally important requirement in this case that the advertising be liked. And the puppy, which first appeared in 1972, has been central to both these requirements. However, the exceptional value of the puppy is really in the way that he has developed over the years and, as a result, achieved valuable consistency, while remaining relevant to successive generations of toilet tissue buyers. In addition to his role, demonstrating the product's softness, strength and length, he has become inextricably linked with the brand, and a metaphor for everything people love about Andrex.

Hence, Andrex advertising is not only exceptionally noticed, it is also exceptionally popular. Millward Brown has found Andrex advertising to be one of the most exceptionally liked campaigns it has ever tracked, with over 85% of respondents saying that they enjoy the advertising (the second highest endorsement of all times on this dimension). The combination of this exceptionally high likeability and the exceptionally high Awareness Index is unmatched by any other brand.

Growing loyalty

The profile of Andrex users is very similar to that of the general population (as would be expected with nearly half the country's households buying), but the profile of its most loyal users tends to be older, probably because of its premium price. Therefore, it is important that non-users of Andrex hold the brand in high esteem, since they must continually be recruited to usership.

Possible threats

As in most grocery markets, Andrex faced the considerable threat of the rise in retailers' own brands. But their growth has been contained by Andrex's market share and policy of continuous advertising. Also the spectacularly fast growth of 'green' issues affected the whole market and, for the first time in its brand history, Andrex was facing an emotional threat. But, in spite of the fact that recycling has consistently been the biggest issue for consumers in this market, Andrex is always seen as a more environmentally friendly brand than even its competitor Kleenex, which offers a recycled variant. And by running advertisements to explain that Scott is a major planter of trees, Andrex was starting to take volume away from recycled products. Lastly, as a premium-priced product, recession might be expected to affect Andrex adversely: when money is tight, buying cheaper toilet tissue would seem an easy sacrifice to make. However, the indications are that Andrex suffers far less than one might expect.

Econometric modelling

In 1974 Scott appointed O'Herlihy Associates (OHAL) to devise modelling for the Andrex brand. The objective was to find out more about what was influencing the brand's performance, and thus to help management make future decisions on budget allocation. OHAL, through a greater understanding of the relationship between advertising and sales by the model, supported that the puppy campaign is the key to the success of the brand. Currently it is estimated that in any one period, advertising accounts directly for between four and five share points of Andrex's 30% volume share: that is, Andrex's share would drop by this amount if advertising stopped for a twelve-month period.

Eliminating other factors

In order to further support our assertion that the puppy advertising has contributed so significantly to the exceptional performance of the Andrex brand it is necessary to briefly isolate and eliminate other factors which, it could be argued, could have made an equally significant or greater contribution.

Distribution: all the major brands in this market (Andrex, Kleenex, own-label) enjoy near-universal distribution and Andrex is far and away the fastest selling brand in the market on this basis.

Promotions: Promotions on Andrex can be divided into those which give extra value to the consumer (extra sheets, money off, etc.) and those designed to reward loyalty (collecting tokens for toy puppies, etc.). It is clearly unlikely that the strong performance of the brand in this period was fuelled by value-giving promotions.

Product quality: has undoubtedly been fundamental to Andrex's success. In order, however, to isolate the effect of advertising, it is necessary to demonstrate that while actual quality is important, consumers' perceptions of Andrex quality exceed the reality.

Packaging: preference alone could not account for the outstanding performance of the brand since 1972. Moreover, in a recent test, when asked what in particular people liked about Andrex, under 1% mentioned Andrex's packaging as a particular 'like'.

Product innovation: Andrex has rarely been the first brand to innovate.

Conclusion

The Andrex puppy campaign began in 1972 and is a classic example of the best of British advertising. It is exceptionally well known and probably the best-loved campaign aimed at a housewife target. The real benefits of the advertising to Scott are the following:

- Toilet paper has not become a commodity market and Scott was able to sustain a premium price for a premium product.

- Andrex is the 'gold standard' toilet paper, as it is seen by housewives to dominate its competitors on all quality dimensions.

- Whilst Andrex is not environmentally 'unfriendly', its 'green' credentials are more complex and harder to grasp than for recycled products. However, the great respect for Andrex, built through advertising, has given it the benefit of the doubt among most housewives and it has been able to retain share against the growth of recycled brands.

- Throughout the two decades of puppy advertising more and more Andrex users have switched to buying just this one brand. The move is two-fold. Some people have become more loyal and new users have joined them.

- Econometric modelling has shown advertising to have had a strong positive influence on Andrex's sales.

Andrex is an exceptional brand. Andrex puppy advertising is, according to all available measures, equally exceptional in its performance, and this case history, we hope, demonstrates what effective advertising can achieve for a product as dull as loo paper. For Scott Worldwide, the parent company of Scott Ltd, proof of their belief in the power of the puppy is shown in the fact that he has been 'exported' to Italy and Spain to advertise their premium product in these markets (Scottex).

Source: WARC, IPA, Advertising Effectiveness Awards 1992, Andrex: Sold on a Pup
Edited by Natalia Yannopoulou

Discussion Questions

1 By using the expectancy-value model, comment on the benefits selected by Scott in order to position Andrex.

2 How do you think routinized response behaviour applies in Andrex's case?

3 Do you think that Andrex has developed an effective positioning statement? Will it help Andrex face the challenges of the future?

4 Imagine being Andrex's main competitor. What steps will you take in order to position yourself as the most preferred brand within the market?

FURTHER READING

- Drawing from the experience of several advertising practitioners, Leslie Butterfield (2003) has edited a volume of empirical examples of the effectiveness of advertising for brands in *AdValue*, Oxford: Butterworth-Heinemann.

- In two other books written by an advertising practitioner, Grep Franzen looks at research methods available to help advertisers develop more effective advertising for brands in *Brands and Advertising*, Henley-on-Thames, UK: Admap publications (1999) and in *The Mental World of Brands* (with Margot Bouwman), Henley-on-Thames, UK: World Advertising Research Centre (2001), which examines in a general way the importance of memory in brand communication.

- *How to Use Advertising to Build Strong Brands* (1999), edited by John Philip Jones, Thousand Oaks, CA: Sage Publications, offers a mix of academic and practitioner thoughts on the role of advertising in various aspects of brand management.

- Papers from the First International Conference on Research in Advertising are collected in Flemming Hansen and Lars Bech Christensen's (2005) *Branding and Advertising*, Copenhagen: Copenhagen Business School Press.

REFERENCES

Baumgartner, H., Sujan, M., and Padgett, D. (1997), 'Patterns of effective reactions to advertisements: the integration of moment-to-moment responses into overall judgements', *Journal of Marketing Research*, 34, 2, 214–32.

Boulding, W., Lee, E., and Staelin, R. (1994), 'Mastering the mix: do advertising, promotion and sales force activities lead to differentiation?', *Journal of Marketing Research*, 31, 2, 159–72.

Dijksterhuis, A., Aarts, H., and Smith, P.K. (2005), 'The power of the subliminal: on subliminal persuasion and other potential applications', in R. Hassin, J. Uleman, and J. Bargh (eds.), *The New Unconscious*, New York: Oxford University Press.

Donaghey, B. and Williamson, M. (2003), 'Thinking through "through-the-line" ', *Admap*, April, 24–6.

Fishbein, M. and Ajzen, I. (1975), *Belief, Attitude, Intention, and Behavior*, Reading, MA: Addison-Wesley Publishing.

Gilbert, D.T. (1991), 'How mental systems believe', *American Psychologist*, 46, 2, 107–19.

Howard, J.A. (1977), *Consumer Behaviour: Application of Theory*, New York: McGraw-Hill.

Interbrand Group (1992), *World's Greatest Brands: An International Review*, New York: John Wiley & Sons.

Kent, R.I. and Allen, C.T. (1993), 'Does competitive clutter in television advertising "interfere" with recognition and recall of brand names and ad claims?', *Marketing Letters*, 4, 2, 175–84.

Kotler, P. (2003), *Marketing Management*, 11th edn, Upper Saddle River, NJ: Prentice-Hall.

Lee, Y.H. and Ang, K.S. (2003), 'Brand name suggestiveness: a Chinese language perspective', *International Journal of Research in Marketing*, 23, 4, 323–58.

Maloney, J.C. (1962), 'Curiosity versus disbelief in advertising', *Journal of Advertising Research*, 2(2), 2–8.

Nelson, P.E. (1970), 'Information and consumer behavior', *Journal of Political Economy*, 78, 2, 311–29.

New Shorter Oxford English Dictionary (1990), Oxford: Clarendon Press.

Percy, L. and Elliott, R. (2005), *Strategic Advertising Management*, Oxford: Oxford University Press.

Rossiter, J.R. and Bellman, S. (2005), *Marketing Communications: Theory and Applications*, Freuchs Forest, NSW: Pearson Education Australia.

—— and Percy, L. (1988), 'Visual communication in advertising', in R.J. Harris (ed.), *Information Processing Research in Advertising*, Hillsdale, NJ: Lawrence Erlbaum Associates.

—— and —— (1997), *Advertising Communication and Promotion Management*, New York: McGraw-Hill.

—— and —— (2000), 'The a-b-e model of benefit focus in advertising', in T.J. Reynolds and J.C. Olson (eds.), *Understanding Consumer Decision Making*, Mahwah, NJ: Lawrence Erlbaum Associates.

Rossiter, J.R., Percy, L., and Donovan, R.J. (1991), 'A better advertising planning grid', *Journal of Advertising Research*, 31, 5, 11–21.

Schacter, D. L. (2001), *The Seven Sins of Memory*, Boston: Houghton Mifflin Co.

Sutherland, M. and Sylvester, A.K. (2000), *Advertising and the Mind of the Consumer*, St Leonard's, Australia: Allen & Unwin.

Warr, P., Barter, J., and Brownbride, G. (1983), 'On the independence of positive and negative affect', *Journal of Personality and Social Psychology,* 44, 8, 641–51.

Wickelgren, W.A. (1977), *Learning and Memory*, Englewood Cliffs, NJ: Prentice-Hall.

Wood, W. and Quinn, J.M. (2003), 'Forewarned and forearmed: two meta-analytic syntheses of fore-warnings of influence appeals', *Psychological Bulletin*, 129, 1, 119–38.

Zajonc, R.B. (1968), 'Attitudinal effects of mere exposure', *Journal of Personality and Social Psychology Monographs*, 9, 2/3, 1–27.

■ INDEX